As a journalist, Keith Smith worked on the *Sydney Morning Herald* and the *Australian* and was a correspondent for Australian Associated Press in London, Saigon and Sydney. With his wife, Irene, he founded *Earth Garden* magazine in 1972. He is well known as an author of many practical books on gardening and self-sufficiency. His book *King Bungaree* was published by Kangaroo Press in 1992.

BENNELONG

THE COMING IN OF THE EORA
SYDNEY COVE
1788–1792

KEITH VINCENT SMITH

Kangaroo Press

First published in Australia in 2001 by Kangaroo Press
an imprint of Simon & Schuster (Australia) Pty Limited
20 Barcoo Street, East Roseville NSW 2069

A Viacom Company
Sydney New York London Toronto Tokyo Singapore

National Library of Australia
Cataloguing-in-Publication data

Smith, Keith Vincent. 1939–
Bennelong
Bibliography
Includes index.

ISBN 0 7318 0969 6

1. Bennelong, ca. 1764–1813. 2. Phillip, Arthur, 1738–1814.
3. Aborigines, Australian – New South Wales – Sydney
Region – Biography. 4. Australia – Discovery and
exploration. I. Title.

305.89915092

Cover design: Wendy Farley, Anthouse

Set in Sabon 10/12

Printed by Griffin Press, Adelaide

10 9 8 7 6 5 4 3 2 1

CONTENTS

DEDICATION

Bennelong is dedicated to my mentors, Dr Frederick David McCarthy (1905–97) and Dr James L. Kohen of Macquarie University, for their encouragement and practical help.

ACKNOWLEDGMENTS

I would like to acknowledge, with thanks, the School of Oriental and African Studies, University of London, for permission to quote from the manuscript notebooks of William Dawes and to reproduce a portion of the text.

Bennelong was researched, for more than seven years, in the Mitchell, Dixson and State libraries of New South Wales, Sydney. My thanks to the library staff for their cheerful cooperation. I am grateful to Richard Neville, curator, Pictures Research, Mitchell Library, for leads to interesting research material.

Thanks, Irene, for listening and for your good advice, and to my friend Peter Brown for reading the manuscript at an early stage.

PREFACE

SEEKING THE ABORIGINAL VOICE

Lured by a shiny fish, a bright-eyed young native man was kidnapped from a beach on the north side of Sydney Harbour in late November 1789. Woollarawarre Bennelong, shaped by his own culture for twenty-five years, was about to encounter an alien world. Unwittingly thrust into history by his abduction, Bennelong would become an important figure in the early days of the convict colony of New South Wales.

Today Bennelong's name lives on at the site of the Sydney Opera House, where Arthur Phillip, the first governor, built him a brick hut. Phillip wanted someone who could be taught to speak English and act as a go-between with the indigenous people. Bennelong was a lucky choice, because he was intelligent and quickly adapted to the ways of the white colonists. He eagerly revealed words, placenames, clan territories and details of the social and cultural life of his people.

Born somewhere along the southern shores of the river which ran from the west into Warrane or Sydney Cove, Bennelong was a wangal, a clan name based on wanne, meaning 'west'. In today's geography, wangal territory ran from Darling Harbour, around the Balmain Peninsula, and along the Parramatta River almost to Parramatta. Collectively the Port Jackson clans called themselves Eora, 'the people'.

This historical reconstruction shows that Bennelong's character was far more complex than it has been previously portrayed. He was a clever and wily politician, who played a double game in his relations with the whites. After five months of detention, Bennelong escaped, to take a leading part in the spirited resistance against those who occupied his country. After deaths and hostility on both sides, the Eora, led by Bennelong, eventually came in peacefully to Sydney Town in October 1790.

When Phillip returned to England on HMS *Atlantic* in December 1792, he took with him Bennelong and his young kinsman Yemmerawanne, who died there two years later of a lung ailment.

At first, Bennelong enjoyed his stay in London. He dressed in a ruffled lace shirt and fancy waistcoat and learned to box, skate, smoke and drink. He met King George III heard debates in parliament and swam in the Thames. He was 'delighted with every thing he sees, and courteous to those who know him', said a newspaper report of the time. Another described him as 'a very merry fellow'.

In September 1795, after a sea journey of seven months Bennelong, ill and broken in spirit by the long absence from his native land, returned to Sydney on HMS *Reliance*, with Governor Hunter, who wrote that 'the coldness of the weather ... has so frequently laid him up that I am apprehensive his lungs are affected'. Also on board were Matthew Flinders and George Bass, who began to learn Aboriginal words from Bennelong. In this second part of his life, Bennelong was a changed man. He abandoned the white settlement, took to drink and was frequently wounded in payback battles. He died at James Squire's orchard at Kissing Point (Meadowbank) on the Parramatta River on 3 January 1813 and was buried there.

That is another story. This account is focused on the young Bennelong and his friendship with Governor Arthur Phillip, whom he attempted to bring into his kinship system, set against the background of the life and culture of the Eora.

*   *   *

It is often said that there is no Aboriginal voice in early Australian history, as the indigenous people did not have writing and the stories they told were not passed on because of the rapid destruction of their society. It is more accurate to say their voice has been 'written out of' colonial histories constructed to make heroes of the English settlers who possessed their land.

If we dig deeply enough, the Aboriginal voice is there for us to unravel. The culture, life and very words and language of the people were preserved by the recorders of the First Fleet, who, like anthropologists in the field, wrote down what they saw with their own eyes and what they were told by the Eora. To find the Aboriginal voice and to recover the Eora presence, we must carefully re-examine the records compiled, for their own purposes, by the English observers whose journals, diaries, official dispatches, private letters and printed histories still survive. 'These officers were the first British ethnologists, whatever their purposes and whatever their prejudices,' writes Aboriginal anthropologist Marcia Langton.

In *Bennelong*, I have tried to return the Aboriginal voice to our shared history by factoring in anthropological concepts of kinship (families and clans), reciprocity (giving and receiving gifts) and vengeance (paybacks).

The insights gained into 'what really happened' are revealing enough to turn the accepted history on its head.

Little attention has been paid to the Eora informants by historians or linguists. In this work, the citations are attributed to them wherever possible.

This is my reading. All readings are valid.

Keith Vincent-Smith
Sydney 2000

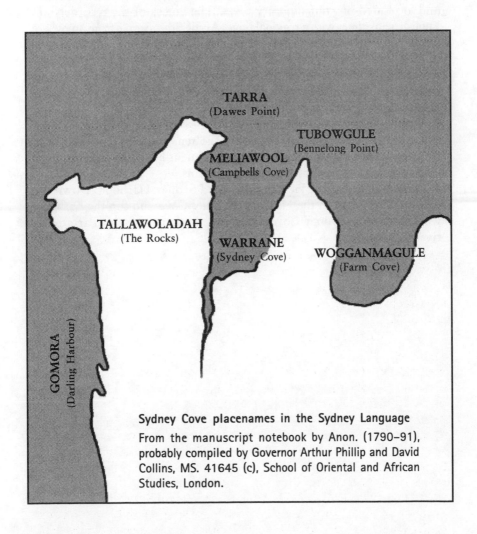

TARRA
(Dawes Point)

TUBOWGULE
(Bennelong Point)

MELIAWOOL
(Campbells Cove)

TALLAWOLADAH
(The Rocks)

WARRANE
(Sydney Cove)

WOGGANMAGULE
(Farm Cove)

GOMORA
(Darling Harbour)

Sydney Cove placenames in the Sydney Language

From the manuscript notebook by Anon. (1790–91), probably compiled by Governor Arthur Phillip and David Collins, MS. 41645 (c), School of Oriental and African Studies, London.

A NOTE ON THE TEXT

Events described in this book took place during the eighteenth century and are based on contemporary texts. The voices of the recorders are English, sometimes with a regional tinge. At the time, people from anywhere in the British Isles called themselves English and their country England.

The words Aborigine or Aboriginal were not yet in use, nor were Australia or Australian. Native meant indigenous, someone from that place so did Indian, and many of the First Fleet diarists had served their king in the former North American colonies.

Abbreviations were often used in hastily written notes — '&c.' for example, meant 'and etc.'. The original, often erratic, spelling has been retained in quoted texts. Units of measurement have been converted to metric with the exception of direct quotations.

At this period, Port Jackson described Sydney Harbour. 'Down the harbour' meant from the Heads to Sydney Cove and 'up the harbour' westwards from Sydney Cove and along the Lane Cove or Parramatta rivers.

PROLOGUE

I

BENNELONG POINT

Fish! – Woollarawarre Bennelong, his little niece perched on his shoulders, watches the *nowey* glide across the water as it rounds the headland of *Tubowgulle* where he stands on the rocks. His new wife Kurubarabulu and his sister Carangarang sing and laugh, beating time with their paddles. To make this new canoe, Bennelong used his hatchet to cut out a strip of bark from a stringybark tree growing by the river which runs to Parramatta. Laughing, he greets the naked young women and joins in their song as they haul the canoe ashore. After stepping out, Kurubarabulu casually urinates against a rock.

The women give Bennelong their catch and sit slightly below him while he cleans the fish and quickly cooks them on the fire. Bennelong's pretty sister Warreweer lies sleeping on a flat rock with her newborn infant in her arms. While Carangarang breastfeeds her child Kah-dier-rang, whom she has taken from Bennelong, Kurubarabulu prises open the shiny shells to feast on fresh rock oysters.[1] After they eat their meal they fall asleep in the sun.

It is an idyllic scene, like a picture frozen in time. This is how families have lived in this place for thousands of years. Why would anybody want to leave?

Not far away – just outside the frame – keenly watching, stands a witness from another culture, Lieutenant David Collins, who wrote down what happened at this 'family party'. That is how we know about it today.[2] A little further inland is the hut, made of fired bricks, built for Bennelong by his friend Governor Arthur Phillip, whom he calls *beanga* or father.

It is almost four years since the eighteenth century came to *Tubowgulle*, which we now call Bennelong Point, and to *Warrane*, which the English settlers renamed Sydney Cove.

Collins does not say when Bennelong's family picnic took place, but it can reasonably be dated to August or September, 'the Season in which they make their new canoes'.[3] The Aborigines living around Sydney Harbour went to Parramatta in spring to obtain the best stringybark (*Eucalyptus obliqua*), which was more easily stripped from the trees after rain. Further, Bennelong's sister Warreweer probably gave birth to her child (whose name is not known) in 1791.

Today on the point of land named after Bennelong the vaulted roof shells of the Sydney Opera House float up like billowing white sails against the blue sky, with glittering water on three sides and the green Botanic Gardens on the fourth. It is the most famous landmark of the city of four million people which grew around the harbour of Port Jackson.

Off this headland on 26 January 1788, HMS *Sirius*, flagship of a convoy of eleven small sailing ships which Australians call the First Fleet, came to anchor after a voyage of more than eight months from Portsmouth in England. From the ships some thousand men, women and children – convicts and marines – soon came ashore to establish what would be the colony of New South Wales.

The commander of these unwilling colonists was Captain Arthur Phillip, aged fifty, a Royal Navy officer with wide experience, who was to be the first governor. Phillip had found Botany Bay, 10 kilometres to the south, unsuitable for a permanent settlement. Instead he chose a small, sheltered V-shaped bay in a harbour which James Cook, passing by in HMS *Endeavour* in 1770, had named Port Jackson.

Fresh water for the new arrivals was provided by a clear creek which ran through thick stands of gum trees and trickled over mudflats into the saltwater cove. This creek, later called the Tank Stream, rose in swamps around what is now Hyde Park and flowed north between the present Pitt and George streets. Soon the sound of iron axes rang out for the first time, chopping out the thick primeval forest beside the stream, where tents were erected for a makeshift camp.

2

SALTWATER ECONOMY

They lived, for tens of thousands of years, in a bountiful environment of blue skies and shimmering waters, a country of sandstone cliffs and ridges, myriad bays and coves, sandy ocean beaches, rocky headlands, mangrove swamps, creeks and tidal lagoons teeming with bird and marine life. United by saltwater, their family groups spread out around the edges of the harbour and along the river running from the west through forests of gum trees. We will call them *Eora*, the people, because that is what they called themselves.

Nature provided the Eora with all their needs: food, water, shelter and tools. Lush vegetation grew in pockets of sand and soil along and between the spiny sandstone ridges. Rain and moisture expanded the clay-cement in the sandstone cliffs, flaking away grains of sand, which built up the thin layer of soil. Over time, rock surfaces eroded to form caves or overhanging ledges which provided natural shelter from the elements.[1]

The Eora exploited the resources of their environment by fishing, gathering plant foods and hunting animals. They had few possessions, yet they lived the 'good life' in the saltwater environment of Port Jackson and along the Pacific Ocean coast, the source of fish and other seafood which they ate fresh each day. When fish were plentiful, which was for most of the year, they could obtain all the food they needed in a couple of hours. This gave them ample leisure time to swim, eat, tell stories, bring up their children, make weapons and to follow a rich cultural and spiritual life filled with singing and dancing.

When the English year of 1788 intersected with their own time, the Eora had developed a refined technology for living lightly in the landscape. Men and women had their own separate tool kits which were superbly fitted to obtain their daily requirements. They could make these implements easily and quickly from materials at hand and showed great skill in using them. The word 'dexterous', referring to both mental and physical skill, was invariably used by early foreign observers. 'In the Summer, the Sea seems to furnish the Natives good subsistence. Fish being then in great plenty in & about the Harbours,' wrote Lieutenant William Bradley of HMS *Sirius*. There were bass, blackfish, bream, flathead, dory, garfish, gurnard, jewfish, kingfish, leatherjacket, mackerel, mullet, perch, red morwong, rock cod, Australian salmon, snapper, sole and tailor. The

From a Sketch by Governor King   Blake Sculp.

A Family of New South Wales

Despite the Europeanised figures and features given to the Aboriginal family, this engraving of a watercolour attributed to Philip Gidley King is full of ethnographic interest. The man carries a bark shield, fishing spear and woomera. The woman's child perches on her shoulder, clinging to her hair. She has a net bag slung around her neck, her fishing line and shell hook in one hand and fish catch in the other, while the son carries four barbed spears and a firestick.

From a sketch by Governor King. Engraved by [William] Blake. John Hunter, *An Historical Journal of the Transactions at Port Jackson and Norfolk Island*, John Stockdale, Piccadilly, 1793.

Eora knew that mullet were running when the coastal wattle (*Acacia sophorae*) was in bloom.

The task of fishing was divided along gender lines and men and women made their own fishing gear. Men speared fish from the rocks or in shallow water, while women used hooks and handlines to fish from bark canoes in the quiet waters of the harbour. The combination of these techniques, together with net fishing and coastal traps, yielded a wide variety of species.

The *nowey* or canoe was about 3 to 4 metres long and about 1 metre in width, shallow and shaped from a straight sheet of bark bunched at each end and tied with cord or vines. Spacer sticks were jammed across the centre to hold the sides apart. Bark for canoes was taken from the stringybark (*Eucalyptus obliqua*) or from the *goomun* or 'fir tree' (*Casuarina* species).[2] Using a stone hatchet to cut out the bark, a canoe could be made in a day.

These canoes were simple but serviceable. The highest part was seldom more than 15 centimetres above the surface of the water.[3] They were 'by far the worst Canoes I ever saw or heard of' said Bradley, yet they could be navigated through a large surf without overturning or taking in water.[4] Surgeon George Worgan of HMS *Sirius* called the native canoes 'contemptible Skiffs', but conceded that they were often paddled 'from one Cove to another even up and down the Coast, keeping as close to the Rocks as possible'.[5] 'Four or five people will go, in the small things, with all their Spears & Emplements [implements] for procuring their subsistence,' observed John Gardiner of HMS *Gorgon*.[6]

When worn and old, canoes began to leak and take in water which had to be baled out by hand with the help of a flat stone or slate.[7] Holes in the bark were patched with strips of paperbark and sealed with the waterproof gum of the grass tree.[8] Canoes used in inland waters such as the Nepean River 'differed in no wise from those found on the seacoast', said Captain Watkin Tench of the Royal Marines.[9]

Narewang or paddles, about 60 centimetres long, were made of wood or bark and shaped like an English pudding stirrer.[10] 'They have two paddles one in each hand with these they make their Canoes go amazingly swift,' said midshipman Henry Waterhouse.[11] In 1770, Joseph Banks had seen canoes at Botany Bay being poled through shallow water and spear throwers were sometimes used as makeshift paddles.[12]

A canoe might also serve as a coffin. Tench mentioned the discovery of a grave of a *gweagal* (Botany Bay clan) warrior whose body was wrapped in a bark canoe.[13] When he died in December 1790, Ballooderry of the *burramattagal* (Parramatta clan) was wrapped in a jacket, woollen blanket and his canoe.

Fishing from their canoes with handlines was an everyday social activity for women. Mothers hugged their youngest children between their knees so their hands would be free to use both paddles. The women sang as they fished, laughed and joked with each other and chewed mussels and cockles, which they spat into the water as berley to attract the fish. 'In general, we observe the canoe occupied by the Women who fish with hook & line, which I never noticed any of the Men to use,' wrote Bradley in October 1788.[14] In the centre of the canoe, a fire built on a bed of seaweed, clay or sand was kept burning to cook fish and shellfish. It was noted that women, who sat in the front of the canoe, often had burn marks in the small of the back.[15]

Hand fishing lines were called *car-re-jun* or *carrigan* because they were spun from the inner bark of the kurrajong tree (*Brachychiton populneus*).[16] Women rolled long strips of bark on the inside of their thighs, wrote Tench, 'so as to twit [twist] it together, carefully inserting the ends of each fresh piece into the last made'.[17] Lieutenant William Dawes, the astronomer and keen linguist, might have been close to the correct pronunciation with his phonetic *dtuuraduralang*, which few would suspect as the origin of kurrajong.[18] To prevent them fraying, the bark lines were soaked in a solution of the sap of the red bloodwood tree (*Eucalyptus gummifera*).[19]

Married women used bark fibre string to make two-ply nets and net bags, in which they carried their fishing lines and other possessions, which hung from their necks or foreheads. These nets were fashioned by 'laying the threads loop within loop something in the way of knitting only very coarse and open, in the very same manner as I have seen ladies make purses in England', wrote Banks.[20] Fishing nets were called *car-rung-un maugro-ma* (a net to catch fish), an indication that they were woven from kurrajong fibre string. Similar cord was used by men to bind spearheads to timber shafts and stone axe heads to wooden handles.

Burra or fishhooks were chipped and ground into a crescent shape from a large shell, usually the turban (*Ninda torquate*), using a long, rounded stone file. The shiny fishhooks did not have a barb to snag the fish and were used without bait, like lures. 'They nevertheless catch fish with them with great facility,' observed Lieutenant David Collins.[21] At Broken Bay in March 1788, wrote William Bradley: 'One of the women made a fishhook while we were by her, from the inside of what is commonly called the pearl Oyster shell, by rubbing it down on the rocks until thin enough & then cut it circular with another [rock] shape[d] the hook with a sharp point rather bent in and not bearded or barbed.'[22] A notch was cut at one end of the curved hook to attach it to the fishing line and the tie or snood was called a *karal*. The sinker attached to a fishing line, a rough, natural stone, was called a *gnammul* or *nammel*, Dawes was told by one of his informants, a young Eora girl named Warreweer.

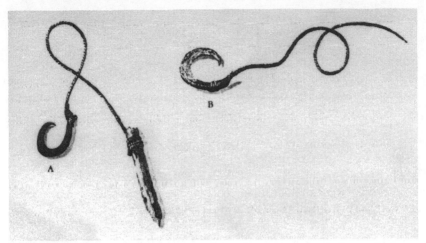

Fish Hooks of New South Wales.
Detail from Plate 36, John White, *Journal of a Voyage to New South Wales*, London, 1789.

The Aborigines of southeastern Australia had fished with hooks and handlines for at least two millennia. A shell fishhook found by archaeologists in the Sydney area was dated to 600 years before the present, while stone files used to shape fishhooks 2000 years old were recovered from rock shelters near Curracurrang Cove in Royal National Park, south of Sydney.[23]

There were inevitably times when fish were scarce, and the women sat in their canoes 'exposed to the fervour of the mid-day sun, hour after hour, chaunting [chanting] their little song', knowing their men would be angry if they came to shore without fish. Their song, Collins perceived, was aimed at 'inviting the fish beneath them to take their bait'.[24] Young men when courting gave presents of fishing tackle to impress their favourite girls.[25]

Men fished with a large spear, rather like a harpoon, but headed with three or four barbed prongs, named a *callarr* (*calara* or *goolarra*), which the English called a fish gig or fizgig (from the Spanish *fisga*, harpoon). The *mooting* was a smaller fishing spear. Fizgig shafts varied from three to 3.5 metres long and were made in the same way as other spears from lengths of the flowering stem of the grass tree (*callun*), glued together with the yellow resin or gum from the same tree. Some fizgigs, according to Collins, were made of wattle (*Acacia* species), about four and a half to 6 metres in length, with a joint in it fastened by gum and armed with four barbed prongs.[26] The wooden prongs were hardened in the fire and headed with animal bone points, sharp fish bones or teeth, or stingray spines stuck on with gum. Fizgigs were always thrown by hand, without a spear-thrower.

When fishing, men walked along the rocks close to the water, said Worgan, 'and strike the fish with their Spears, and at this, they are very dexterous, seldom missing their Aim. They used canoes mainly to cross from one cove to another.[27] 'In these canoes they will stand up to strike fish at which they seem expert,' wrote Bradley.[28] This technique was used in deeper water to take fish like mullet as they leapt from shoals. 'Baneelon has been seen to kill more than twenty fish by this method in an afternoon,' wrote Tench.[29]

Fish were sometimes preserved by drying them in the sun or over a smoky fire. A 'quantity of dried fish' was seen at a large gathering of some 200 people near Botany Bay in May 1788.[30]

Shellfish were an important part of the Eora diet, as were crabs (*kera*) and crayfish or lobsters. Women and children gathered bivalve molluscs such as mud oysters (*dainia*), rock oysters (*patanga*), mussels (*dalgal*), cockles (*kaadian*) and pipis (a Maori word) and dived for submerged rock oysters and abalone. Shells of the *kaadien* or Sydney cockle (*Anadara trapeza*) were used to sharpen spear heads. Men quickly shaped shell spear points by biting off the cutting edge with their strong teeth. Both men and women could stay underwater for a long time, according to John Harris. 'They take down a Stone and thump [shellfish] of[f] the rocks nor do they ever come up without an arm full,' he wrote.[31] 'Where they find most Oysters or the best fishing there they take up their Residence in the hollow of a Rock till they have cleared the Neighbouring Rocks of the Oysters & other shell fish which adhere to them & then seek some other place,' David Blackburn, master of HMS *Supply* told his sister.[32] Shellfish were levered from the rocks and opened with the shell at the butt end of a *womerra* or spear-thrower. Bradley saw one man open oyster shells with his thumb 'as fast as we could with a knife'.[33] Mussels and other shellfish were roasted on the fire.

Discarded shells of edible molluscs piled in heaps or middens on rocks and beaches mark the site of many ancient meals. Recent research by archaeologist Dr Val Attenbrow of the Australian Museum in Sydney confirms that 400 such sites have survived in the Sydney area. Some 80 of these have been excavated and Attenbrow has established that Aborigines occupied coastal Sydney 10 000 years ago.[34]

It was not long before the new settlers began to exploit the numerous middens, sending women convicts around the nearest coves to collect oyster shells which were burnt to make lime to build 'a small house for the Governor on the eastern side of the Cove'.[35] 'They have no resource but in burning Oyster & Cockle Shells, for no Stone has been yet discovered that will do for Lime,' wrote Worgan.[36]

'The Craw fish, and lobsters they catch in small hoop nets the making of which shews some art,' Governor Arthur Phillip noted while at Broken

Bay in March 1788.[37] The Reverend Lancelot Threlkeld (1825) said that on calm days the *awabakal* (Lake Macquarie clan) dived in the sea from canoes to pull craw-fish (lobsters) from holes in the rocks.[38] A young whale cast ashore near Botany Bay in 1788 was soon cut into pieces and 'laid upon the fire only long enough to scorch the outside'.[39] A stranded whale was usually the occasion for a feast attended by clans from far and wide, as at Manly Cove in September 1790. 'Porpoises are never refused,' wrote Threlkeld, who also saw whale feasts at Lake Macquarie.[40]

The Eora squeezed out the oil from fish entrails and rubbed it over their heads and faces and into their skin. This provided them with a natural insect repellent against flies and mosquitoes, but the colonists complained about the stench they gave off in hot weather.[41]

'They barely warm their victuals,' Gardiner complained. 'I have seen a Young girl take a fish of at least two pounds thus dress'd & devour it intrials [entrails] & bones with as much ease as if it had been scarce an ounce.'[42] The Eora, however, taught Tench and others to appreciate the 'delicacies' of the *wallumai* or snapper fish (*Chrysophyrs auratus*). The English called older snapper 'light-horseman' because they developed a characteristic forehead bump, like the helmet worn by soldiers. 'No epicure in England could pick a head with more glee and dexterity than they do that of a light-horseman,' Tench wrote.[43] When hungry, women would cook fish on the fire in their canoes, but they usually brought the catch ashore to eat with their families and share with others. 'After a meal of this kind they generally sleep,' declared Gardiner.[44]

Burra or short-finned eels (*Anguilla australis*) were plentiful in the inland fresh waters. Eels, which have elongated bodies and two fins immediately behind the head, are often represented in the stone engravings still found around Sydney. In April each year, the 'woods' natives camped at lagoons, where, wrote Collins, 'they subsist on eels which they procure by laying hollow pieces of timber into the water, into which the eels creep, and are easily taken'. Freshwater mullet, silver perch, catfish, blackfish, mud crabs, yabbies, tortoises, mussels and crayfish were also plentiful. Long slimy *cobra* grubs or shipworms (*Teredo* species), obtained from waterlogged timber, were described by Collins as 'loathsome worms' but were considered a delicacy, especially by the *cabrogal* (Cabramatta-Liverpool clan), who took their name from them. Large grubs from the dwarf gum tree, the larvae of moths and beetles, which we call *witjuti* grubs today, were eagerly sought. Collins's servant told him they were 'sweeter than any marrow he had ever tasted'.[45]

1788–1789

Arthur Phillip Esq. Frontispiece in *The Voyage of Governor Phillip to Botany Bay,*
John Stockdale, Piccadilly, 1789.

3

A LINE IN THE SAND

Early in the afternoon of 22 January 1788, two cutters and a longboat came into the harbour from the sea. Hoping to find a better site for a settlement, Captain Arthur Phillip, accompanied by Captain John Hunter of HMS *Sirius*, sailing masters James Keltie and David Blackburn and their boat crews, had left Botany Bay that morning to explore Port Jackson, an opening named by Lieutenant James Cook, who sailed by in HMS *Endeavour* in 1770.

Finding a spacious harbour, the boats ran along the west side of Middle Harbour and then circled to go ashore on the north side at a cove which Phillip called Manly Bay.[1]

'When I first went in the Boats to Port Jackson, the Natives appeared armed ... and were very vociferous,' Phillip told Lord Sydney in his first dispatch to London in May 1788. As they passed a headland, some twenty men put down their spears and waded into the water unarmed, curiously examining the strangers and their boats and taking the beads and soft red stuff like paperbark which they gave them. Phillip was impressed by the courage of these people. 'Their confidence, and manly behaviour made me give the name of Manly Cove to this place,' he wrote.[2]

The Eora did not attempt any opposition. In fact, they were in festive mood and very friendly. It was high summer, a time when people traditionally feasted on fish, shellfish and other seafood, which were plentiful, and gathered for the initiation of young men and other celebrations. One of the native men had rubbed white pipeclay over his face so that it looked like a mask, while a woman standing on the rocks had white markings on her face, neck and breasts. In later years, initiation ceremonies, attended by men and women painted with white designs, were held at about the same time around the shores of Port Jackson.

Messengers would have already brought the news of the arrival of the strangers in their *murry nowey* (big canoes) at Botany Bay to the south. Well-beaten tracks ran along the coast between the two harbours. Now they saw the boats pass through the gap between *Carangel*, the rocky northern headland, and the southern headland called *Tarralbe*.[3]

The young men ran towards the sandy, curved shore of Kayyemy, where the boats landed.[4] On the beach, Captain Phillip met an older native 'who appeared to be the Chief, or Master of the Family' and persuaded him to pass through a group of marines armed with muskets to where the boat crew was boiling meat in a pot. When the elder realised that he would be separated from his people by the redcoats, he stopped, wrote Phillip, and 'with great firmness seemed, by words & actions to threaten them, if they offered to take any advantage of his situation'. The warriors soon arrived, armed with spears, while two carried shields and wooden clubs. 'As their curiosity made them very troublesome when we were preparing our Dinner, I made a circle round us; there was little difficulty in making them understand that they were not to come within it, and they then sat down very quiet,' wrote Phillip.

The 'Indians' wrote Watkin Tench (who had served in North America), received the landing party with great cordiality and acknowledged their authority by allowing a boundary to be 'drawn in the sand, which they attempted not to infringe, and appeared to be satisfied with'.[5] Although he admired the conduct and physique of the native men he met, Arthur Phillip had drawn a line in the sand at Manly Cove. This line, secured by marines armed with superior weapons, was both a physical and symbolic barrier which segregated black and white at their first meeting in Port Jackson.

After their meal, the explorers rowed to a small beach to the south of the harbour entrance (Camp Cove) where they pitched their tents for the night. Next day they surveyed the harbour, seeking a suitable place for a settlement.

Phillip was able to tell Lord Sydney that he had 'the satisfaction of finding the finest Harbour in the World, in which a thousand sail of the line may ride in the most perfect security'. Late on 23 January, Phillip sailed south to Botany Bay, which he had decided to abandon. Two days later, he returned to Port Jackson on board the *Supply*. For the first settlement in New South Wales, he fixed on a small cove with the best spring of water, in which ships could anchor close to the shore.[6]

As the remaining ships set sail from Botany Bay on the morning of 26 January 1788, two large vessels of the French expedition to the South Seas commanded by Comte Jean de La Pérouse came into the bay. All the ships of the First Fleet were safely moored in Sydney Cove that night.

The presence of large numbers of indigenous people along the coast from Botany Bay to Sydney Cove was marked by 'a great number of fires', observed Marine Lieutenant Ralph Clark on *Friendship*.[7] They crowded the high cliffs as the ships sailed into the sheltered harbour. 'The natives on shore hollered Walla Walla Wha or something to that effect, and brandished their spears as if vexed at the approach,' said Robert Brown, captain of the storeship *Fishburn*.[8] 'All the natives which were seen when we first arrived at Port Jackson' danced violently, shouting '*woroo woroo*, go away,' wrote Philip Gidley King.[9] These were the first words ever spoken to Europeans by the native people of southeastern Australia. In April 1770, James Cook had received the same warning at Botany Bay. 'They threatened us ... often crying to us, Warra warra wai,' said the Scots artist Sydney Parkinson who accompanied Cook on his first landing.[10] John Easty, a marine private aboard the transport *Scarborough*, saw 'a great many of the nativs as we Came in att 1/2 Past 7 ... Came to anchor opposite a littel Cove nameed Sidney Cove'. In his journal, Easty had crossed out the words 'Phillips Cove'.[11] Clark said the ships were roped to 'Trees on Shore both sides of Governours Cove ... about five miles from the entrance'.[12]

Convicts were sent ashore in a longboat from the *Scarborough* next day to help cut down trees, clear the ground and pitch tents. The native people of Sydney Cove seemed to have melted away into the bush. 'None of them has appeared since we anchored,' commented Arthur Bowes Smyth, surgeon of *Lady Penrhyn*.[13] Fishing boats sent 'down the harbour' to the Heads had some good catches with their seine nets. The north shore natives were friendly and helped to haul the laden nets ashore, 'for which kind office they were liberally rewarded with a Portion of the fish', wrote Surgeon Worgan. Governor Phillip issued orders that the natives should be treated with friendship and not be molested. 'In case of their stealing any thing,' wrote Worgan, 'mild means were to be used to recover it, but upon no account to fire at them with Ball or Shot.'[14]

4

MEN'S BUSINESS

'Dexterity in throwing, and parrying the spear, is considered the highest acquirement,' wrote Watkin Tench of the Eora. Spears dropped to the ground during combat were quickly grasped between the toes and lifted up ready to throw, without causing any distraction from the fight.[1] In punishment rituals, a man stood alone to defend himself from a shower of spears which he deflected with only a bark or timber shield. 'Their war spears have only one point, and that commonly jagged, so as to be very destructive,' wrote Daniel Southwell.[2] A man who ran away when a spear was thrown at him in a ritual punishment was a coward (*gee-run*) and bad (*wee-ere*).[3]

When hunting kangaroos, wallabies and small game, men launched their spears with great velocity, harnessing the powerful lever action of the *womerra* (woomera) or spear-thrower, a short wooden shaft of split wattle (*Acacia* species) about 60 to 75 centimetres in length. A hook at the butt end of the *womerra* fitted into a hole made in the end of the spear. 'After poising it for some time, and measuring with the eye the distance from the object to be thrown at, the spear is discharged, the throwing-stick remaining in the hand,' wrote Collins.[4] A sharpened clam shell or *kaadien* (Sydney cockle) was set into the front end of the *womerra* to use as a knife, scraper or adze and for opening oyster shells.

Spear-throwers, clubs, flexible handles for stone hatchets and digging sticks for collecting roots and tubers were usually fashioned from knobbly tree and mangrove roots.

The *eleemong*, a shield used in combat, was made of gum tree bark.[5] In 1770 at Botany Bay, Joseph Banks picked up an oblong bark shield which had been dropped by 'a man who attempted to oppose our landing'. Banks noticed that many trees had been cut to the shape of a shield and lifted with wedges, but not removed, 'which shews', he wrote, 'that these people certainly know how much thicker and stronger bark becomes by being suffered to remain upon the tree some time after it is cut round'.[6] A shield cut from a solid piece of wood and hardened in the fire was called an *arragong*.[7]

The Eora adapted the most basic of natural materials, the stones from the ground, and put them to good use. They produced sharp-edged flakes by striking different kinds of stones against each other. Hand-held cutting stones were used to chop wood or to scrape, straighten and sharpen weapons and tools and to slice and cut meat. The *mogo*, a hatchet with a head made of hard, durable stone, sharpened at one end, was used to strip sheets of stringybark from trees to make canoes or bark shelters, to carve battle shields, to cut toeholds for climbing and to enlarge holes in trees to catch possums and obtain edible grubs and honey. To make a *mogo*, a stone weighing about 1 kilogram was ground to a sharp cutting edge by rubbing it over coarse sandstone, lubricated by water from a nearby source such as a rock pool or creek. It might take a full day to shape the stone. Hatchets were kept sharp by the same method. Short, curved, shallow stone hatchet grinding grooves can still be seen in many places around Sydney and in the Blue Mountains, often near stone engravings. Stone hatchets were hafted, that is, fitted with a flexible handle, which was made by splitting and scraping the bark from a green sapling branch using a stone flake. The handle was wrapped around the head, bound with bark fibre cord and cemented in place with grass tree resin or beeswax.

Fire or *gwee-yang* was a tool of great value to the Eora.[8] They used fire to cook fish, kangaroos, kangaroo rats and other small game, to dry fish and to smoke gliders and possums out of trees, to drive game from cover and for night fishing. Spear shafts and heads, other weapons and bark sheets were shaped over fires, and grass tree resin was melted in the heat. Camp fires in the open outside huts or rock shelters kept people warm at night and scared off malevolent spirits. The hearth was the true home of the family group, giving light and warmth, while fire smoke deterred mosquitoes and other insects. Finally, fire burnt the bodies of the dead to ashes and consumed personal belongings which might bear traces of a dead person's spirit or essence.

To obtain fire, the pointed end of a stick was pushed into a hole in a flat piece of wood and twirled rapidly around between both hands, sliding them up and down. When the operator was tired, wrote Philip Gidley King, 'he is relieved by another of his Companions, who are all seated for the purpose in a Circle, & each takes his turn untill fire is procured'.[9] From King's journal it is clear that it was 'Wolarewarre' (Bennelong) who demonstrated this fire-making technique, probably to a group of interested officers.[10] Tench said the base plate used was a reed (probably the stalk of the grass tree) shaved on one side to make it flat.[11]

As the process of making fire was tedious and time-consuming, men usually took firesticks – *gerubber* or *gooroobeera* – with them wherever they went.[12] They were rarely seen 'without either a fire actually made, or a piece of lighted wood, which they carry with them from place to place, and even in their canoes', said Phillip.[13]

In windy weather, large groups would come together to set the bush on fire over areas of several kilometres. 'This, we generally understood, is for the purpose of disturbing such animals as may be within reach of the conflagration and thereby have an opportunity of killing many,' wrote Hunter.[14] More fires were seen in winter and one at North Head in July 1788 covered an area of about 2 hectares Hunter's theories about firing the landscape have been confirmed in recent years by Aborigines in other parts of Australia, who regard burning as 'looking after' country. Many Australian native trees and plants are adapted to fire and recover quickly from bushfires, which spread seed in fertile ashes to regenerate after rains. According to anthropologist Rhys Jones (1968), what he termed Aboriginal 'firestick farming' produced, over thousands of years, 'widespread ecological changes in the vegetation, and hence in the animals'.[15] These regular small fires thinned out the eucalypt forests, kept the undergrowth sparse, promoted the growth of plant foods and native grasses, which encouraged grazing animals like kangaroos. Over a long period, fire shaped the face of the landscape, altering the mix of vegetation species. The First Fleet recorders often remarked on the open, 'park-like' nature of the country around Sydney Cove and at Parramatta.[16]

'Of land animals they probably eat every kind they can kill,' wrote Joseph Banks after spending several weeks ashore on the eastern Australian coast at Botany Bay and the Endeavour River in 1770.[17] 'The pat-ta-go-rang or kangaroo was (bood-yer-re) good, and they ate it whenever they were fortunate enough to kill one of these animals,' wrote Collins. Though rarely seen near Sydney Cove after the settlement, there were always mobs of kangaroos in the inland grasslands and open woodlands.

Explorer Francis Barrallier said natives could only catch kangaroos by uniting 'in great numbers to hunt it'.[18] Writing in 1804, George Caley, a botanist employed in New South Wales by Sir Joseph Banks, described this hunting technique, called *walbunga*, which, he wrote, meant 'catching kangaroos by setting the place on fire, and by placing themselves in the direction the animal is forced to pass, and throwing spears at it as it passes along'.[19]

The 'woods tribes', as the English called the natives who lived inland, climbed trees to hunt furry marsupials such as brushtail and ringtail possums, koalas, flying foxes, sugar, pigmy and yellow-bellied gliders, white-footed tree rats (now extinct), brown marsupial mice and boobook owls. Game which could be flushed out by fire and speared or felled with a club or digging stick included wallabies, swamp wallabies, red-necked pademelons, brush-tailed rats, wombats, spotted rats and kangaroo rats. Groups of men hunted through the long grass for bandicoots, about the size of a rabbit, which they killed with one blow of a well-thrown stick called a *waddi* or *woodah*.

A small cloak was found which had been made from the skins of possums and gliders. Phillip said it was 'very neatly sewed together, the inside ornamented in diamonds of curved lines, by raising the skin with the point of a small bone, which is made sharp for that purpose. This cloak they put over their heads when they sleep.'[20]

The flesh of echidnas was considered a delicacy and the natives used short spears to strike platypus when they came to the surface of rivers and lakes. *Weereammy*, flying foxes or fruit bats, still feed voraciously on Port Jackson figs and can eat as many as 800 ripe fruit in one night's feeding, ranging over 100 kilometres. 'Their smell is stronger than that of a fox; they are very fat, and are reckoned by the natives excellent food,' wrote Phillip, who kept a pet female fruit bat in his house which he fed on rice.[21]

The Eora speared or trapped a wide variety of birds, especially wild ducks, teals, swamp hens and black swans which inhabited streams, lagoons and swamps. They ate cockatoos, hawks, cranes, pelicans, pigeons, herons and emu (*marryang*). On the Hawkesbury River, quails (*beeanbing*) were caught in narrow traps, 9 to 15 metres long, made of reeds and branches and covered with earth.[22]

Undoubtedly the most useful plant which grew along the coastal strip was the *goolgadie* or grass tree (*Xanthorrhea* species), also called the gum or gummy plant or blackboy. Heated in a hot fire or with a firestick, the yellow or red resin found in the trunk of the tree melted and solidified into almost pure lumps which were used as a waterproof, all-purpose adhesive.[23] Most of the grass trees in the bush around Port Jackson had been burnt until the stumps were charred black (a possible source of charcoal). The gum, observed Henry Waterhouse, was 'very servisable to the Natives':

> it is with this Gum they fasten the Bull rushes [grass tree stalks] together to make their spears & stop any holes in their Canoes or Water Vessels as water will not dissolve it[.] it is remarkable that this tree is always burnt to a cinder on the outside ... [while] the heart of the tree is perfectly sound & good & the top is allways green.[24]

The flowering spike (*yegali*) of the grass tree produced nectar and was soaked in water to make a sweet drink. The edible worm or grub found in the grass tree was called *tangnoa*.[25] At Lake Macquarie in 1825, the Reverend Lancelot Threlkeld watched in astonishment as his *awabakal* guide (probably Birabran) obtained his breakfast by kicking a grass tree with his bare foot and breaking it in two, then picking from its centre several 'fine large maggots, commonly called *cobra*'. Threlkeld expressed his surprise: '"Oh!" says my guide, "all the same as an oyster to you, and just as nice".'[26]

The soft tissue of the paperbark or tea tree (*Melaleuca* species) protected the Eora at birth and death. Sheets of finely layered paperbark were wrapped around newborn babies and around dead bodies for burial.[27]

Yellow Gum Plant
The Voyage of Governor Phillip to Botany Bay, John Stockdale, Piccadilly, 1789.

Bark sheets, usually of stringybark (*Eucalyptus obliqua*), were used as *gonye* or shelters and for temporary windbreaks. Tench described 'hunting huts' at the Nepean River, which were: 'Nothing more than a large piece of bark, bent in the middle, and open at both ends, exactly resembling two cards, set up to form an acute angle.'[28] At Botany Bay in 1770, Joseph Banks had noted small, rounded and domed huts made with a framework of bent saplings set in the ground and covered with cabbage palm leaves and pieces of bark. A fire burned at the entrance.[29]

After huts, canoes and cord, the bark outer skin of trees was used to make shields, baskets, water containers and carrying dishes. Bark fibre was woven into headbands worn by young men following their initiation and, in cooler areas, cloaks were made of beaten bark.

5

RESISTANCE

Captain John Hunter and Lieutenant William Bradley began a survey of Port Jackson on 29 January 1788. The next day they landed at Spring Cove, south of Manly Bay and just inside North Head, where about twelve natives crowded around the boats. Three of them, noted Bradley, still had the 'trinkets &c. hanging about them' which Governor Phillip had given out the previous week. The sailors mixed with the men, who were 'quite sociable, dancing and otherwise amusing them', but kept their women well away. 'The Governor's plan with respect to the Natives, was, if possible to cultivate our acquaintance with them having an Idea of our great superiority over them, that their Confidence & Friendship might be more firmly fixed,' wrote Bradley. Not surprisingly, the whites could not persuade any of the natives to return with them to the settlement at Sydney Cove.[1] During the survey Hunter found the Port Jackson inhabitants a 'very lively and inquisitive race'. They were straight, thin, well made, rather small-limbed, but active and very curious about the newcomers. 'They examined with the greatest attention, and expressed the utmost astonishment, at the different coverings we had on; for they certainly considered our cloaths as so many different skins, and the hat as part of the head,' he wrote.[2]

The idea that the Aborigines of the Sydney area did not fiercely resist the invasion of their country by English settlers in 1788 is a myth that should be set to rest. Spirited opposition was widespread and Manly and the northern area of the harbour were the initial focus of guerilla attacks by the clans which gathered there.

After the arrival in Port Jackson of the ships of the First Fleet in January 1788 there was a constant traffic of boats from the tents in Sydney Cove, to and fro down the harbour to the area around North Head and Manly. While the indigenous people shunned the settlement after February 1788, contact between the two races was a daily occurrence on the water. Boats from the ships moored in Sydney Cove were sent to fish with nets near the Heads, expeditions to Broken Bay landed at Manly before walking overland and the two boats skippered by Hunter and Bradley were surveying and mapping the harbour.

Longboats were regularly sent to the north harbour in quest of tall, straight trunks of cabbage tree (*Livistona australis*) which were used to build the first slab huts in Australia for convicts and marines. Cut into lengths, the soft timber was found 'very fit for the purpose of erecting temporary huts, the posts and plates of which being made of the pine of this country [*Casuarina*] and the sides and ends filled with lengths of the cabbage-tree,' wrote David Collins. These huts were roofed with a thatch of grass tree leaves and, plastered over with clay, made 'a very good hovel', Collins judged.[3] Cameragal clans in the north harbour and on the coast at Manly, which was first called Cabbage Tree Beach, resented these constant intrusions into their territory. When some of the fishing crews stopped sharing their catch with them, they began to retaliate with a shower of stones whenever they had the chance.

The native people quickly developed a great fear of the foreigners' firearms and from the earliest contact were awed by the red-coated marines armed with long-barrelled Brown Bess muskets. Four companies of Royal Marines, more than 200 men, were commanded by Major Robert Ross, who refused to allow his troops to guard the convicts. On the second day at Botany Bay, 21 January 1788, the inhabitants, although 'funny and friendly', to quote George Worgan, already seemed to be afraid of the soldiers and 'made signs for us to take them away before they would venture to come near Us ... One of them was bold enough to go up to a Soldier and feel his Gun, and felt the point of the Bayonet, looked very serious & gave a significant Hum.'[4]

'I am well convinced that they know and dread the superiority of our arms,' wrote John White on 23 January. 'From the first, they carefully avoided a soldier, or any person wearing a red coat, which they seem to have marked as a fighting venture.' White noted that many of the Botany Bay warriors were painted with stripes across the chest and back 'which at some little distance appears not unlike our soldiers cross belts'.[5]

The inquisitive English officers were to find that *gerubber* or *gerebar*, the word for a 'firestick', which the natives gave to their muskets, was also one of the names they called the white invaders.[6] *Gubba* or *gubber*, used today by Aborigines everywhere to mean any white person, and sometimes said to be derived from 'government man' (a euphemism for convict), is more likely to have come from this usage.[7]

On 4 February, a boat crew from *Lady Penrhyn* and another boat fishing in a cove near the Heads were pelted with stones. The natives 'seem'd to threaten throwing their lances [spears],' said Bowes Smyth.[8] Some boats continued to share their fish. In another cove on 15 February, native men and women helped with the seine net and were 'very thankful' when given fish.[9] The Eora were probably catching less fish than usual because the whites were netting large catches, but they still expected to receive their fair share of the fish.

There was strong resistance at Botany Bay to the presence of the French ships. Three French seamen who came to Port Jackson said that the natives had attempted to steal several things and they were 'obligd to fire on them once or twice' and French officers said the Botany Bay natives were 'exceedingly troublesome there & that whenever they meet an unarmed Man they attack him'.[10]

THE RAGE FOR CURIOSITY

A further reason for conflict between the indigenous people and the new occupants of their land and harbour involved the acquisition of native weapons and other implements, which Daniel Southwell called 'the rage for curiosity'.[11] There was both official and unofficial trafficking in artefacts, which Governor Phillip was obliged to dispatch to King George, Lord Sydney and his powerful patron Sir Joseph Banks. Officers sought curios, whatever was strange and new, to send to family, friends and influential contacts at home in England.

Typical of these private collectors was Bowes Smyth, who at Botany Bay exchanged a mirror for a heavy bludgeon (club). In late February 1788, Bowes Smyth went with Midshipman Holt in the *Sirius* pinnace to a cove a 'great distance' from Sydney, where he saw many men, women and children and was given a stone axe. The Eora were 'very social' and were given some fish for helping with the nets.[12] The surgeon was acting against the orders of Governor Phillip, who had banned trading in weapons with the natives while the transport ships were still in Sydney Cove. To maintain a 'friendly and desirable intercourse' with the natives, wrote David Collins, 'it was strictly forbidden to take away their spears, fizgigs, gum, or other articles, which we soon perceived they were accustomed to leave under the rocks or loose and scattered about upon the beaches'.[13]

Sailors on the ships which had transported the convicts to the penal colony were also keen to acquire weapons and implements, not for aesthetic reasons, but because they would fetch a good price in England. The convicts, many of them habitual thieves, picked up anything the Eora put down. Selling weapons and curios to seamen was one of the few things a convict could do to improve his lot. These activities angered the Eora, who in return began to steal implements from the Europeans, especially iron axes, hatchets, picks, shovels and other metal tools. They also started to retaliate with spears: one unarmed convict was the same as any other to them.

When a group of natives appeared in their canoes at a point close to Sydney Cove (Bennelong Point) on 18 February, a boat landed and gave them some fish, which they eagerly accepted. The next day four canoes passed through the moored ships and one joined the others. From there, some twenty to thirty men went in canoes to the island where the *Sirius* crew had established a garden (now Garden Island) and stole two iron shovels and a pick axe. The gardeners forced them to bring back the pick axe and drew the first blood. 'The shovels the[y] escaped with but not without their skin being well peppered with small shot,' wrote Bradley.[14] The incident outraged Clark, who wrote in his diary: 'They are the greatest thefs that ever lived I think that we are in a fine state. We brought nothing but thefs out with us to find nothing but thefs.'[15] Collins blamed the convicts, who were 'every where straggling about, collecting animals and gum to sell to the people on the transports, who at the same time were procuring shields, swords, fishing-lines, and other articles from the natives, to carry to Europe'.[16]

The French ships at Botany Bay were preparing to sail. After a visit there on 8 March, John Shea told Ralph Clark that the French 'had often been obliged to fire on the Natives, for that they are become most daring and troublesome'.[17] On 9 March, Duncan Sinclair, master of the *Alexander* transport, recorded in his log: 'A man found in the woods quite naked, being stript by the natives'.[18] Peter Scriven, a sailor from *Lady Penrhyn*, was attacked with stones but escaped by hiding in dense rushes. The French ships sailed away from Botany Bay on 10 March 1788 and were not heard of again for many years.

When Phillip talked to groups of natives at Botany Bay and during his expedition to Broken Bay in March 1788, they regarded him as an initiated warrior. According to George Worgan, the natives would sometimes thrust their fingers into the white men's mouths to see if they had a missing tooth. 'The Governor happens to want this Tooth, at which they appear somewhat pleased & surprized.'[19] This tooth, the upper right incisor, was knocked out in initiation ceremonies. 'Most of the Men want the Right front tooth in the upper Jaw,' Phillip wrote to Lord Sydney. 'On my showing them that I wanted a front tooth it occasioned a general clamour, and I thought gave me some little merit in their opinion.'[20]

THE RUSHCUTTERS

On 15 March 1788, some natives threw spears at four convicts who were cutting rushes 'some distance from the Governor's Farm', possibly at the present Rushcutters Bay, wounding one man on the collarbone. The Eora wanted their iron tools and threw spears and stones when they refused to give them up.[21] Five days later, Captain James Meredith talked to some natives on the shore opposite Dawes Island (now Spectacle Island) and gave them some small presents. A spear passed close by as the boat left and Meredith fired at the natives, who were hiding in the trees. The same day, natives used their spear-throwers to severely beat a convict gathering greens. His companion escaped by running into thick undergrowth. Natives threw stones at convicts working at the Brick Fields, 1.5 kilometres south of the settlement, on 26 March.[22] On 14 April, 'Two natives landed on the pt. of the Cove where the Observatory is fixed [Dawes Point], but could not be persuaded to go into Camp', wrote Bradley.[23]

Revenge and retaliation hardened into outright murder for the first time on 21 May 1788. That day William Ayers, a convict recovering from a long illness, wandered to the 'cove beyond the farm' (Woolloomooloo) to pick greens and sweet tea or sarsaparilla (*Smilax australis*), which was eagerly sought by patients recovering from scurvy in Surgeon White's hospital. That evening, Ayers stumbled into the camp with the jagged barb of a spear protruding from his back. He said that natives had first thrown stones at him and another convict named Peter Burn. When they threw the stones back, the natives hurled their spears. Burn was stripped, beaten and killed and his body was dragged away. Surgeon White cut out the spearhead, which had penetrated nearly 8 centimetres into his body. A few days later, a soldier found a shirt, hat and a piece of Burns's jacket pierced by spears in a native hut in the bush.[24]

The murder of two convicts on 30 May 1788 while cutting rushes is often supposed to have taken place at Rushcutters Bay. However, William Bradley clearly stated that Captain James Campbell went by boat to 'the SW [southwest] arm' of Port Jackson, where he found the two bodies. Both Watkin Tench and George Worgan used the term 'up the harbour', meaning to the west of Sydney Cove.[25] This makes it clear that the convicts, William Okey and Samuel Davis, had been cutting rushes for thatching huts in the swamps around Long Cove, now Darling Harbour. The territory of the *wangal* started at Darling Harbour and continued along the south shore of the Parramatta River almost to Parramatta. 'Finding some blood near the Tent, [Campbell] followed it to the Mangrove bushes and found both Men dead & laying at some distance from each other.'[26] Okey had been beaten to death; his eyes were torn out and his brains flowed from his split skull. Midshipman Newton Fowell thought Okey's skull had been smashed with his own metal axe.[27] Davis, a young man, was killed by a single blow to the forehead.[28]

A few days earlier at the farm belonging to Lieutenant Governor Major Robert Ross on the eastern peninsula of Balmain (now called Peacock Point), a soldier had wounded and possibly killed a native.[29] Witnesses questioned about the incident by Judge Advocate Collins stated that some natives had come to the farm and stolen a jacket belonging to Morty Lynch, a marine in Captain Meredith's Company. The following day, Lynch tried to retrieve the jacket from a native in a canoe, but the man beat him on the arms and wrists with his paddle, so Lynch slashed his knife across the man's stomach. Convicts James Strong and Jesse Moloch (or Mocock) and Elias Bishop, a marine in Tench's Company, claimed they had seen the native paddle away in the canoe.[30] The grisly murders of Okey and Davis were payback killings by the Eora. In the English camp, Worgan heard a rumour that 'some of the Convicts had murdered two of the Natives'. The natives had not interfered with their tent, but took all their metal tools: an axe, two billhooks and two scythes.[31] Richard Williams of the transport *Borrowdale* thought the motive had been 'thro' revenge for taking away one of their canoes'.[32] It was even possible, said Hunter, that the rushcutters 'might have been rash enough to use violence with some of the natives, who had been numerous there'.[33] Bradley wrote:

> I have no doubt but this Native having been murdered occasioned their seeking revenge & which proved fatal to those who were not concerned. They have attacked our people where they met them unarmed, but that did not happen until they had been very ill treated by us in the lower part of the Harbour & fired upon by the French.[34]

In search of the killers of the rushcutters, Governor Phillip, Surgeon White and Lieutenants George Johnston and Robert Kellow set out on 31 May with six marine privates and two armed convicts. They first went to the scene of the murder, then followed a native path to the northwest arm of Botany Bay, where they pitched their tents for the night. In the morning the party counted forty-nine canoes drawn up on a deserted beach. In a nearby cove, they had a friendly meeting with more than 200 Aboriginal men, women and children. Each man was armed with a spear, *womerra*, shield and club or stone hatchet, but Phillip advanced towards them unarmed and gave them fishhooks, beads and other presents. One man showed Phillip a wound on his shoulder apparently caused by an axe.

It was the largest gathering of native people the colonists had ever seen. Governor Phillip gave orders when he returned to Sydney that no group of less than six armed men was to go into the bush 'on account of the Natives being so numerous'. In a letter to the Marquess of Lansdowne, Phillip said he had been determined, from the time he landed, 'not to fire on the natives but in a case of absolute necessity' and was fortunate to have so far avoided it. 'I think better of them having been among them,' he added.[35]

'I am still persuaded the natives were not the aggressors,' Phillip wrote on 9 July 1788. He suspected that they had acted in self-defence or 'in defending their canoes'.[36]

Twice during July natives attacked and beat the crew of the *Sirius* fishing boat and took fish. 'The temptation was great, for the quantity caught was considerable, & fish is now very scarce,' Phillip advised Lord Sydney.[37] Aggression also continued against stragglers in the bush. On 19 July, convicts gathering sweet tea near Botany Bay were chased for 3 kilometres by natives armed with spears and clubs. Two convicts gathering greens were attacked at Botany Bay on 27 July. One got away, but the other was speared in the chest and over the left ear. He escaped by swimming across an arm of the bay while 'the natives stood on the bank laughing at him'. Next day a sailor lost in the bush was stoned by natives, but had the presence of mind to point a stick towards them 'in manner of a Musquet'. This halted the attackers and saved his life.[38]

'Their numbers [of Natives] in the neighbourhood of the Settlement, that is within Ten Miles to the northward, and Ten Miles to the Southward, I reckon at fifteen hundred,' Phillip told Lord Sydney.[39] On 17 August, Phillip and Hunter set out to make a census of the number of canoes and natives on the harbour north and south of Sydney Cove. They found a total of 67 canoes, 94 men, 34 women and 9 children. As Hunter was talking to some natives on the shore, one threw a spear over the boat. George Johnston fired a musket loaded with small shot into the bushes. 'It was perhaps fortunate that my gun did not go off,' wrote Hunter, 'as I was so displeased at this treachery, that it is highly probable that I would have shot one of them.'[40]

Such incidents became common. In August natives collecting bark beat and stripped a convict, but ran off when they heard musket shots. Some warriors landed at Dawes Point, menaced a seamen with spears, then killed a goat and took it away from the hospital, towards Long Cove (Darling Harbour). On 25 September, natives threw spears at a fisherman who had given them some small fish, but would not give them the larger fish they wanted.[41] 'It was much to be regretted,' wrote Collins, 'that none of them would, place a confidence in and reside among us; as in such case, by an exchange of languages, they would have found that we had the most friendly intention towards them.'[42]

The natives, Clark wrote on 1 October, were ready to attack convicts in the woods 'whenever they think they may get the better of them, but they never meddle with a red coat'.[43] Cooper Handley, a convict, was killed near Botany Bay when he strayed from a marine guard in search of greens on 2 October 1788.[44] 'Latterly, they have attack'd almost every person who has met with them that has not had a musquet,' wrote Bradley. He did not doubt that some natives had 'been killed by Musquet balls, both at Port Jackson by our People & at Botany Bay by the French'. When natives threw spears at a convict on 24 October, Phillip immediately went to the place, and ordered his troops to open fire – 'it having become absolutely necessary to compel them to keep at a greater distance from the settlement', said Collins.[45]

One week later, Governor Phillip turned his mind to the establishment of a farming settlement at the head of the river running to Sydney from the west. This invasion was carried out in orderly military style. On 2 November, Phillip with surveyor Augustus Alt, two officers and a party of marines went to the Crescent 'to choose the spot, and mark out the redoubt and other necessary buildings'.[46] An earthwork fort was built and more troops and convicts were sent up on succeeding days to the place, which was at first named Rose Hill (Parramatta).

'The Natives were very numerous at the Time at all parts of the Harbour and very troublesome to Boats going up and Down the Harbour & would as they passed near a Point throw a Speer at them & then retire to the Woods,' Newton Fowell wrote in a letter from Batavia (Jakarta) shortly before his death.[47] 'They have lately been Very troublesome to our fishing and foraging partys ... so that we have been oblig'd to go Well Armd as they have Several Times come down in a body of 60 or so & throw Stones & Spears at us whilst fishing & Even attempted to take the fish from us,' David Blackburn wrote.[48]

Phillip had not been able to make friendly contact, or persuade any of the indigenous people to live in the settlement. 'The natives now avoid us more than they did when we first landed,' Phillip advised Lord Sydney in November, 'and which I impute to the robberies committed on them by the convicts, who steal their spears and fish-gigs which they frequently leave in their huts when they go out a-fishing ... though every precaution has been taken to prevent it.'[49]

Word was brought on 18 December that a large force of natives had assembled at the Brick Fields. A marine patrol set out immediately and returned with the news that about fifty natives had run into the woods when the convict workers pointed their spades and shovels at them as if they were guns.

Fearing further attacks, the English colonists began to feel the isolation and remoteness of their new colony. HMS *Sirius*, ordered to the Cape of Good Hope for supplies, left port on 1 October and at the end of November the last transport ships set sail, leaving only the brig HMS *Supply* at anchor in Sydney Cove. They had lived in Port Jackson for almost one year, but no natives had come into the camp since February. Tired of this state of 'petty warfare', wrote Tench, Governor Phillip was 'determined to capture some of them and retain them by force, which would either inflame the natives to vengeance or promote an intercourse'.[50]

6

ARABANOO

At Manly Cove on 30 December 1788, two unlucky men were ambushed by Captain Henry Ball of HMS *Supply* and Marine Lieutenant George Johnston. One escaped, but the other was captured by a seaman, who threw a rope around his neck and dragged him into the boat. Hearing his cries of distress, his friends ran from the bush and attacked. 'They threw spears, stones, firebrands, and whatever else presented itself ... nor did they retreat ... until many musquets were fired over them,' wrote Watkin Tench. When the boat pulled off, the rope was tied to the captive's leg and he was given some cooked fish and 'sullenly accepted to his destiny'.[1] 'The terror this poor wretch suffered, can better be conceived than expressed; he believed he was to be immediately murdered,' commented John Hunter.[2]

The native man, well built but not tall, was brought up the harbour to the governor's temporary canvas house near the stream at the head of Sydney Cove. His hair was cut and combed and his beard shaved off. Determined to find the true colour of the man's skin, Tench plunged him into a tub of soapy water and scrubbed him from head to toe, concluding that he was 'as black as the lighter cast of the African negroes'. He was then dressed in a shirt, jacket and a pair of 'trowsers'.

As he would not reveal his name, Governor Phillip called the captive Manly, after the cove where he was caught, but later he told them his name was Arabanoo. Newton Fowell wrote it as Arooboonoo and Arooboonen, Daniel Southwell as Araboonoo, Elizabeth Macarthur as Arrabason and Henry Waterhouse as Harrabanu.

An iron handcuff attached to a rope was fastened to Arabanoo's left wrist. This delighted him at first and he called it *ben-gad-ee*, meaning an ornament, 'but his delight changed to rage and hatred when he discovered its use', wrote Tench.[3] Arabanoo was locked up that night and the following morning his convict keeper reported that he had slept well and did not attempt to escape. Thus was the first of the Eora introduced to the benefits of European civilisation.

To try to shake off his obvious sullenness and dejection, Arabanoo was led around the camp and then to William Dawes's observatory on the western point of Sydney Cove (Dawes Point). There he looked across to the north shore at smoke from a camp fire and sighed '*gwee-un*' (fire).[4]

He would also have seen the carving of a sperm whale on the rock face on the opposite point, which was removed by quarrying in the mid-nineteenth century.[5]

For three months, Arabanoo remained a prisoner, constantly guarded and locked up each night in a hut made of bush timber and bark near the Guardhouse.[6] Hunter found Arabanoo to be 'a good natured talkative fellow' and 'fairly good-looking.'[7] Newton Fowell said he was a very good mimic and had become 'much attached to several particular People'. One of these was Tench, who said Arabanoo had a soft, musical voice and quickly became 'extraordinarily courteous' to the ladies.

At first, Arabanoo had an enormous appetite. For breakfast he would eat eight fish, none less than half a kilogram in weight, and for dinner (the midday meal) three kangaroo rats and more than a kilogram of fish. After his first meal, Arabanoo turned his back on the fire and sat so close to the flames that his shirt caught alight. It was soon extinguished, but Arabanoo was so terrified that it was difficult to persuade him to put on another shirt. He dined with Governor Phillip, but at a side table, heartily eating fish and duck, but would not touch wine and smelled bread and salt meat with suspicion and put it aside. 'When he was first taken he had a voracious Appetite but as he found he got his Meals regular that Appetite wore off. He was very fond of Bread & Vegetables,' wrote Fowell.[8]

New Year's Day 1789 must have been very strange for Arabanoo, who joined the officers at Governor Phillip's new brick house overlooking Sydney Cove and the sandhills at Cockle Bay (Darling Harbour). Arabanoo had to be prevented from throwing his plate out the window after his meal of fish and roast pork. He stretched out on his wooden chest by the window, put his hat over his face and was soon asleep, oblivious of the band playing loudly in the next room.[9] Fowell, who confused New Year's Day with Christmas (before Arabanooo had been captured), wrote that 'Arooboonen was Vastly Frightnd so much so that His Appetite failed him. After Dinner he Appeared more Chearful and it was afterwards learnt that he supposed it was intended to Eat him.'[10]

Arabanoo's captivity did not deter the Eora from their resistance. At the end of January, north shore natives took three jackets from a boat in a bay where convicts were cutting rushes for thatching. The coxswain chased two men in a canoe to a small island nearby, and towed away their canoe, which they had left on the rocks. The Eora followed and one hurled a spear at the coxswain which wounded him in the arm. 'They must have known that at that time we had one of their people in our possession, on whom the injury might be retaliated,' wrote Collins. 'He, poor fellow, did not seem to expect any such treatment from us, and began to seem reconciled to his situation.'[11] Jacob Nagle said the coxswain recovered from his wound. 'The natives ware now so troublesome that we ware allow'd a musket in the boat, as we were constantly up and down the harbour,' said Nagle.[12]

Arabanoo was taken 'down the harbour' to Manly, where he was allowed to talk to his friends. He was heard to repeat the word Weerong, the native name for Sydney Cove, doubtless, wrote Tench, 'to inform his countrymen of the place of his captivity'. When he went there again two days later, no natives would talk to him, but he left them a present of three birds, which he placed in a bark basket.

In the settlement, Arabanoo made friends with the children and, if he was eating, always gave them the choicest food. He began to relish bread and drank tea avidly. In February, Phillip took Arabanoo aboard HMS *Supply*, which was leaving for Norfolk Island. At the first chance, Arabanoo dived overboard, but soon discovered that his clothes kept him afloat and that he could not even submerge his head. He was sullen when brought back to the ship but soon cheered up when Phillip called him to get into the boat to go ashore.[13]

On 3 March 1789, sixteen rebellious convicts from the brickmaker's gang at the Brick Fields, 1.5 kilometres from the camp at Sydney Cove, armed themselves with their working tools and large clubs and set off on the track to Botany Bay. Their aim, wrote Tench, was to attack the natives there and to steal their spears and fishing tackle. However, the convicts were ambushed by some fifty natives, who killed one man and wounded seven others as they fled back to Sydney. A detachment of marines recovered the body of the dead convict, which had been stripped and lay on the path to Botany Bay. Some of the convicts claimed they had been quietly picking sweet tea in the bush when they were suddenly attacked by the natives, but others said that they were seeking revenge for the murder of a convict killed while picking sweet tea.[14]

The troops also found a young boy, stripped and left for dead, with his left ear nearly cut off. In a show of force, two armed parties were sent out, one to Botany Bay. The wounded convicts were taken to the hospital, while seven who were healthy were tied up in front of the provisions store and given 150 lashes each in front of the assembled camp.[15] 'Arabanoo was present at the infliction of the punishment; and was made to comprehend the cause and the necessity of it,' wrote Tench, 'but he displayed on the occasion symptoms of disgust and terror only.'[16]

SMALLPOX

The Small Pox raged among them with great Fury and carried off Great Numbers of them. Every boat that went down the Harbour found them laying Dead on the beaches and in Caverns of Rock forsaken by the rest as soon as the Disease is discovered on them.

– Newton Fowell, Batavia, 31 July 1790[17]

A deadly epidemic of smallpox broke out among the native population of Port Jackson in April 1789, about fourteen months after the arrival of the First Fleet and La Pérouse's ships at Botany Bay. It spread like wildfire, infecting and killing hundreds of men, women and children around Sydney, but no white settlers were infected.

Smallpox is a highly contagious virus which takes twelve days to incubate. It starts with an irritating skin rash and is followed by sores filled with pus. Its victims suffer from alternating hot and cold fevers and cry out for water. A few recover in five or six weeks, but the majority sicken and die, leaving a stench of rotting flesh.

Captain John Hunter was shocked by the sight of bodies floating in the water and lying unburied on beaches and in caves all round the harbour, where previously whole families used to shelter in wet weather.[18] Not a single fishing canoe was seen in the harbour. The Eora fled from the pestilence, inland and to the north, leaving the victims with some water and a small fire burning beside them.[19] Some were found with their dead children; others lying dead between a cave and running water.[20]

'Repeated accounts brought by our boats of finding Indians in all the coves and inlets of the harbour, caused the gentlemen of our hospital to procure some of them for the purposes of examination and anatomy,' wrote Watkin Tench. 'On inspection, it appeared that all the parties had died a natural death: pustules, similar to those occasioned by the small pox, were thickly spread on the bodies.'[21] Phillip sent boat crews down the harbour to collect the bodies and bury them.

On 15 April 1789, Sergeant Scott wrote in his journal:

> I went with a party to Cut Grass tree for Lt. Johnstone. Found three Nativs Under a Rock, Vis, a man and two Boys (of Which One Boy Was Dead). The Govorner being Acquented with it, order'd the Man & Boy to the Hospital Under Care of the surgion the[y] having the Small pox.[22]

Governor Phillip immediately set out for the cove by boat, taking Surgeon John White and Arabanoo. They found an old man, very ill, stretched beside a fire and a boy nine or ten years old pouring water from a shell over his head. Nearby lay a dead woman and her baby girl. 'Eruptions covered the poor boy from head to foot,' wrote Tench. Arabanoo buried the child, scooping out a hole in the sand with his hands. He lined the grave with grass and put in the body, covering it with more grass and a mound of sand.

The sick man and boy were taken to an empty house near the hospital on the west side of Sydney Cove. When offered fish, the old man turned his head away, but the boy, who was called Nanbarry, immediately leapt up and began to cook some. The patients were washed in a warm bath, given clean shirts and blankets and put into their beds. The old man, whose name may have been Cud-dur, suffered from shivering fits and, because of his obstructed throat, cried out for water.[23] He lived only a few more hours. Arabanoo placed his body in a grave dug by a convict in the presence of Phillip, Tench, Ball and a few others. That evening, Ball and Tench crossed the harbour and buried the corpse of the woman on the beach. In time, Nanbarry recovered and was adopted by Surgeon White.[24]

Two more smallpox victims, a young man and a girl, about fourteen years of age, were brought into the settlement in the governor's boat and taken to the hospital hut. 'The sympathy and affection of Arabanoo, which had appeared languid in the instance of Nanbaree and his father, here manifested themselves immediately,' wrote Tench. The young man died after three days, but the girl (who might have been his sister) eventually recovered and was taken into the family of Mrs Johnson, the chaplain's wife. The girl's name was Boorong or Booron, but from a mistake in pronunciation she was at first called Abaroo.[25]

When Arabanoo was taken by boat to look for his friends, not one living person could be found. Appalled by the sight of decaying bodies all around the harbour, he cried out 'All dead! All dead!', then hung his head and said no more.[26] It is conceivable that six men with 'DD' ('deceased') written after their names in the anonymous language notebook (probably by Phillip and Collins) were among those who died of smallpox. They were: Gomil, Gora-moa-bou, Gnoo-lu-mey, Yendaw, Yarre-a-rool and Baid-do. The last man is more likely to have been crying for water than giving his name, as *bado* is the Sydney language word for water.[27]

The only non-Aboriginal victim of the smallpox was a North American seaman from the crew of HMS *Supply*, who, wrote Collins, 'was seized with it, and soon after died'. This sailor had visited Nanbarry and Boorong in the hospital when they were ill.[28] Many of the English children had been to see them, but none caught the disease.[29]

From their experience in England, the First Fleet surgeons were convinced that the disease was smallpox. 'That it was the smallpox there was no doubt; for the person seized with it was affected exactly as Europeans are who have the disorder,' wrote Collins, 'and on many that had recovered from it we saw the traces, in some the ravages of it on the face.'[30] There is no satisfactory explanation of how the disease had been introduced and spread so widely. When first questioned, Arabanoo and the children called the illness *galgalla*, which 'seemed to indicate a preacquaintance with it', wrote Collins.[31] Fowell said it was 'Conjectured that it was among them before any Europeans visited the Country as they have a Name for it'.[32] John Hunter, however, stated that 'we had reason to suppose they have never before been affected by it'.[33]

Phillip informed Lord Sydney in London that until the outbreak in 1789 smallpox had 'never appeared on board any of the ships in our passage, nor in the settlement'. Phillip posed the question 'Whether the small-pox, which has proved fatal to great numbers of the natives, is a disorder to which they were subject before any Europeans visited this country, or whether it was brought by the French ships, we have not yet attained sufficient knowledge of the language to determine'.[34] The two ships had anchored at Botany Bay for six weeks from 26 January to 10 March 1788. No cases of smallpox were reported, but the ships had previously called at Macau, the Philippines, Formosa (Taiwan) and Samoa.

One possibility, which does not seem to have been fully investigated, is worth examining. It is conceivable that smallpox could have lain dormant in the colony if a 'carrier' who was resistant to it was aboard any of the European ships and unknowingly spread the disease to an Aborigine, who could not resist it. There might also have been smallpox cases in the settlement which were so mild that they had not been noticed or diagnosed. Many among the convicts and ships' crews had contracted smallpox at some time. For example, at her trial at the Old Bailey in London in 1792, Mary Bryant, who had escaped from Sydney, was said to be 'marked with smallpox'.[35] In support of this theory, the First Fleet accounts contain evidence of widespread sickness among the indigenous people around the settlement in the winter of 1788, about six months after the arrival of the French and English ships. The diarists thought these people were starving, which is unlikely, considering the wide range of food resources available to the Eora. The smallpox outbreak might have been confined to groups which had little contact with others, until the winter of 1789, when it became general.

On 18 May 1788 a party visiting coves 'down the Harbour' met natives who 'seemed to be very badly off for food not having any Fish'. At another cove a family was seen chewing 'a root much like fern'.[36] Fish were often scarce in winter, when fern roots were normally part of the diet. Lieutenant Ralph Clark noted that 'the poor wrechd Inhabitance [sic] ... live on limpets and fern roots'.[37] Asked in 1845 what his people at Botany Bay lived on, Mahroot (also called Boatswain) replied: 'Generally on the sea coast side fish, and fern root.'[38]

Weak from starvation, Edward Corbett, a convict who had run off into the bush on 5 June 1788, returned to the camp at Sydney Cove on 24 June. Corbett reported seeing four natives dying in the woods, who made signs for something to eat, as if they were perishing from hunger.[39] Corbett was hanged the following day. If the sick native men he saw had contracted smallpox they were probably seeking water.

On 20 June, Bradley found an old man 'nearly dead', being cared for by some young men and women who lit fires on each side to keep him warm.[40] Phillip told Sir Joseph Banks that, following heavy rains, 'few fish were caught & the Natives [were] very much distressed for food, several have been seen dying in the Woods, & visibly for want of food'.[41] At Camp Cove on 14 July 1788, Bradley met a man feeding a boy and girl 'who appeared to be starving' with roasted and pounded fern root. 'The Man had many sores about him & was really a miserable object,' Bradley noted. He eagerly ate some salt beef that was offered to him.[42]

Sustained contact between the Eora and the convicts occurred during July 1788, when one clan took up residence in 'one of the adjoining coves'. Collins said they were 'visited by large parties of the convicts of both sexes on those days in which they were not wanted for labour, where they danced and sung with apparent good humour and received such presents as they could afford to make them; but none of them would venture back with their visitors'.[43]

In 1882, Obed West, an elderly Sydney resident, passed on an oral tradition told to him by Aboriginal elders from Botany Bay, 'some of whom were very strongly pockmarked'. From what they told him, said West, 'I gathered that they contracted the disease [smallpox] from the men of La Perouse's ships'.[44]

On Friday, 8 May, Captain John Hunter returned to Sydney Cove after a stormy circumnavigation of the globe at low latitudes in HMS *Sirius*, bringing back enough flour from the Cape of Good Hope for four months rations. On landing, he went to see Governor Phillip who was:

> sitting by the fire drinking tea with a few friends; among whom I observed a native man of this country, who was decently cloathed, and seemed to be at much at his ease at the tea table as any person there; he managed his cup and saucer as well as though he had long been accustomed to such entertainment. This man was taken from his friends by force ...[45]

The following day, Hunter welcomed Arabanoo aboard the *Sirius* to eat dinner with Governor Phillip.

Arabanoo, who had nursed Boorong and Nanbarry through their illness, caught the smallpox himself, probably through his close contact with them or the child he had buried. He allowed the doctors to bleed him and confidently took all the medicines they gave him.[46] 'It happened as the fears of every one predicted; he fell a victim to the disease in eight days after he was seized with it, to the great regret of every one who had witnessed how little of the savage was found in his manner,' lamented Collins.[47]

Poor Arabanoo died on 18 May 1789 and was buried in the governor's garden. Phillip, 'who particularly regarded him', attended the funeral, wrote Tench.[48] Fowell said 'he was regretted by everyone as it was Supposed he would be of great Service in Reconciling the Natives to Us'.[49]

On 2 June 1789 a group of twenty canoes passed Sydney Cove going down the harbour. 'This was the first time any number of them had been seen together since the Small Pox having been among them,' Bradley noted.[50] The epidemic had spread north to Broken Bay, west to the Hawkesbury River and south to Botany Bay. 'On visiting Broken Bay … in many places our path was covered with skeletons,' wrote Collins.[51] At the end of September 1789, Captain John Hunter returned after surveying Botany Bay, where he had seen skeletons, bones and bodies of many people killed by smallpox in some of the caves.[52]

As severe as it was, smallpox did not halt the Eora resistance. In August 1789, an English boat party with the little boy Nanbarry went 'down the harbour to take a Native if a good opportunity offered'. They talked to a group of men on the north shore who did not take much notice of Nanbarry, nor he of them. 'They were a considerable time with them but had not an opportunity of taking one,' wrote Bradley.[53] On 1 September, a native hidden behind a tree threw a spear at a convict at Ross's farm and immediately ran away.[54] On the north shore, while Commissary John Palmer was cutting cabbage tree trunks on 24 September, some Eora men stole his metal axes and ran off, probably as revenge for the theft of their weapons by convicts. They left behind two children, one aged about seven and the other about two years old, who went to sleep in the ship's boat. The men appeared again and after some parleying returned the axes in exchange for the children. The following day, natives threw spears at the fishing boats when the crew would not give them a large fish they wanted, although they had been given some small fish.[55]

Two days later Henry Hacking, quartermaster of HMS *Sirius*, was hunting game at Middle Harbour, when a stone whizzed past his head. Turning, he saw three men armed with spears and clubs coming towards him. Hacking fired small shot from his musket, which halted the attackers, who shouted in surprise. Hacking later claimed he had been set on by a mob of forty men 'making a great noise'. He reloaded his musket with heavy buckshot, waited until the warriors were within 50 yards and fired into the thick of them. Two fell, dead or wounded, while the others ran off, taking their injured companions.[56]

7

TAKING A NATIVE

Fish! On the beach at *Kayyemy* (Manly Cove), a seaman held up two large fish, tempting two native men from a large group, who clambered over the rocks, dropped their spears and came to the boat. The date was 25 November 1789. 'They eagerly took the fish,' wrote First Lieutenant William Bradley; 'they were dancing together when the Signal was given by me, and the two poor devils were seiz'd & handed into the boat in an instant.' The captives were quickly bound with ropes and tied to the boat, which pulled away without a shot being fired. When they realised that their friends had been taken, the Eora rushed from the bush and ran to both headlands of the cove, angrily shaking their spears and clubs.[1] Spears flew through the air and one, wrote Philip Gidley King later, 'went through four folds of the boat's sail and struck the apron of the stern with sufficient force to split it'.[2] It was too late, wrote Bradley in his journal: 'The noise of the men, crying & screaming of the women and children together with the situation of the two miserable wretches in our possessions was really a most distressing scene; they were much terrified.' The captives cried for help. The older man shouted angrily at those on the shore, while the younger one trembled with fear.

At Sydney Cove, a curious crowd of convicts, seamen and marines gathered at the Governor's Wharf to see the natives as they came ashore. The two native children in the settlement, who had recovered from the smallpox, were delighted to see them. Nanbarry came down to the wharf, shouting 'Colby' and 'Bennelong'. He had often spoken about Colby, his uncle, as a great warrior and a leader of his people. The abducted men were led up the hill to the governor's house, where they were met by Boorong, who was 'frantic with Joy'. Once inside they were shaved, washed and dressed. To stop them escaping, each man had an iron shackle put on one leg, with a rope tied to it, which was held by a convict keeper.

'It was by far the most unpleasant service I was ever ordered to Execute,' wrote Bradley, who found the whole incident distasteful. Although the children told them they would be well treated and eventually allowed to leave, Bradley realised that 'all that could be said or done was not sufficient to remove the pang they naturally felt at being torn away from their Friends; or to reconcile them to their situation'.

Bennelong and Colby were sullen and shaky, traumatised at being torn from their kin and companions. Fear did not affect their appetites and they easily polished off 5 kilograms of fish in a single meal. Being locked into a cave-like room at night must have been terrifying to men used to sleeping under the stars. Every night they tried to escape by chewing through their ropes, but whenever they broke free they were caught by their captors as they blundered about in the dark, not knowing how to unlock and open the doors and windows.[3]

The First Fleet recorders were full of curiosity about the two natives. Watkin Tench judged Bennelong to be 'about twenty-six years old, of good stature, and stoutly made, with a bold intrepid countenance, which bespoke defiance and revenge'.[4] John Hunter thought Bennelong was 'a very good looking young fellow, of a pleasant, lively disposition' and about twenty-five years old,[5] while King estimated his age at about twenty-eight.[6]

Colby, said Tench, 'was perhaps near thirty, of less sullen aspect than his comrade' and much shorter and thinner.[7] Hunter named Colby as a chief 'of the tribe of Cadigal' and said he was about thirty-five years old.[8] Both men had suffered from smallpox and recovered and Colby's face was heavily pockmarked. Midshipman Newton Fowell described him as 'the principal one of the two' and said he was called Gringerry Kibba Coleby,[9] while Daniel Southwell gave his name as Kebada Colby.[10] *Gibba, kibba* or *kebah* was the word for a rock or stone, while *kebara* was a name given only to initiated men, indicating that their front teeth had been knocked out by a stone.[11]

Elizabeth Macarthur, who did not arrive at Port Jackson until June 1790, more than six months after the event, gave this account of what she had heard about the capture of Bennelong and Colby in a letter written on 7 March 1791:

> Despairing to gain their Confidence by fair means, the Govr. ordered that two men should be taken by force. This was done, the poor Fellows, I am told exhibited the Strongest marks of terror and Consternation at this proceeding, believing they were certainly meant, to be sacrificed. When they were taken to the Govrs. House and immediately clean'd and Cloth'd their astonishment at every thing they saw was amazing. A new World was unfolded to their view at once.[12]

The governor gave orders to guard the two captives strictly, but to treat them indulgently. After several attempts, Colby escaped on the night of 12 December. While Bennelong and their keepers were eating their supper, Colby, sitting just outside the door, pulled the rope from his leg shackle and in a moment jumped the paling fence and ran into the bush. 'We saw him no more,' wrote Hunter. 'However, we heard afterwards that he had joined his friends again ... his friends would certainly be something surprized to see him so well cloathed, for he carried off his whole wardrobe.'[13]

Given a further minute, Bennelong would have followed his companion.

'He was much alarmed,' wrote Bradley, 'no doubt expecting punishment or to be put to death.'[14]

Kidnapping a person seems a strange way to begin a relationship, but it is true to say that, in time, a close friendship did develop between Bennelong the native and Captain Arthur Phillip, governor of the English colony of New South Wales. In his three voyages around the Pacific, Captain James Cook had established a tradition well known in the Royal Navy of abducting or detaining native 'chiefs' and holding them until stolen property was returned. This tactic met with mixed success and, finally, to Cook's death. At Matavai Bay in 1763, as HMS *Endeavour* was about to leave Tahiti after observing the transit of Venus, Joseph Banks persuaded Cook to take on board Tupia, a high priest from the island of Raiatea, as a pilot and translator. Banks did not hesitate to add a human being to his natural history collection. 'I do not know why I may not keep him as a curiosity, as well as some of my neighbours do lyons and tigers at a larger expense than he will probably ever put me to,' Banks wrote in his journal on 12 July 1769, adding, 'the amusement I shall have in his future conversation ... will I think fully repay me.'[15]

Phillip had instructions from King George III to 'endeavour, by every possible means, to open an intercourse with the natives, and to conciliate their affections, enjoining all our subjects to live in amity and kindness with them'.[16] He could not comply with these orders when there was no contact with the native inhabitants, who had kept well away from Sydney Cove after the first weeks of settlement in 1788.

Within a few days of Colby's escape, Bennelong seemed more resigned to his situation and Phillip began to take him on excursions around the harbour of Port Jackson. Bennelong was taken on a tour of HMS *Sirius*, where, said Bradley, 'He looked with attention at every part of the Ship & express'd much astonishment particularly at the Cables'.[17] Two days later, Phillip ordered Colby's guard William Moore to be given 100 lashes for his carelessness in letting him escape. In place of a rope, a metal chain was attached to link the iron shackle on Bennelong's leg to the wrist of his keeper.

On Christmas Day 1789, only one month after his capture, Bennelong dined with Phillip and his officers on a turtle which the *Supply* had brought from Lord Howe Island.[18]

Bennelong seemed to be liberated by Colby's escape and, wrote Newton Fowell, 'he became very lively & very intelligent'.[19] Hunter said he was 'much more chearful after *Co-al-by's* absence, which confirmed our conjecture, and the children's account, that he was a man more distinguished in his tribe than *Ba-na-lang*'.[20]

'The other [Bennelong] lives with me,' Phillip advised Lord Sydney, '& will soon be able to inform us of their Customs & Manners.'[21]

A MERRY FELLOW

The likeness of Bennelong, as engraved (and written) in colonial histories and school books, is a stereotype: a cowed-looking black man with cropped hair wearing a Beau Brummell suit, waistcoat and ruffled lace collar.[22] This received image is not true of the Bennelong of the period between 1789 and 1792. He is about twenty-six years of age, handsome and at the peak of his young manhood. He is about 170 centimetres tall, wiry and muscular. He has a flat nose and a mischievous twinkle in his large dark eyes. His skin, after being vigorously scrubbed, is shiny black and pitted by the marks of smallpox, initiation and battle wounds.

Bennelong sings, dances and capers. He is always smiling and laughing and ready for a joke, even against himself. 'He is a very good natured fellow, & has a good deal of humour, being seldom angry at whatever jokes are passed on him,' noted Philip Gidley King in his journal.[23] 'He is a Merry fellow & does not Seem inclin'd to go away,' wrote David Blackburn, master of HMS *Supply*, from Batavia (Jakarta) in August 1790.[24] The English officers would find that at times Bennelong could also be angry and excessively violent.

Woollarawarre Bennelong is an initiated man, a warrior, skilled fisherman and hunter. His first wife has died some time before his capture, possibly from smallpox. He has two sisters, Carangarang and Warreweer, and is related to Worogan.

He is both clever and cunning (as we shall see) and the English officers regard him as a reliable informant. 'He lives with the Governor, & is a very intelligent Man, much information can be got from him when he is better understood,' said King.[25] 'His powers of mind were certainly above mediocrity,' observed Watkin Tench. 'He acquired knowledge both of our manners and language, faster than his predecessor [Arabanoo] had done.'[26]

Bennelong attempts to find a place for Governor Phillip and his officers in the traditional kinship system of his people. 'He calls the Governor Beanga (Father) and names himself Doorow (Son) and calls the Judge [David Collins] and Commissary [John Palmer] Babunna (Brother).'[27] He has five names, written with many variations in spelling and order by the recorders, for instance: Bannelon, Wollewarre, Boinba, Bunde-bunda, Wogeltrowey (King) Wogultrowey, Wolarrabarrey, Baunellon, Boinba, Bundebunda (Phillip) and Wollarawery Ocultroway Benallon (Southwell). He prefers Woollarawarre and 'as a mark of affection and respect to the governor, he conferred on him the name of Wolarawaree ... adopting to himself the name of governor. This interchange of names,' said Tench, 'we found is a constant symbol of friendship among them'.[28]

He is a great womaniser and boasts about it. 'Love and war seemd his favourite pursuits ... in both of which he has suffered severely,' wrote

Tench.[29] *Boon-alliey* means 'to kiss', Bennelong tells King, 'which he says the Natives do i.e. the Men kiss the Women'.[30]

Bennelong's body is like a map of his life which records his battles with his enemies. Initiation scars line his chest and upper arms and he is proud of a spear wound in his arm and another through his leg. Half of one thumb is missing and he has a scar on the back of his hand.

'How did you get that?' Tench asked Bennelong.

> He laughed, and owned that it was received in carrying off a lady of another tribe by force.
> 'I was dragging her away; she cried aloud, and stuck her teeth in me.'
> 'And what did you do then?'
> 'I knocked her down, and beat her until she was insensible, and covered with blood. —Then—.'[31]

Bennelong will not take cheek from a mere boy and once slapped Nanbarry, Colby's nephew. Nanbarry spoke 'Pretty good English' and David Blackburn thought he might forget his native tongue because he was so young, 'as Mr Bennelong does not like to talk with him'. At first Bennelong refused to answer any questions that Nanbarry was instructed to ask him.[32] As an initiated man, Bennelong cannot consider Nanbarry, a boy with all his teeth, as an equal.

This is the natural man. Bennelong must now comply with the constraints of the culture of his captors, especially in social behaviour and clothing. They dress him in a pair of 'trowsers' and a red jacket of kersey, a coarse, ribbed woollen cloth originally made in Kersey, Suffolk. Governor Phillip makes Bennelong wear the thick garment, says King, so 'he may be so sensible of the Cold as not to be able to go without Cloaths'. On Sundays, Bennelong wears a suit of buff yellow nankeen cotton cloth from China. Soon Bennelong is not 'the least awkward in Eating & considering the state of nature he was brought up in he may be called a polite man As he performs every action of bowing, drinking healths, returning thanks &c. with a scrupulous exactitude'.[33] He is taught to raise his glass and drink a toast to 'The King', which he associates forever after with a glass of wine.

'Bannylong,' according to Elizabeth Macarthur, 'appeared highly pleas'd with our people and manners, taking it as a great compliment to be call'd White man.'[34] Southwell and other English gentlemen marvel at his extraordinary appetite: 'Tis certain he can manage the share of six men with great ease at one meal.' At a time of near famine in the infant colony, Bennelong eats one week's normal rations in a day and quickly learns the difference between full and short allowances.

Already in these first reports there is conflict over whether or not Bennelong liked to drink hard spirits. Watkin Tench says he does. After Colby's escape, wrote Tench:

He quickly threw off all reserve; and pretended, nay, at particular moments, perhaps felt satisfaction in his new state. Unlike poor Arabanoo, he became at once fond of our viands, and would drink the strongest liquors, not simply without reluctance, but with eager marks of delight and enjoyment. He was the only native we ever knew who immediately shewed a fondness for spirits: Colbee would not at first touch them.[35]

However, writing at the same time as Tench (April 1790), Philip Gidley King said Bennelong was fond of wine, which he drank with water, but could not bear even the smell of spirits. 'It has often been tried to deceive him by mixing very weak rum or brandy & Water, instead of Wine & Water, but he instantly finds the trick out, & on this occasion he is angry.'[36]

A particular interpretation of Bennelong's character has been constructed from the only sources available: the subjective, racially and culturally arrogant descriptions which survive in journals, letters and books of men (and one woman) from the colonial elite of early Sydney. Tench's account of his drinking habits has prevailed over King's version and Bennelong is thought of as a good-natured drunk and a collaborator with the whites.

In *Rum, Seduction and Death: 'Aboriginality' and Alcohol*, anthropologist Marcia Langton, herself an Aborigine, identifies the lingering racist image of the 'drunken Aborigine' which, she charges, 'is a colonial construction, predating the ready availability of alcohol to Aboriginal people'.[37] The story of Bennelong, argues Langton, 'was the first reconstruction of an Aboriginal person as a "drunken Abo", and from there the stereotype was developed'.[38] It is important to stress that, in the period covered in this book (1788–92), Bennelong is not presented as a drunk who is easily affected by alcohol, but as a person who drinks socially and holds his liquor well. Tench says as much: 'Nor was the effect of wine or brandy on him more perceptible than an equal quantity would have produced upon one of us, although fermented liquor was new to him.'[39]

The lingering image of Bennelong as the first 'drunken Aborigine' is based on the stories about his behaviour after his return to Sydney in 1795, which followed three years of long sea voyages and exile in England.

Like many of his people, Bennelong was a clever mimic, 'readily imitating all the actions & gesture of every person in the Governors family', according to Philip Gidley King. He would occasionally re-enact his capture, as Southwell stated:

Benallon relates, with a great deal of humour (chiefly by gestures and signs), the manner of his being caught – for he was decoyed with a fish – and says 'beial, beial' – very good, very good; and so it was, for he gets plenty [of fish] without the trouble of spearing them now![40]

A tragic irony here underlies the general misinterpretation by the Europeans at Sydney Cove of the meaning of the word *beial*, *beal* or *bial* as 'good'.

Southwell later concluded that *beal* could mean either 'yes' or 'no' and noted: 'Beal seems to signify both good or bad.'[41] Correctly interpreted *bial* meant, emphatically, 'No'. In miming his story, however humorously, Bennelong was crying out, 'no, no' – quite the opposite of 'very good' – as he relived the terror of his abduction.

On 3 February 1790, Governor Phillip took Bennelong by boat to the Look Out Post at South Head, which had been established by John Hunter in late December 1789. While there, Bennelong threw a spear nearly 90 metres against a strong wind 'with great force and exactness'. Returning to Sydney Cove the boat stopped at a point near Rose Bay on the eastern side of the harbour, where Bennelong talked a long time with a native woman he said he was 'very fond of' called Barangaroo. Still hindered by his leg shackle, Bennelong was forced to ask her to come down to the boat. An English jacket and other gifts were thrown from the boat to Barangaroo and other women, who said Colby was fishing on the other side of the hill, and had not been able to remove the shackle from his leg.

At the Look Out a few days later, Nanbarry played a game in which he acted out the Eora burial ceremony. He dug a hole, then pretended to set fire to a dead body and heaped up earth in the shape of a burial mound. He tried to show how his people made fire by friction using two sticks, but was not yet strong enough to do it. Nanbarry stayed for a few days, wrote Southwell, who was in charge at South Head, but would not go outside in the dark for fear of seeing 'some of the departed'. The Eora called this rocky headland *Woolara*. It was a burial ground, regarded as a sacred place and was also famous, said Nanbarry, for 'great engagements' or ritual battles.[42]

THE INFORMANT

Arabanoo, wrote William Bradley, had been 'quite familiarised & very happy quite one of the Governors family & had got some of our language as well as communicated much of theirs'.[43] At Governor Phillip's house, it was a favourite amusement, after dinner, wrote Watkin Tench, to make Arabanoo 'repeat the names of things in his language, which he never hesitated to do with the utmost alacrity, correcting our pronunciation when erroneous'.[44]

Some of the words obtained from Arabanoo during 1789 can be gleaned from Tench's *Complete Account of the Settlement at Port Jackson* (1793), for example, *ben-gàd-ee* (ornament), *gweè-un* (fire) and *Weè-rong* (Sydney).[45] John Hunter must have been amused when Arabanoo called the 512 ton HMS *Sirius*, a large ship for the times, a big *nowee* (canoe).[46] Arabanoo pleased his captors by being able to recognise the difference between pictures of birds and animals and those of humans. When shown a 'handsome print' of the Duchess of Cumberland, he called out 'woman', a name he had just been taught to call the female convicts.[47]

Acquiring knowledge of the language spoken by the indigenous people was a crucial part of Arthur Phillip's plan to 'reconcile' them to the occupation of their country and to persuade them to come and live among the colonists. Linguist Jakelin Troy has characterised the capture and 'training' of Arabanoo as 'the first linguistic experiment'.[48] 'Much information relating to the customs and manners of his country was also gained from him,' said Tench. For some reason, perhaps the difficulty of acquiring English or 'the unskilfulness of his teachers', Tench concluded that 'his progress in learning ... was not equal to what we expected'.[49]

Bennelong quickly proved to be much more cooperative and informative than Arabanoo. 'He willingly communicated information [and] told us all the customs of his country and all the details of his family economy,' wrote Tench.[50] According to Elizabeth Macarthur, Bennelong 'furnish'd our people with the native names for animals, birds, fish &c.'.[51]

Bennelong attempted to convey to Phillip some idea of the scale of the devastation caused by the smallpox. On 13 February 1790, Phillip was able to inform Lord Sydney:

> It is not possible to determine the number of natives who were carried off by this fatal disorder. It must be very great; and judging from the information of the native now living with us [Bennelong], and who has recovered from the disorder before he was taken, one-half of those who inhabit this part of the country died.[52]

This figure of 50 per cent of deaths caused by smallpox is often quoted in history books but is, of course, usually attributed to Phillip himself. In the same dispatch, Phillip made the first reference to the settlement at Rose Hill by its native name, Parramatta. With some sensitivity, Phillip took due note of this information, obviously obtained from Bennelong, and officially renamed Rose Hill on the King's Birthday, 4 June 1791.[53]

It was Bennelong who told David Collins that one clan, the *cadigal*, had been reduced by smallpox to only three persons: Colby, his nephew Nanbarry and another man. This meant that perhaps fifty or more men, women and children alive in 1788 had perished from the disease. To prevent their extinction, the *cadigal* were compelled to unite with another group.[54] The third survivor was probably Caruey (Carraway), who Collins said was 'a relation of Colby'.[55]

Bennelong also told Phillip the native names for the stars and the four winds. However, the most valuable information the English settlers learned from him (despite a few misunderstandings) was the name and territory of the major clans in the Sydney area, which Phillip called tribes.

The Natives live in Tribes, which are distinguished by the Name of their Chief, who probably takes his Name from the District in which he resides. About the North West Part of this Harbour there is a Tribe which is mentioned as being very powerfull; either from their Numbers or the Abilities of their Chief. The District is called Cammerra – the Head of the Tribe is named Cammerragal, by which Name the Men of that Tribe are distinguished – a Woman of that Tribe is called a Cammerragalleon ...

From the Entrance of the Harbour, along the South Shore, to the Cove adjoining this Settlement: the District is called Cadi, & the Tribe Cadigal – the Women, Cadigalleon.

The South Side of the Harbour from the above-mentioned Cove to Rose-Hill, which the Natives call Parramatta, the District is called Wann, & the Tribe, Wangal.

The opposite Shore is called Wallumetta, & the Tribe, Wallumedegal.

The other Tribes which live near us, are those of Gweagal, Noronggerragal, Borogegal, Gomerrigal, & Boromedegal.[56]

In April 1790 the shackle was removed from Bennelong's leg. He was no longer physically restrained and could walk about freely with Governor Phillip, who, to demonstrate his trust, unbuckled the short sword or dagger he usually wore at his side and gave it to Bennelong 'who puts it on & is not a little pleased at this mark of Confidence'.[57]

On 5 April, Philip Gidley King returned to Port Jackson on HMS *Supply*, bringing news of the wreck of the First Fleet flagship HMS *Sirius* at Norfolk Island. Three days later, King travelled with Phillip from Sydney to Rose Hill. After eating, they walked to Prospect Hill, 6 kilometres away, through 'a pleasant tract of country' with well-spaced trees, grassy slopes and gentle hills and dales, which 'appeared like a vast park'. Phillip and King were accompanied by Bennelong, who seemed to have a good knowledge of the area. King noted in his journal that Bennelong frequently stumbled over tree roots as they returned in the dark, exclaiming *Were wade* and *wade were*, 'bad wood or roots' (changing the word order)'.[58]

King thought it was remarkable that 'the natives divide the district between Rose Hill & Prospect, which is only four miles, into eight ... districts'. King himself did not record the names of these places, nor do they appear in the published version of his journal in John Hunter's *An Historical Journal* (1793). However, they are found, listed as 'Names of Places', in an entry in the anonymous language notebook but in what looks like Arthur Phillip's 'fair' or formal handwriting.[59]

After the sinking of the storeship *Guardian* in December 1789 and the loss of HMS *Sirius* at Norfolk Island in March 1790, the colonists at Sydney and Rose Hill were faced with reduced rations and possible starvation. In this emergency, officers, including the surgeons and Chaplain Richard Johnson, volunteered to supervise night fishing while convict and marine marksmen were sent out to shoot kangaroos. HMS *Supply*, the colony's only remaining vessel, sailed to Batavia for supplies. Officers invited to dine with Governor Phillip were asked to bring their own bread. Phillip and others feared that the natives might cause trouble if Bennelong discovered the dire state of affairs and told them about it. Tench wrote:

> Our friend Baneelong, during this season of scarcity, was as well taken care of as our desperate circumstances would allow. We knew not how to keep him, and yet were unwilling to part with him ... Every expedient was used to keep him in ignorance; his allowance was regularly received by the governor's servant, like those of any other person, but the ration of a week was insufficient to have kept him for a day; the deficiency was supplied by fish, whenever it could be procured, and a little Indian corn, which had been reserved, was ground and appropriated to his use. In spite of all these aids, want of food has been known to make him furious, and often melancholy.[60]

1790

8

PAYBACK

At Governor Phillip's house Wolarawaree Bennelong slept in an upstairs room, which he shared with the governor's steward, the Frenchman from Lille, Bernard de Maliez. At two o'clock in the morning of 3 May 1790, Bennelong woke de Maliez, told him he was sick, and begged to go downstairs. The unsuspecting steward opened the door to let him out.

Once outside, Bennelong stripped off his English clothes, jumped onto an empty water butt and leapt the paling fence to freedom. When he did not return, de Maliez called out for Bennelong. When there was no reply he had to tell the governor the unwelcome news.[1]

John Hunter later observed facetiously that Bennelong had taken 'French leave'.[2] The general feeling in Sydney was that Bennelong must have been planning his escape for some time. Phillip, who treated his captive with genuine affection and generosity, believed that Bennelong's main reason for running off was to look for a woman. The governor did not relish the task of capturing and training another go-between, as he told Sir Joseph Banks in a letter:

> Our native has left us, & that at a time whe[n he] appeared to be happy & contented. This too is unlucky for we have all the ceremony to go over again with another, & I think that Mans leaving us proves that nothing will make these people amends for the loss of their liberty. The Girl [Boorong] who still remains says he went after a Woman, he had often mentioned & who I had as often told him to bring to live with him.[3]

Daniel Southwell said the 'fam'd charmer' Bennelong was seeking was called 'Odooradah', whom he spoke about 'in raptures'. The Eora treated Bennelong's escape as a great joke against the whites. When the officers called from their boats for Bennelong, the women laughed and mimicked them, shrilly repeating his name, Southwell told his uncle.[4]

'The natives continue to shun us,' wrote Captain William Hill of the New South Wales Corps at the end of July. 'I have not seen one yet, except a boy and a girl we have in the colony, who begin to speak our language and have no wish to leave us.'[5] Boorong and Nanbarry were happy for the moment to stay with their guardians and told them that Bennelong would not return.

*   *   *

A huge sperm whale came in from the sea, through the Heads, and into the harbour of Port Jackson. Sailors from the convict transport ships went after it with harpoons, but the whale escaped unhurt.

After breakfast on 17 July 1790, Midshipman James Ferguson and three marines stationed at South Head Lookout went fishing off Bradley's Head in a flat-bottomed punt they had leased from Marine Lieutenant John Poulden. Suddenly, the whale surfaced, 'spouting and dashing about' and splashing water into the punt. The marines baled out the water and rowed away, but the whale came up again, this time half filling the vessel. 'With their hands against the whale did they bear the boat off,' wrote Southwell. 'In vain they thro' out their hats, the bags for our provis's [provisions], and the fish they had caught, in hopes to satisfy him or turn his attention.'[6]

Twice the whale rose from the water with the punt on its back, then, finally, it tossed the fragile timber vessel into the air. 'Slipping off, she dropped as from a precipice, and immediately filled and sunk,' wrote Tench. 'The midshipman and one of the marines were sucked into the vortex which the whale had made, and disappeared at once.' The other two marines swam for shore, but only one reached safety.[7]

John Wilkins, the survivor, told Sergeant James Scott that he rode on the back of the whale for some time before he swam about a kilometre and got ashore on the rocks near Rose Bay.[8] Midshipman Ferguson and the two privates, John Bates and Thomas Harp, were drowned. The whale was so badly injured that by August it had 'run itself ashore in Manly Cove', said John Harris.[9] Collins said the natives had killed the whale, which 'was the cause of numbers of them being ... assembled to partake of the repasts which it afforded them'.[10]

On the morning of Tuesday 7 September 1790, a party landed at Manly Cove, planning to trek overland to shoot game around Broken Bay. The hunters included Surgeon John White, Captain Nicholas Nepean and Lieutenant Edward Abbott of the New South Wales Corps, surgeon's mate John Harris, the governor's game shooter John McEntire, and Nanbarry.

The crescent-shaped sandy bay, backed by thick undergrowth, was swarming with groups of Eora gathered around fires cooking pieces of *garuma* (blubber) cut from the dead whale, which by this time, wrote Watkin Tench, was 'in the most disgusting state of putrefaction'. About 200 natives were feasting on the whale flesh 'with the most extravagant marks of greediness and rapture'.[11] In the opinion of the (unnamed) surgeon of the whaling ship *Britannia*, who visited Sydney in 1793, whale blubber was the favourite food of the natives, who 'devour it in a most voracious manner, untill they can eat no longer.' He added: 'Indeed, Blubber has the same effect upon their Constitutions as Spirituous Liquors has upon an Europeans. It makes them compleatly drunk, after which they fall asleep.'[12]

At the approach of the boat the feasters rushed to pick up their spears. While the crew rested on their oars, Nanbarry stood up to tell them that their visitors were friendly. Surgeon White called for Bennclong, who came down to the water, but was 'so greatly emaciated, and so far disfigured by a long beard' that it was difficult to recognise him. In his half-forgotten English, Bennelong asked after Governor Phillip. Colby soon joined them, pointing to his leg to show that he had at last freed himself from the iron shackle still attached when he escaped from Sydney.

Governor Phillip, accompanied by Judge Advocate David Collins and Lieutenant Henry Waterhouse of HMS *Sirius*, had gone to South Head that morning to give directions for a column to be built as a landmark for ships at sea. When told that Phillip was nearby, Bennelong said he would look for him and go on to Sydney if he did not find him.

Bennelong also asked if they had brought any hatchets with them. There were no hatchets to spare, so the officers gave Bennelong and Colby some shirts, handkerchiefs, knives and other gifts. Bennclong tried to put on a shirt, so clumsily that Surgeon White asked McEntire to help him. 'This man who was well known to him, he positively forbade him to approach,' wrote Tench, 'eyeing him ferociously, and with every mark of horror and resentment.'[13] Bennelong was given a pair of clippers and began to cut his hair. All this time, the women and children, more than fifty of them, stood apart at a distance and would not come any closer.

– Which of them is your old favourite, Barangaroo, of whom you used to speak so often? they asked Bennelong.

– Oh, he answered, she is become the new wife of Colby, but I have got *Bulla Muree Deein* [two big women] to compensate for her loss.

Bennelong had obviously not lost his quick sense of humour, although he had acquired a spear wound through his upper arm and a large scar over his left eye from a club. Perhaps, Tench speculated, the wounds had been inflicted during a conflict over the two fat ladies.

Acting as interpreter, Nanbarry kept close to his guardian, Surgeon White. Asked why so many people were gathered at Manly Cove, Bennelong pointed to the dead whale and Colby made signs that at such feasts they often ate until they were sick. When Bennelong again requested hatchets, the officers asked why he had not brought his own. He replied that whale blubber was usually cut up with the shell attached to the end of the *woomerra*. The boat put off and the shooters set out for Broken Bay after ordering the coxswain to find Governor Phillip and tell him they had spoken to Bennelong. The Eora crowded around the boat as it was leaving and brought down three or four large 'junks' (chunks) of blubber. Bennelong said that the largest piece should be sent to Governor Phillip as a present from him.

Phillip was just leaving South Head when the boat arrived from Manly.

The coxswain told him that the gentlemen going to Broken Bay had had a long conference with Bennelong and Colby, who had inquired about everyone they knew in the settlement, especially Phillip. Bennelong had sent him a piece of whale and promised to return to Sydney with the governor if he would come to meet him. Phillip returned to South Head to collect some gifts for Bennelong – 'every little thing which was likely to please' him. They took four muskets and a pistol, but only two would fire when they were tested.

At Manly Cove the Eora were still gathered around their fires on the beach near the stranded whale. As the governor's boat came into the bay, several natives retreated into the bush. Standing in the boat, Phillip called out for Bennelong, using all five of his names.

– I am here, replied a man some distance away.

– It is *beanga*, said Phillip.

Phillip ordered Waterhouse and Collins to stand by the boat with their muskets at the ready. He stepped onto the beach, taking only one unarmed sailor, who carried some beef, bread and small presents. He held out his arms as a sign of friendship and to show he did not have a musket, but kept his pistol and his dagger or short sword. One man came forward to pick up the presents which were placed on the ground.

– Where is Bennelong? Phillip asked the man.

– I am Bennelong, he replied.

Phillip had not seen Bennelong for four months. He had changed so much that he could not believe it was really him. Bennelong looked 'poor and miserable' with long hair, a beard and a fresh gash over his forehead. However, when a bottle of wine was held up, he eagerly made his accustomed toast: 'The King'. This was enough to convince Phillip that it was, indeed, Bennelong. The governor followed him into the bushes behind the beach, out of sight of the boat, where they talked. Bennelong was pleased to see Phillip and constantly called him Governor and *beanga* and the two men shook hands. Phillip uncorked the wine bottle and poured out a glass, which Bennelong drank with his usual relish and good humour. Bennelong asked by name about everyone he could remember in Sydney, including the French cook and steward de Maliez, always the butt of his ridicule while he was a reluctant guest at the governor's house. Once again, Bennelong imitated the Frenchman's voice, walk and other peculiarities, accurately and drolly.

Colby joined them and took a glass of wine. Phillip gave Bennelong and Colby hats, knives, some bread, and pork. Laughing, Colby mimicked Bennelong's escape, placing his head on his hand, closing his eyes and saying '*Governor nangorar*' (asleep) and pretending to be Bennelong scampering into the bush. Both men constantly asked for hatchets and Phillip promised to bring them one each when he returned in two days with the clothes Bennelong used to wear. Bennelong said he would sleep by the same camp fire until then. Phillip went back to the boat and brought Collins with him to the bushes.

Waterhouse recalled:

> As they went up, I frequently heard a man on the right of them call out 'Bennalon' - & told him of something either what we were doing in the Boat or something he had observed as we kept the Boat on her Oars (which might reasonably occasion some mistrust as the same precaution was [made] when they were forcibly taken away and in the same Cove where the Boat was now laying.[14]

Bennelong asked for Waterhouse and a man was sent to fetch him. At the top of the strip of sand, Waterhouse observed several natives on each side and eight or ten of them in front, all armed with spears, except for Bennelong and Colby, who were deep in conversation with Phillip. As they went up the beach, wrote Watkin Tench, many of the 'Indians' filed off to the right and left 'as if in some measure to surround them', so the party drew back slightly.[15] Waterhouse too had trouble recognising Bennelong until he was pointed out. He shook hands with Bennelong, who was wearing two English jackets, one given to him by Phillip and one by Collins. Colby shook Waterhouse by the hand and asked for help with his jacket, which he could not manage to put on. Bennelong asked particularly about an English woman (probably one of the governor's servants) 'from whom he once ventured to snatch a kiss'. Told that she was in good health, he grasped Waterhouse by the neck, laughed and kissed him, to show he still remembered her.

While walking up, Phillip had seen Bennelong holding an unusual and 'remarkably good' spear and asked him for it. Bennelong, according to Waterhouse, 'either could not, or would not, understand him but took the Spear & laid it down in the grass, during all which time perfect Harmony subsisted'[16]

Tench described the weapon as a 'very fine barbed spear of uncommon size'.[17] Phillip said the spear was 'longer than common, and appeared to be a very curious one, being barbed and pointed with hard wood'.[18] This kind of spear, with one barb cut from the wood, was called a *bil-larr*. Instead of the spear, Bennelong gave Phillip a short spear (or a throwing stick) and a club.

Bennelong then began the customary ceremony of introducing the governor to the strangers, starting with 'a stout, corpulent native' who had been standing nearby, showing 'strong marks of fear'. When Phillip spoke to him in a friendly way, this man pointed out a spear wound in his back. In return, Bennelong proudly showed off his new wounds, which he said he had received in combat at Botany Bay. By this time, the Eora had formed a rough arc around Phillip, Collins, Waterhouse and the sailor.

There were some nineteen armed men close by and more out of sight in the undergrowth. Four men were in front, others grouped to the right and left and still more between them and the beach. This manoeuvre, said Phillip, had been directed by Bennelong and Colby, who waited until it was made before they came close enough to shake hands.[19]

Just as the officers were about to leave, Bennelong introduced another stranger.

'And this is my very intimate friend,' said Bennelong, pointing to a short, sturdy, older man who had been standing 20 or 30 metres away.[20]

Phillip advanced to meet him with his hands outstretched, but the stranger seemed to be afraid and made signs for the governor to stay where he was. Phillip threw his short sword to the ground and held out his hands, but kept his pistol. Collins followed close behind. As Phillip approached, the man suddenly picked up the spear with his toes, fixed it to a *womerra* and stood his ground. It was the same long, barbed spear that Bennelong had put down. Phillip motioned for the man to drop the spear, calling out *Weree weree* ('bad; you are doing wrong' in Tench's translation).

Instead, the warrior suddenly stepped back on his right leg and hurled the spear at the governor with great force. The shaft struck Phillip's right shoulder near the collarbone and came out about 8 centimetres lower, close to the backbone and behind the shoulderblade.

The attacker kept his eye on the spear until it struck and then dashed into the bush. Bennelong and Colby had disappeared. 'Instant confusion on both sides took place,' observed Tench. At that moment, Waterhouse thought Phillip was dead and saw no chance of escape. Waterhouse was close behind Collins as they ran for the boat. He saw Phillip attempting to run, struggling with both hands to hold up the spear, which Waterhouse thought was about twelve feet long, to stop it dragging along the ground, which must have caused great pain.

'For God's sake haul out the spear,' Phillip begged Waterhouse.

Knowing that it was dangerous to remove the barb, Waterhouse tried unsuccessfully to break off the spear shaft. While he was doing this, another spear took off the skin between the thumb and forefinger of his right hand. 'I own it frightened me & I believe added to my exertions,' he admitted later. At the third attempt, Waterhouse broke off the shaft, leaving the point embedded in Phillip's shoulder. Spears were now flying thickly and one fell at Collins's feet. Freed at last from the long spear, Phillip ran down the beach, firing his pistol, while his coxswain, Henry Hone, came from the boat and blasted his musket at the attackers. None of the other muskets would fire.

Phillip, weak and bleeding heavily, was lifted into the boat, which pulled out quickly and covered the 8 kilometres to Sydney Cove within two hours. William Balmain, the first surgeon to meet the boat, quickly extracted the wooden point from Phillip's shoulder and said he would not die from the wound. Despite the agonising pain, Governor Phillip gave explicit orders 'to prevent any of the natives being fired on, unless they were the aggressors, by throwing spears'.

*   *   *

Lieutenant John Long, adjutant of HMS *Sirius*, was sent with a group of armed marines to meet the shooting party and guard them on their return trip to Sydney. Long reached Manly after sunset and pushed on to find Surgeon White's party at two o'clock the following morning, camped about 19 kilometres further north.

Back at Manly Cove, the hunters questioned three Eora men standing on a rock. They asked, through Nanbarry, who had wounded Governor Phillip? The Eora told them that it was a man from the *carigal*, 'a tribe residing at Broken Bay', who was later identified as Willemering.[21] One officer asked them for a spear, which was immediately given to him.

Bennelong and Colby had just left Manly Cove after a friendly meeting with the boat crew. 'Like the others they had pretended highly to disapprove the conduct of the man who had thrown the spear, vowing to execute vengeance upon them.'[22] There was no sign of Bennelong or Colby for more than a week. Phillip, recovering from his wound, was still eager to renew their friendship. To this end, he sent his most trusted officers up and down the harbour to search for Bennelong.

EXHIBIT A

A fresh examination and analysis of the Manly whale feast spearing exposes it as a ritual punishment against Governor Arthur Phillip, instigated and organised by Bennelong as a payback for his abduction and capture in 1789. It was just one of a series of defiant challenges posed by Bennelong against English authority, which greatly increased his influence and power among his own people. This crucial event in cross-cultural relations at Port Jackson would lead to the Eora 'coming in' to live peacefully in the Sydney settlement. Bennelong's actions question the persistent notion that he was a willing collaborator with the invaders of his country and reveal him as a clever politician, whose character was far more complex than it has been previously portrayed.

In evidence, we have the actual words of three eyewitnesses, principally Henry Waterhouse, third lieutenant of HMS *Sirius*; Governor Phillip himself; and, to a lesser extent, his secretary David Collins. Waterhouse's account survives in letters to his father purchased in 1998 by the Mitchell Library, Sydney, and in slightly varying statements he made to Watkin Tench and William Bradley. Phillip's version of the incident appeared (edited into the third person) in John Hunter's *An Historical Journal*

(London, 1793). This narrative was based on Phillip's official reports and makes a nonsense of the frequent claim that he did not mention that he had been wounded in his dispatches. This account relies on all these original sources.[23]

Many historians agree with his principal biographer Isadore Brodsky that 'Bennelong can be seen to have had no culpable part in this sensational incident'.[24] They frequently echo David Collins, who wrote: 'No other motive could be assigned for this conduct in the savage, than the supposed apprehension that he was about to be seized by the governor, which the circumstance of his advancing toward him with his hands held out might create.'[25] The inference is usually drawn that Willemering threw the spear at Phillip from fear that he might be abducted in the same way as Bennelong and Colby.

Among the doubters, anthropologist Isabel McBryde in *Guests of the Governor* (1989) suspected power plays 'within the local Aboriginal society involving interaction with the European community' and suggested that closer anthropological analysis 'could well be rewarding'.[26]

What really happened at the whale feast? Looking at the historical evidence, it becomes clear from a close reading of Waterhouse's eyewitness account that Bennelong was the mastermind behind this violation. Bennelong chose the time and place by asking Phillip to come to see him at Manly Cove. Bennelong and Colby directed the movements of the armed men who encircled Phillip. Bennelong handled the unusually long barbed wooden spear (which he refused to give to Phillip) and put it down on the ground. This was the spear that Willemering picked up and threw at Phillip. If Bennelong had been brought to trial, the spear which wounded the governor would have been marked as 'Exhibit A', but there was never any attempt to charge him with a crime.

The action of the avenging party in forming a half circle to ambush Phillip fits all the precedents for ritual punishment under Aboriginal law, in which the victims are often wounded or killed by deceit or trickery. In these cases, a *kadaicha* man, equivalent to the Sydney area *carradhy* or *koradgee*, is often brought in to do the spearing. Willemering, who threw the spear, was a *koradgee* from Carigal or Gurugal on the south shore of Broken Bay near the present West Head in Ku-rin-gai National Park.

A spear wound would be sufficient to satisfy Bennelong's grievances. Atonement was necessary before he could resume a friendly dialogue once more with Phillip.

In the published account based on his dispatches to London, Phillip questioned Bennelong's behaviour, which, he said, was 'not so easily to be accounted for; he never attempted to interfere when the man took the spear up, or said a single word to prevent him from throwing it'. Almost in the same breath, Phillip excused Bennelong, because 'he probably did not think the spear would be thrown, and the whole was but the business of a moment'. Two pages later, Phillip reflects that his life must surely have hung in the balance: 'Though Bannelong probably might be glad that Governor Phillip was not killed, yet there is no doubt that the natives throw their spears, and take a life in their quarrels, which are very frequent, as readily as the lower class of people in England strip to box, and think as little of the consequences.'[27]

'There are different opinions as to Colby or Benallon being accessories to this assault, which I cannot but mistrust was the case,' wrote William Bradley, who did not hear about the incident until his return from Norfolk Island, where HMS *Sirius* was wrecked in March 1790.[28] In his account, published in 1798, Collins criticised Phillip for placing 'too great a confidence in these people, under an idea that the sight of firearms would deter them from approaching', adding that the governor had been taught a lesson that he would never forget.[29]

'The deeper motive of the attack remains a mystery,' wrote the eminent anthropologist W.E.H. Stanner in his analysis of the event. 'Historians tend to regard the assault as the act of a frightened man. That seems improbable.' Stanner put forward six possible major grievances which might have been expressed in the attack, one of which, 'by Benelong, his relatives and friends', seems most plausible. To Phillip's credit, wrote Stanner, 'he allowed no retaliation, and harboured no resentment'.[30]

The wound in Phillip's shoulder healed quickly and he was 'perfectly recovered' within six weeks. Having no go-betweens as interpreters, apart from the two children Boorong and Nanbarry, Phillip was determined to find Bennelong and to be reconciled to him at any cost.

9

COMING IN

'Scenes of bloodshed and horror' might have been expected after the attack on Governor Phillip at the whale feast, wrote Watkin Tench.[1] Reprisals against the natives by armed marines would certainly have followed if Phillip had not recovered from his spear wound. What did happen seems, even in hindsight, much more unlikely.

One week later, on 14 September 1790, Lieutenant William Dawes and Chaplain Richard Johnson, accompanied by Boorong in a boat, met her father Maugoran, an elder of the *burramattagal* (Parramatta clan), with another man (possibly Boorodel). They revealed that the man who had speared the governor was called Wil-ee-ma-rin and seemed happy when told that the governor was likely to recover. Maugoran and his companion complained about the number of whites who had settled in their territories, wrote Tench.[2] In his dispatches, Phillip gave Maugoran's words a stronger emphasis: 'If this man's information could be depended on, the natives were very angry at so many people being sent to Rose-hill [Parramatta],' he wrote, adding, 'certain it is that wherever our colonists fix themselves, the natives are obliged to leave that part of the country.' Phillip's immediate reaction to Maugoran's protest was to reinforce the detachment at Rose Hill the next day.

After the attack on Phillip, Maugoran had been wounded at Manly Cove in a dispute over sharing the whale blubber. He told the surgeon who dressed his wounds that several men had been killed in this battle. When Boorong spoke to her father about a young man at *Kay-yee-my* (Manly Cove) who wanted to marry her, he ordered her to stay away from the north shore. The *cameragal*, Maugoran warned, were ready to 'throw spears' and would attack any white man.[3]

The next morning (15 September) several officers, including Surgeon John White and Commissary John Palmer, found Bennelong and Barangaroo among a group of Eora on the north shore. Bennelong came down to the boat and shook hands with several people. He asked if Governor Phillip was dead, and when told he was not, promised to come to see him at Sydney Cove. Bennelong claimed he had beaten Willemering. The conversation was interpreted by the two children, Boorong and Nanbarry, who were also in the boat. This group, unlike most other natives, did not show any signs of fear of the English muskets. Boorong asked to stay with her father, but they would not permit it. White and Palmer urged Bennelong to arrange a husband for Boorong, someone who would be free to come and go from the settlement. They invited Yemmerrawanne, 'a slender fine looking youth … about sixteen years old', to approach Boorong, but, said Tench, she 'disclaimed his advances, repeating the name of another person, who we knew was her favourite'.

That afternoon, an English party went ashore without arms to meet their Eora friends as arranged. 'Several little presents, which had been purposely brought, were distributed among them.' Bennelong was given an iron hatchet and some fish. A group of shy children were persuaded to join the men. Someone brought out a bottle of wine and Bennelong called loudly for bread and beef and began to eat and drink. Two of his friends tasted the meat, but none would touch the bread. Bennelong's face was shaved 'to the great admiration of his countrymen, who laughed and exclaimed at the operation', wrote Tench. The others refused to be shaved, but did not mind having their beards trimmed with scissors.

Boorong was sent to fetch an Eora woman, who Bennelong said was his wife Barangaroo, 'notwithstanding he had so lately pretended she had left him for Colbee [Colby]'. Boorong put a petticoat on Barangaroo and brought her to them. 'But this was the prudery of the wilderness, which her husband joined us to ridicule,' wrote Tench, 'and we soon laughed her out of it.' Barangaroo dropped the petticoat and stood naked from head to toe. She was delighted at having her hair cut and combed, but refused to taste the wine and turned away from it with disgust, though Bennelong urged her to drink 'by example and persuasion'.

Yemmerrawanne again flirted with Boorong, who now seemed to welcome his attention. The English visitors began to 'play and romp' with the Eora. In a feat of strength, a sailor from the boat crew easily lifted two Eora men off the ground, though not one of them could budge him. They called him *murree mulla* ('big man'). Boorong was instructed to take Barangaroo aside and urge her to visit Sydney, with the intention of attracting Bennelong and others there. The two women wandered off talking together, but even from a distance the officers could see that Barangaroo's arguments in favour of Boorong rejoining her people were more forceful than the girl's attempt to get her to 'come among' the whites. Afterwards, the moody Boorong wanted to stay with Barangaroo and sat in the boat sulking.

Bennelong complained that some of the foreigners had recently stolen spears, fishing spears and other weapons. He asked for these items to be returned and said that if they were, he would give back the governor's dagger (left on the beach at the whale feast) if they came to the same place.

The following day (16 September) an English party crossed the harbour in boats to return the stolen property, but Bennelong and Barangaroo were out fishing. As soon as the boat landed, Yemmerrawanne came forward and claimed a club. Showing off to Boorong, he brandished the weapon and battered a grass tree with it, shouting, gesturing and calling on everyone to look at him. 'Having conquered his enemy,' said Tench, 'he laid aside his fighting face, and joined us with a countenance which carried in it every mark of youth and good nature.' After that, Yemmerrawanne ignored Boorong. Though too young to grow a beard, he delighted in having his hair clipped and combed.

An older man took a fishing spear from the bundle, while another, aged between thirty and forty, with a face marked by smallpox, stood apart 'in a musing posture, contemplating what passed'. He seemed happy enough and shook hands with anyone who approached him. Around his neck hung a *gwee-rang*, a necklace made of pieces of dried reed threaded on string, which Tench wanted to swap for a 'stock' (a woollen stocking or sock). Although he smiled in a good-natured way, the man would not part with his beads, but Yemmerrawanne snatched them off and put them around Tench's neck. 'I feared he would be enraged,' said Tench, 'but he bore it with serenity, and suffered a gentleman present to fasten his black stock upon him, with which he appeared to be pleased.'

An hour later the boat party left to look for Bennelong and Barangaroo. When they found them on a beach cooking some fish over a small fire, the couple ran away, but returned when their names were called. The rest of the stolen implements were returned to Bennelong. Barangaroo reclaimed a net containing fishing gear which she slung around her neck. Bennelong asked after Phillip, but did not produce the governor's dagger and pretended to know nothing about it, changing the subject by asking for wine, which they gave him to drink.[4]

Nearly 4000 sea salmon, each weighing about 2 kilograms, were caught in two hauls of the seine net by the English fishing boats that day. Some were issued as rations at Sydney and Rose Hill. 'Thirty or forty were sent as a conciliating present to Bennillong and his party on the north shore,' Collins recorded.[5] Bennelong's visitors had given him some of the fish and further supplies were brought by Phillip's orderly sergeant, who Bennelong regarded as his great friend. As they left, the English officers pressed Bennelong to say when he would come to Sydney, where he would be well received and treated kindly. Bennelong insisted that Phillip must first come to see him, and they promised he would.[6]

'The Governor Walks Out and is getting Quite the better of his Wound,' wrote Sergeant Scott in his journal on 17 September 1790.[7] That morning, Phillip and Boorong went by boat to the cove opposite Sydney where Bennelong and his wife had set up camp in a rock overhang. The Eora there said that Bennelong was fishing. Phillip gave an iron hatchet and some fish to Boorong's father Maugoran, who, in exchange, gave the governor a short spear. Instead of the usual shell, this spear was pointed with a metal knife, the first record of such an innovation by the Eora.

As the boat party set out to look for Bennelong, they saw four canoes coming towards them and rowed back to the cove. This significant moment is captured by the artist known as the Port Jackson Painter in the watercolour *Ban nal lang meeting the Governor by appointment*. It shows the encounter between Bennelong, another man and two women (in separate canoes), with Phillip and an officer (wearing tall hats) and eight oarsmen in their boat. Bennelong, in the nearest canoe, holds out a paddle as a signal to the boat. The woman in the second canoe is probably Barangaroo.[8]

Pulling his canoe up the beach, Bennelong came to the boat. He greeted Phillip and asked about his wound. 'Bennillong then repeated his assurances of his having, in conjunction with his friend Cole-by, severely beaten Wil-le-me-ring,' wrote Collins, 'and added that [Willemering's] throwing the spear at the governor was entirely the effect of his fears, and done from the impulse of self-preservation.'[9] When told that Willemering would be executed for his treachery, Bennelong 'desired it might be done', wrote Phillip.

Phillip presented Bennelong with a hatchet and fishing lines and Barangaroo with a petticoat (which the Eora called a *matty*) and other gifts. Bennelong was especially pleased when the red jacket with a silver epaulet which he used to wear at the governor's house was returned to him. He agreed to have dinner with Phillip the following day and promised to bring Barangaroo. He pointed out a youth and two men who had been given hatchets (probably Boorong's brothers) and said he would bring them with him.

However, Bennelong did not keep this appointment until some three weeks later.

The early spring weather was dry and some natives could be seen on the north shore opposite Sydney Cove burning the undergrowth to catch 'rats and other animals' while the women were fishing. Bennelong played a waiting game. Although he did not come to Sydney, he and Barangaroo paddled in their canoe to parley with the crew of the longboat of HMS *Sirius* on the harbour.

While there was the least chance of Bennelong coming in voluntarily, Phillip wrote, he was not willing to take him by force again as 'it was likely he would soon be reconciled to pass a considerable part of his time at Sydney, when he found he could be his own master, and come and go when he pleased'.[10]

Towards the end of September, as Phillip was going to Rose Hill by boat he hailed a native on one of the harbour headlands. Asked where

Bennelong was, the man replied 'Memilla' (at Me-mel or Memill, now called Goat Island, opposite the Sydney suburb of Balmain). They rowed to the island and Bennelong and Barangaroo came down to talk to Phillip, who gave them some bread. 'From the confidence Bannelong now placed in his visitors, there was no doubt but he would soon come to the settlement as usual,' Phillip commented.[11] When Phillip returned two days later, Bennelong had left the island. Bennelong told David Collins, the colony's chief legal officer, that Me-mel was his property and that it had once belonged to his father and he intended to give it to his affiliate Bigon. Bennelong and his family often feasted and fished there. Bennelong said that other Eora 'possessed this kind of hereditary property, which they retained undisturbed'.[12]

On the morning of 8 October, a plume of smoke was seen on the north shore opposite the settlement, a prearranged signal that Bennelong would welcome visitors. 'Various parties accordingly set out to meet them, provided with different articles, which we thought would prove acceptable to them,' Tench wrote. They were welcomed by Bennelong, Barangaroo, a young woman and six men, while an older man stood apart from the group.

When they saw that their visitors had brought hatchets and other articles, the Eora took out spears, fishing spears and fishing lines to exchange. 'It had long been our wish to establish a commerce of this sort,' wrote Tench in a footnote. 'It is a painful consideration, that every previous addition to the cabinet of the virtuosi, from this country, had wrung a tear from the plundered Indian.' Tench had an old blunt spear which needed repairing. One man took it to the fire, tore a piece of fish bone from a fishing spear with his teeth and stuck it to the spear with yellow gum which he heated on the fire. Tench gave the man an iron hatchet for his trouble. He asked a barber who was shaving the Eora men to try to obtain a fine barbed spear, but the man who held the weapon would only part with it for a hatchet. 'In vain did I tempt him with a knife, a handkerchief, and a hat, nothing but a hatchet seemed to be regarded. *Bulla Mogo Parrabugo* (two hatchets tomorrow), I repeatedly cried; but probably having experienced our insincerity, he rejected the proposal with disdain.' Keen to acquire the spear, Tench took a boat back to Sydney Cove to find a hatchet.[13]

While Tench was away, Bennelong had seen Phillip returning from Rose Hill by boat and called to him repeatedly. White persuaded Bennelong and three other natives to cross the harbour in his canoe to visit the governor. Coming back, Tench was surprised to see the boats with Bennelong and his friends heading in the direction of Sydney Cove. He quickly swapped his iron hatchet with a man in a canoe, who held out the spear he wanted and gave him a throwing stick as a bonus.

Barangaroo angrily resented Bennelong's decision to visit the settlement.

She cried hysterically, scolded and threatened him, stamped her feet and tore at her hair. When Bennelong insisted, she snatched one of his fishing spears and broke it against the rocks. To calm her, Chaplain Johnson and Boorong agreed to remain with Barangaroo as 'hostages' until Bennelong returned. A convict called 'Stogdale' (John Stockdale) was also obliged to stay, 'as a pledge that Banalong & the Other three, Return'd', wrote Sergeant Scott.[14]

The boats and canoe tied up on the east side of Sydney Cove at the Governor's Wharf, opposite the hospital. As they set off for Phillip's house, a curious crowd flocked around to see Bennelong and the others, who fearlessly marched through them. Bennelong was delighted to be reunited with Phillip and pleased that he had recovered from his wound. He told the governor that Willemering was at Broken Bay. The native guests were served with bread and beef, but there was no fish, which they had been promised to tempt them across the harbour. Each man was given a hatchet, while petticoats and some fishing lines were sent across to Barangaroo and another woman.

Bennelong soon felt at home again in the governor's two-storey residence. As soon as the formalities were over, he ran from room to room with his friends and introduced them to the household servants 'in the most familiar manner'. He kissed Phillip's orderly sergeant 'with great affection' and also kissed a kitchen maid. As usual, Bennelong demonstrated his particular dislike of the governor's gamekeeper, John McEntire, and would not let him come near him.

Bennelong showed his friends all the strange new objects, but confused them when he called a pair of candle snuffers in English 'Nuffer for candle'. Attempting to explain, he used the big finger of his left hand to represent a candle and mimed the operation of extinguishing the flame. When his friends still did not understand, he threw down the snuffer in disgust and walked away, telling them that they were stupid. Tench noticed that Bennelong had quite forgotten the soft, gentle tone of voice he had been taught to use, although, like Arabanoo, he showed great affection for the white children who were brought to see him. Bennelong, said Phillip, 'appeared very much at his ease, and not under the least apprehension of being detained; promising, when he went away, to bring his wife over, which he did two days afterwards'.[15]

In order to banish all appearances of restraint, wrote Tench, Bennelong and his companions were taken back to the north shore by Surgeon White and others as soon as they wanted to leave. There they found Boorong and some women fishing from a canoe, while Chaplain Johnson sat by the fire with Barangaroo, who was making shell fishhooks. Nearby, on higher ground, an Eora man with a spear watched over them. Barangaroo had continued to whine and rebuke Bennelong while he was away, but when he returned, she quietly went about her work. Bennelong was furious when he saw she had broken his fishing spear and threatened to hit her with the pieces, but White restrained him and Barangaroo said she was sorry. Then Barangaroo refused to return his embraces, 'elated by his condescension, and emboldened by our presence, and the finery [petticoats] in which we had decked her'. Subdued, Bennelong seemed 'anxious only to please her'.

'Thus ended a day,' wrote Tench, 'the events of which served to complete, what an unhappy accident had begun. From this time our intercourse with the natives, though partially interrupted, was never broken off. We gradually continued, henceforth, to gain knowledge of their customs and policy: the only knowledge that can lead to a just estimate of national character.'[16] 'This accident gave cause to the opening of a communication between the natives of this country and the settlement,' commented Collins, 'which, although attended with such an unpromising beginning, it was hoped would be followed with good consequences.'[17] Just five months had passed since Bennelong's escape from the governor's house in May 1790.

Two days later (10 October), Bennelong brought one of his sisters and three men into the settlement. They were given blankets and clothing and each ate 'a belly-full' of fish. Bennelong 'sat down to dinner with Governor Phillip, and drank his wine and coffee as usual'. Phillip acquired a spear from one of the visitors (probably in exchange for a hatchet) and tried to make them understand that spears, lines, birds or whatever they brought with them should always be purchased. He promised Bennelong a shield in return for a spear, 'as accustoming these people to barter was judged the most likely means of bringing them to reside among the colonists'.

Boorong joined Bennelong's sister and some other young people in their canoe. She had now lived one year and three months with the Reverend Mr Johnson and his wife Mary and was so keen to go away that she was now given permission. Next day Boorong was seen naked in a canoe, but she put on a petticoat when Johnson arrived. Encouraged by her example, Nanbarry asked to spend the night with the Eora and was left with them. The following morning, however, he came to see White and did not seem to want to go back. A large group of Eora visited Sydney to collect the shield that had been promised to Bennelong, but it was still not ready.

'The natives now visited the settlement daily,' wrote Phillip. On the morning of 17 October, Bennelong came to the governor's house for the first time for several days, but left soon after breakfast. He told Phillip that he was going 'a great way off' with two young men and would not come back for three days. It was assumed that Bennelong was going somewhere to fight, most likely to Botany Bay.

Colby, Nanbarry's uncle, was also drawn into the peace agreement.

On 18 October 1790, the day HMS *Supply* returned to Sydney from Batavia (Jakarta), Phillip met him 'at the next cove' (Farm Cove) with two little girls and two young men who had already been into the settlement. 'A hatchet, was, as usual, desired and given, and Colebe promised to come to dinner the next day.'[18]

A convict had been missing for some time and it was believed that he had been killed by the natives. Military patrols met with two large groups of Eora, one of about forty and the other of less than twenty men. While out searching for the convict on 19 October, a sergeant and three soldiers met Bennelong and Colby at the head of a band of men and boys. Bennelong tried to persuade the marines to go with him to kill a man 'well known for having lost an eye, and who was supposed to be a leader of the tribe that reside about Botany-Bay', an obvious reference to the *bidjigal* warrior Pemulwuy. However, the soldiers took no notice of Bennelong's plea. While some of the Eora continued on their way, Colby returned to Sydney Cove to eat with the governor as he had promised and Bennelong and several others decided to come with him.

While at Botany Bay, Bennelong had fought with a man who had previously wounded him, probably Mety. He said his spear had gone through both the shield and hand of his opponent and claimed that the clan he had been fighting had murdered the escaped convict.

Boorong came back to Sydney after an absence of eighteen days. According to Hunter, 'she appeared to have fared badly, and had been beat by her friend Colebe'. This might indicate either a paternal or sexual interest in Boorong on Colby's part. Two days later, however, Boorong 'returned to her companions' on the north shore.

By the end of October 1790, wrote Phillip, 'They [the settlers] were frequently visited by many of the natives, some of whom daily came to the barracks: all of them were very fond of bread, and they now found the advantage of coming among the settlers'.[19]

RECONCILIATION

The peaceful coming-in of the Eora to Sydney in October 1790 was skilfully and equally devised by two men, Arthur Phillip and Woollarawarre Bennelong. On the one hand it was a triumph of Phillip's diplomatic skill and his ready gifts of iron hatchets and other goods. The governor assured Bennelong and his people that they would not be forcibly captured, manacled or held against their will, but could come and go from the settlement without restraint. They would be provided with plenty of fish, bread and meat, blankets, hatchets and other European goods. Bennelong was promised a tin shield and asked Governor Phillip to build him a brick house.

The Eora, for their part, would put an end to active resistance and live on a friendly basis with the white people who had occupied their country. This was a triumph for Bennelong, who had been a leader of the Eora resistance and now promoted reconciliation and coexistence. Nothing was ever put into writing, but it is obvious that a verbal peace agreement had been reached between the two parties. This was the result of negotiations conducted through Boorong, with Bennelong and her father Maugoran and his family, and through Nanbarry, with Colby and his affiliates.

While the treaty might have been verbal, in the eyes of the Eora it was binding and had been sealed with handshakes, friendly meetings and symbolic gifts of iron hatchets, knives, metal fishhooks, European clothing, blankets, fish, bread, meat and wine. While the English officers might regard such gifts simply as bribes, the indigenous people saw them as symbolic and reciprocal; in effect drawing the colonists into a web of binding social obligations. Traditionally, gifts were given to settle grievances or debts, and, in this case, they could be seen as compensation for the loss of Eora territory.

Bennelong throughout these meetings had demonstrated his skill as a wily politician and a master of adaptation and improvisation when confronted with the superior technology of a powerful and alien culture.

In recognition of the new understanding between the two races, Governor Phillip built Bennelong a brick hut at *Tubowgullee*, 'the extremity of the eastern point of [Sydney] Cove', now known as Bennelong Point and the site of the Sydney Opera House. Bennelong had chosen the place himself, wrote Watkin Tench. Bennelong's hut had a tiled roof and was about 3.5 metres square.[20] It had an exterior brick chimney, which is shown clearly in contemporary views of Sydney Cove.[21]

'A House of Bricks was Run up for a Chief calld Bennelong ... where his Wife Children and Relations often Come & stay a Day or two – Since When, Many More Men Women & Children are Come Among Us, & are Sometimes quite familiar,' wrote Midshipman David Blackburn.[22] Bennelong and Barangaroo came into town each day with half a dozen friends and several children. They seemed to have adopted two children whose parents had died. Colby, said Phillip, 'was generally one of the party'.[23]

In December 1790, however, Phillip 'began to suspect, though very unwillingly, that there was a great deal of art and cunning in Bennelong; he had lately been at Botany Bay, where, he said, they danced, and that one of the tribe had sung a song, the subject of which was, his house, the governor, and the white men at Sydney'.[24]

In Aboriginal culture, songs relate people to each other and to their totems and country. By telling Governor Phillip of the song about his house in Sydney, Bennelong asserted ownership of the site, although it lay in *cadigal* territory. The corroboree at Botany Bay celebrated peace with the *gweagal*, who, said Bennelong, 'would not throw any more spears, as they and the Cammeragals [*cameragal*] were all friends and were good men; this was only a few days after he had said that he liked his house at the point, because the Botany-Bay men and the Cammeragals would not come to it on account of the white men; and had, as usual, whenever those tribes were mentioned, requested the governor to kill them all'.[25]

Just as Phillip's house overlooking Sydney Cove symbolised the power of the whites to the Eora, it could be said that Bennelong's hut, a make-believe governor's house, was in a sense the first Aboriginal Embassy in Australia. Some other Eora also settled there, according to historian J.P. McGuane. 'For Bennelong and three more blacks huts were built on the point of land now bearing his name,' wrote McGuane. 'Biscuits steeped in molasses, a plentiful supply of fish, and Phillip's protection, were inducements which soon tempted other blacks to dwell in the vicinity,' he added.[26]

However, by May 1792, neither Bennelong nor his family lived permanently in their 'very neat brick hut', according to George Thompson. 'They will sometimes stay at the place for a day, then make a fire on the outside of it. In short, they prefer living in the woods and going naked to the best house or clothes in the colony.' The Eora, Thompson pointed out, 'cannot bear to be confined to a hut or tent'.[27]

A reference to Bennelong Point was made in about 1793 by convict artist Thomas Watling, who arrived in Sydney in October 1792. Watling added the caption 'A View of the west Side of Sydney Cove taken from Too-bay-ulee, or Bannellongs Point' to a pencil, ink and wash illustration.[28] In *An Account of the English Colony in New South Wales* (London, 1798), David Collins mentioned salt-making operations at 'Bennillong's Point (as the east point of the cove had long been named)'.[29] According to the *Sydney Gazette*, 'Bennelong's Point' was the scene of Aboriginal hostilities in October 1804.[30]

SPEAR AND SHIELD

On 8 April 1998, Christies, the London auction house, offered for sale a metal blade, 7 cm long and 0.6 cm wide, with an accompanying label ('in late nineteenth-century hand') reading: 'Spearhead – taken out of Govr. Phillips shoulder by Captain Henry Waterhouse – NSW'.[31]

In the same lot was a fourteen-page notebook which included Lieutenant Henry Waterhouse's description of the incident in which Governor Arthur Phillip was speared at Manly Cove in September 1790. The notebook was purchased by the Mitchell Library, State Library of New South Wales, while the spearhead was sold to a private collector.

This metal blade could not have been removed from Phillip's shoulder because it was never there. As we have seen, the spear which struck Governor Phillip on 17 September 1790 was a *billarr*, with a wooden shaft and a barbed wooden point, as he and other eyewitnesses state, which was removed from Phillip's shoulder by Surgeon Balmain. In a letter written in March 1791, Dr John Harris said 'the Barb was sawn of[f] and extracted early'.[32] The auctioned blade is, however, consistent with the description of a 'short spear that had been pointed with a knife' which Phillip exchanged with the *burramattagal* elder Maugoran in return for an iron hatchet and some fish on 17 September 1790. By using a knife blade as the point of a spear, Maugoran had incorporated an English artefact into an Eora one, which he now returned. There must have been other similar spears, because Phillip said that the natives liked to use a knife to point their spears 'when they could procure one, in preference to the shell'.[33]

Both Bennelong and Colby had been given English knives at the whale feast at Manly Cove. As the Eora often exchanged weapons and other goods among themselves, it is likely that one of these knives was used by Maugoran to make the hybrid spear. Otherwise, Maugoran could have obtained a knife from his daughter Boorong, who lived with Chaplain Johnson and his wife and was often at the governor's house. According to John Harris the Eora had begun to use glass from English bottles for spear barbs in place of shell, wood or bone.[34]

Bennelong had developed the agility of slipping easily from the conventions of one culture to the other. At Phillip's house, he was expected to wear the foreign jackets and clothing he had been given, but he took them off as soon as he left the settlement. 'One day he would appear in them; and the next day he was to be seen carrying them in a net, slung around his neck,' wrote Tench.[35] 'However well you may cloathe these people,' wrote Phillip, 'they generally return naked the next day.' Bennelong, said Phillip, had kept very few of the clothes and other articles that had been given to him. 'His shield, and most of his cloaths, were, by his own account, sent a great distance off; but whether he had lost them, or given them away, was uncertain.'[36] Bennelong was probably putting the gifts he received to good use, by exchanging them to seal agreements with his friends and affiliates and to forge new alliances with former rivals.

Bennelong's shield is a saga in itself. Phillip had first promised Bennelong a shield 'for which he was to bring a spear in return' on 10 October 1790.[37] The next day a large group of Eora, including Ballooderry and his brother, came to Sydney to collect the shield, but it was not finished.[38] Bennelong was given the shield a few days later, when he came to dine with Governor Phillip. He 'left the place highly delighted with his shield, which being made of [shoe] sole leather and covered with tin, was likely to resist the force of their spears'. Barangaroo and one of Bennelong's sisters, with two men, came in their canoes to collect him. 'There was every appearance of these people being perfectly reconciled,' Phillip commented, 'and no doubt could be entertained but that they would visit the settlement as frequently as could be wished.'[39]

After Bennelong returned from the ritual battles at Botany Bay, he told Phillip at dinner on 19 October that his shield was *boojery* (good).[40] 'Elated by these marks of favour' (the hut and shield), Bennelong, said Tench, understood that his importance with his own people 'arose in proportion to our patronage of him, [and] warmly attached himself to our society'.[41]

Bennelong took his leather and tin shield to the Manly area, but returned to Sydney without it, claiming he had lost it. However, the shield was neither lost nor passed on in exchange. The *cameragal* had ruled that Bennelong would have an unequal advantage in parrying spears in ritual battles. 'In fact,' wrote Collins, 'it had been taken from him by the people of the north shore district and destroyed; it being deemed unfair to cover himself with such a guard.'[42]

10

GETTING WORDS

In November 1790, one month after Bennelong and the friendly Eora began to frequent the settlement growing around Sydney Cove, William Dawes, a young marine officer from Portsmouth, opened a small notebook and began to write down words and phrases from their language. Dawes (1762-1836) had a classical education and was a skilled surveyor, engineer, and map maker. He had seen active service in North America and was wounded at Chesapeake Bay in 1781. He supervised the building of the first earthwork redoubt on the eastern side of Sydney Cove, laid out the Government Farm (present Royal Botanic Gardens) and streets of Sydney Town and Parramatta. Dawes had been trained as an astronomer and lived in a hut next to his observatory, built in 1788 on a sandstone outcrop on the western point of Sydney Cove, near the southern pylons of today's Sydney Harbour Bridge, now named Dawes Point in his honour.

In his notebook, Dawes often acknowledged his informants, who were among the first indigenous Australians to become familiar with the English way of life. He recorded the meaning of words and phrases they told him in their own language and struggled with the unfamiliar verb system.[1] The children Nanbarry (written as Nanbarri and Nanbarree) and Boorong are mentioned on 19 and 25 November, Bennelong (Benelong) and his wife Barangaroo (Berangaroo) on 23 November and Colby (Kolby) on 21 December 1790. Others noted in this early contact period were Boorong's brothers Yeranibe (Yirinibe) and Ballooderry (Baluderri), two young men, Angangan and Kooroooda (Goorooda), and a young girl, Warreweer (Warwiar the less).

Some of the dialogues in Dawes's first notebook, like the first words most people learn in a foreign language, concerned eating and drinking. For example:

Bye & bye Patabangoon } Bye & bye We Dawes
Dawes, Benelong   } and Benelong shall eat

This was said by Benelong a little before dinner on 23d Novr 1790[2]

Patalieba   He will eat

Benelong a little after the above, having observed that I ate nothing & being told by me that I was going on board the Supply repeated what I said to him, to his wife and added Patalieba or He will eat signifying that I was going on board to dinner.[3]

Widabangoon tea } We shall drink tea
touga   } and sugar

Bennelong, who had obviously become fond of his cup of tea, told Dawes that same day.[4]

'The natives never use the letter S, and find some difficulty in pronouncing it,' wrote Arthur Phillip in February 1790.[5] Because of this, stated Watkin Tench, the Eora, who could otherwise perfectly mimic anything said to them, struggled to repeat some English words. 'When bidden to pronounce sun, they always say tun; salt, talt; and so on of all words wherein it occurs.'[6] Later, Tench wrote: 'The letters s and v they could never pronounce, the latter became invariably w, and the former mocked all their efforts, which in the instance of Baneelon has been noticed.'[7]

Governor Phillip had been instructed to 'endeavour, by every possible means, to open an intercourse with the natives'. This had led to the capture of Arabanoo and then Bennelong and Colby.

Official efforts to obtain the language of the native people around Sydney were pursued by Phillip himself, his secretary David Collins and other officers. In his journal, dated 9 April 1790, Philip Gidley King included a 'very Correct Vocabulary' of the native language of the Sydney area, which, he wrote, 'I got from Mr. Collins & Governor Phillip, both having been very assiduous in getting words to compose it, which they compare'.[8] This word list was the basis for the vocabulary, 'very much enlarged by Captain Hunter', printed in *An Historical Journal* (1793), which King says 'Mr. Collins permitted me to copy'.[9]

King's list of words, as language scholar Jakelin Troy (1993a) points out, is very similar to the content of the third unpublished notebook held in the Marsden Collection at the School of African and Oriental Studies in London, which is very different to Dawes's two informal notebooks.[10] Much of the manuscript is written in neat copperplate, but there are entries in several hands, among them, says Troy, the 'rough hand' of Arthur Phillip. Based on a study of handwriting styles, Troy has argued convincingly that this notebook was compiled by Phillip, Collins and Hunter.[11] At the time of writing this book, Phillip's formal handwriting can be compared with the original text of his letters to Sir Joseph Banks on the State Library of New South Wales Internet website.

From its third page and throughout, the anonymous manuscript lists Eora names of individuals who came into the settlement after October 1790. Therefore King copied his vocabulary in April 1790 from a word list that preceded the existing manuscript. This original list must have been gathered by the executive officers from Arabanoo, Nanbarry and

Boorong. However, the majority of the words and phrases in the existing anonymous manuscript were gleaned from Bennelong, who was quizzed regularly during his five months of captivity in 1789-90 and during his regular visits to Governor Phillip after October 1790. Phillip spoke Portuguese and French and owed his skill in foreign languages to his father Jacob, a German-born language teacher.

A great deal of information obtained from Bennelong was incorporated into the First Fleet journals and, subsequently, the first histories written about Australia. 'Man is inseparable from language and language implies society,' Claude Lévi-Strauss realised after his travels in South America with the Nambikwara.[12] At Sydney Cove, Bennelong had become a cultural mediator, responsible, in large part, for preserving vital knowledge about the social life of his people, in their own words and through their own language.

EORA

Entries in the language notebooks, including a second notebook by William Dawes, provide conclusive evidence that the indigenous people living around Port Jackson and along the Parramatta River called themselves Eora, 'men or people'.

In his journal, King gives 'Eo-ra – Men, or People',[13] while 'Eo-ra (or) E-o-rah' is the translation for 'People' in the anonymous 'Vocabulary' probably preparred by Phillip and Collins.[14] Dawes has the sentence: 'Yenmaou mullnaoul naabaou eéora', which means, he says, 'In plain English: I will go tomorrow morning to see the people'.[15] 'Yo-ra. A number of people' occurs in the vocabulary printed in Hunter (1793).[16] In his published vocabulary (1798) David Collins listed 'Eo-ora The name common for the natives'[17] and in the Appendix Collins writes: 'I then asked him where the black men (or Eora) came from?'[18]

Dawes, writes James Kohen (1988), indicates that the root of the word is *ora*, meaning 'a place' or 'country'. The prefix *E-e* is given by Daniel Southwell as the word for yes. 'The Eora, then,' writes Kohen, 'were the people from the country where the word for "yes" was "e-e", that is the Sydney coastal region.'[19]

11

ABDUCTING A WIFE

Bennelong had received a bad gash to his forehead in November 1790 while fighting a ritual duel at Botany Bay with 'an old man named Me-ty'. He returned to Sydney with Mety's daughter, who he had abducted by force. David Collins gave the girl's name as Go-roo-bar-roo-bool-lo,[1] but William Dawes preferred to spell it phonetically as Kurubarabulu and said she was about seventeen years old, while Phillip estimated her age at about fifteen.[2]

This account only partly explains the ensuing puzzling and violent behaviour by Bennelong against Kurubarabulu, his wife Barangaroo, and Governor Phillip, which remains as confusing today as it was to the First Fleet observers. In the long run, these events would culminate in Bennelong taking the girl as his second wife (she was to stay with him for the next two years). Taking a second wife was not unusual among the Eora, but capturing a woman from a hostile group during a revenge expedition seems to have been rare. However, Spencer and Gillen (1899) noted abduction as one of four methods used to obtain a wife in Central Australia, a practice described in the Kimberleys (Western Australia), said A. P. Elkin (1966), as 'pulling a woman'.[3] It seems that in Bennelong's case, his abduction of Kurubarabulu was a hostile act which was later ratified or legalised by the giving of gifts or the conclusion of peace between the clans.

According to William Dawes, Kurubarabulu was the younger sister of Colby's *damelian* or namesake Warungin or Botany Bay Kolbi and the elder sister of a boy called Karangarany (possibly Punangan or Anganangan).[4]

'The governor's wound is quite healed, and he feels no inconvenience whatever from it,' wrote Watkin Tench about 12 November 1790. 'With the natives we are hand in glove. They throng the camp every day, and sometimes by their clamour and importunity for bread and meat (of which they now all eat greedily) are become very troublesome. God knows we have little enough for ourselves.'[5] Bennelong, Tench mocked, had recently become 'a man of so much dignity and consequence' that it was 'not always easy to obtain his company'.[6]

Early in the morning of 13 November 1790, sixteen Eora visitors sat down by a fire in the yard at the governor's big house 'in great good humour' to cook some fish they had been given. A few who had not been to the settlement before were elated by the new things they saw around them. One of the women, noted Phillip, had 'pleasing features' and bright copper-coloured skin, free from dirt and smoke. 'Had she been in a European settlement, no one would have doubted her being a Mulatto Jewess,' he wrote. While this group was eating, Bennelong returned from Botany Bay with Barangaroo, who had fresh head wounds and looked ill. He declared that he had beaten her because she had broken a fishing spear and a *womerra*. After breakfast, the Eora crossed the stream to the hospital on the west side of the cove so the surgeons could treat Barangaroo and another woman with a gashed head. They later returned to the governor's house and sat down again in the yard.

Bennelong was angry. Grasping an iron hatchet, he went into the house and sat beside Governor Phillip, who was writing. Several times Bennelong threatened to use the hatchet (which he frequently tested for sharpness) against Kurubarabulu. The two men argued and Bennelong got up saying he was going to beat Kurubarabulu. Phillip insisted on going with Bennelong and they set off down the hill to his hut. On the way they were joined by David Collins and Bennelong's friend, the governor's orderly sergeant.[7] Bennelong spoke wildly and threatened to kill the girl. They took the hatchet from him and gave him Phillip's walking stick as a substitute, but then took that away as well.

Outside Bennelong's hut, five Eora men, two youths, several women, including Kurubarabulu, and some children were sitting around a fire and on the grass near the door. These people, said Tench, were 'full of bustle and agitation' and frequently called out 'Bennelong' and '*dee-in*' (*gin*, or woman). Suddenly, Bennelong snatched a wooden club and twice struck Kurubarabulu on the head and once on the shoulder before they could take it from him. He next seized a hatchet, but it was also wrestled away. The girl now lay unconscious on the ground. Bennelong grabbed another club, but Collins held him back. 'In vain did the governor in turns soothe and threaten him,' wrote Tench. 'In vain did the serjeant point his musket at him; he seemed dead to every passion but revenge; forgot his affection to his old friends; and, instead of complying with the request they made, furiously brandished his sword at the governor, and called aloud for his hatchet to dispatch the unhappy victim of his barbarity.' Bennelong's friends shook their spears menacingly in his support and one of them constantly urged Phillip to give back Bennelong's weapons.

Surgeon White and Lieutenant Henry Ball saw the struggle from HMS *Supply*, picked up their muskets and rowed ashore in a boat. Bennelong was not intimidated and boldly demanded custody of his victim, threatening to cut off her head. The Eora held back while the whites put Kurubarabulu into the boat to take her to the ship. Boorong's brother,

Ballooderry, an ally of Bennelong, then asked if he could go with the girl in the boat. He claimed he was her husband, which she said was true. Tench described Ballooderry as 'a fine well grown lad' about nineteen or twenty years old. Ballooderry, however, made no attempt to protect Kurubarabulu from Bennelong's abuse.

Phillip, Bennelong, Collins and the sergeant returned to the governor's house. When Bennelong had cooled down a little, Phillip told him he was very angry with him for attacking the girl. Bennelong, however, was still furious that she had been taken away. He said she was his, that her father had cut him above the eye, that all her clan were bad and that Phillip must realise that he would kill her. He accused the girl of attacking him at Botany Bay while 'under the lance of his antagonist' (her father Mety) in battle. Tench quotes Bennelong in melodramatic terms: 'She is now my property. I have ravished her by force from her tribe: and I will part with her to no person whatever, until my vengeance be glutted.'[8]

Collins warned Bennelong that if he killed the girl, Governor Phillip would have him executed. Bennelong replied by indicating which parts of her body – head, breast and arms – he would strike before he cut off her head. He threatened to go to the hospital to kill her. Phillip told him that if he did, he would be shot immediately.[9]

That same day a small boat was sent out with a crew of five convicts to fish near the Heads of Port Jackson. Returning under sail loaded with fish, she was blown against the rocks below Middle Head and wrecked, with all hands drowned. Colby and some others, who were on the spot, managed to save the seine fishing net which was caught in the rocks as well as the boat's rudder, a mast and an oar. They were rewarded with blankets and some clothing. In David Collins's opinion, Colby's actions were a striking example of the good relations and understanding which now existed between blacks and whites around Sydney.[10]

In the evening, Kurubarabulu was taken from the *Supply* to Surgeon White's house near the hospital. Ballooderry, who had treated her gently, asked if he could stay with her. Several Eora came to see the girl and urged her to return to Bennelong's hut, where, she said, she wanted to go. Although a sentry was posted outside the door, Ballooderry and Kurubarabulu attempted to escape during the night. Asked where they could find shelter, they replied that they would be safe with the *cameragal*. Next morning, Yemmerrawanne joined the young couple, saying he was afraid of what Bennelong might do. Soon after, a group of Bennelong's allies, led by Bigon, entered the hospital garden and tried to carry off all three by force. The governor's guard drove them off, but Bigon continued to defy them.

Two days later (15 November), Bennelong appeared at Governor Phillip's house brandishing a spear and tried to push past a sentry. He calmed down when the guard turned out with muskets and he and Barangaroo were allowed to go inside.

Bennelong promised Phillip that he would not attack Kurubarabulu again. He confessed that he had again beaten Barangaroo about the head and said she had clubbed him on the shoulder in return. Phillip suggested they should both go to the hospital to have their wounds dressed, but Bennelong refused. He said he was afraid of Surgeon White and would not sleep at his hut at *Tubowgullee* because he thought White might shoot him during the night. Phillip soon convinced Bennelong that he would be shot only if he killed Kurubarabulu or threw spears at the settlers. When he was finally persuaded that White was still his friend, Bennelong said he would go to him to get a plaster for his shoulder and one for Barangaroo's head. Instead, Phillip sent for the surgeon. When they met, Bennelong was friendly, shared some of the food he was eating with White, and walked back with him to see Kurubarabulu at the surgeon's house.

Bennelong, according to Tench, entered the house in sullen silence, but suddenly had an emotional about-turn. Instead of attacking Kurubarabulu as he had threatened, Bennelong took her by the hand and spoke to her quietly, saying he was sorry for what he had done. His actions irritated Barangaroo, who flew into a rage and hit the girl over the head with a club she snatched from an Eora man. Barangaroo abused both Bennelong and Kurubarabulu 'with great bitterness' and threw stones at the girl. Bennelong did not try to stop his wife's frenzied attacks until the officers rebuked him. He then gave Barangaroo 'a pretty smart slap on the face'. She left, crying tears of rage.

For her own protection, the injured girl was taken from the surgeon's house to a maidservant's room at the governor's. Bennelong seemed happy about this arrangement and asked if Ballooderry could stay with her.

Outside in the yard, Barangaroo continued to scream abuse. She seized Bennelong's spears and refused to surrender them to a marine, who took them by force. Bennelong grabbed the spears and gave them to Phillip, making signs for them to be kept inside the house. He seemed ready to use his club against the soldiers who stopped him going inside and one of his comrades was ready to help. Exasperated, Phillip ordered that all the natives, except Bennelong and Ballooderry, be sent out of the yard. Barangaroo left with the others, but came to eat dinner as if nothing unusual had taken place.

That evening, when Bennelong was leaving, Ballooderry said he would go also. Kurubarabulu began to cry and forced her way out of the maid's room to go with Bennelong. She was brought back and told that Bennelong would beat her. However, Bennelong promised he would not attack the girl and said Barangaroo was no longer angry with her. Ballooderry also pressed Governor Phillip to release Kurubarabulu, saying that Barangaroo would not beat her any more and was now 'very good'. Phillip thought that the information that Barangaroo's anger had ebbed could only have been brought by a boy who returned to the house that afternoon, and he was not at first inclined to let Kurubarabulu go.[11] This boy was probably Nanbarry, who, in company with Ballooderry, had spoken to William Dawes that day. Dawes recorded this exchange:

Boobanga meedyung – Cover thou my sore
Or in plain english, Put a plaster on my sore.
This Baluderri [Ballooderry] said to me on the 15 Nov.r 1790 & was clearly explained by his own gestures as well as positively in words by Nanbarri [Nanbarry].[12]

Phillip knew he could not detain Kurubarabulu against her will without locking her up. 'There appeared so much sincerity in Bennelong's countenance when he said she should not be beat,' wrote Phillip, who decided to allow her to leave. 'The moment the girl was without the gate,' he wrote, 'she ran towards Bennelong's hut, without waiting for those who were going along with her.'

Despite the general feeling that Bennelong would kill the girl, Phillip believed that he would keep his word. A large number of Eora gathered at Bennelong's hut that night, which gave rise to fear and rumours in the English camp. However, Bennelong came to eat with Phillip the next day (16 November) and told him that he had sent Kurubarabulu back to her father at Botany Bay, a fact confirmed by other natives. 'How Bannelong got this girl in his possession could not be learnt,' Phillip wrote: 'when she went away her wounds were in a fair way of doing well; fortunately, for her, the weapon which had first presented itself when Bannelong beat her was a boy's wooden sword, and made of very light wood.'[13]

Tench thought that Bennelong's brave indifference to personal risk – 'nay of life' – in confronting Governor Phillip and his armed guard merited admiration, 'though it led us to predict that this Baneelon, whom imagination had fondly pictured, like a second Omai, the gaze of the court, and the scrutiny of the curious, would perish untimely, the victim of his own temerity'.[14] Omai, a handsome young Polynesian from the South Pacific island of Raiatea near Tahiti, was taken to Britain in 1773 where he met King George and was lionised by London society. Like Omai, Bennelong would one day meet 'King Tosh' at St James's Palace.

A few days later, Bennelong asked to go with Governor Phillip to Rose Hill (Parramatta). However, when the governor's boat stopped at the point to pick up Barangaroo from their hut, she refused to go and persuaded Bennelong to stay with her. When Phillip returned, he was told that Bennelong was mourning the death of his 'brother' or close relative (possibly a brother of Barangaroo) who had been killed by the *cameragal*. Bennelong had breakfast with some officers who had gone to his hut on hearing the cries of the women mourners. They took him in their boat to the north shore, where he was seen not long after, collecting wild bushfruits with some *cameragal*. Bennelong's behaviour confused the English observers, who wondered why he was so frequently with the *cameragal* when he often said they were 'bad people' and asked Phillip to kill them.

There was more friction at Bennelong's hut, perhaps over Kurubarabulu, on the night of 21 November, when Bennelong and Barangaroo were forced to seek Phillip's protection. Bennelong told the governor that there were a great many people at his hut and asked if he could stay at his house that night. He claimed that the *cameragal* had killed one of his friends or relations and had burnt his body. When told that Phillip would send soldiers to punish them, he pressed him to do so – 'indeed, from the first day he was able to make himself understood, he was desirous to have all the tribe of Cammeragal killed, yet he was along with that tribe when Governor Phillip was wounded'.

After eating, Bennelong and Barangaroo went to bed in a back room. He asked anxiously for Phillip to lock the door and put the key safely in his pocket. Boorong left with them the next day and slept at Bennelong's hut that night, but was brought back to the settlement the following morning.[15]

Bennelong seems to have been quite sexually active at this time. Although Barangaroo was pregnant, he had presumably slept with his new wife Kurubarabulu, while an entry in Dawes's notebook (with a cryptic blank space) indicates that Ballooderry's sister Boorong was also one of his partners:

Mooroomadióra Boorong
I was angry with Boorong.
Note this was said by Berangarro [Barangaroo] after she told me that benelong had   Boorong.[16]

Two otherwise obscure sentences in the language notebook attributed to Phillip and Collins refer to a conflict some time during 1790 in which Bennelong wounded Boorong's brother Yeranibe with a double-headed short spear called a *doo-ul*.

Doo-ul — the spear by which Yer-ren-iby was wounded.
Mur-ra-mur-rong — the reason given for Bennelong's wounding Yer-ren-i-bey[17]

The 'reason' Yeranibe was wounded is likely to have been a person – Bennelong's brother-in-law 'Collins' or Gnunga Gnunga, whose name was also Mur-re-mur-gan.[18] There were two men named Yeranibe in early Sydney and Bennelong and Gnunga Gnunga were allies of the 'other' Yeranibe, who was killed in a ritual punishment in 1795.

I2

DEATH OF A GAME SHOOTER

John McEntire was one of three convicts allowed to keep a musket and to come and go from Sydney Cove to shoot wild game for the officers' tables. McEntire had been convicted of robbery at Durham in northern England in 1785 and was sentenced to seven years transportation.

In time, McEntire became the personal game shooter for Governor Arthur Phillip. In this role, his musket and his sour disposition made him a fearful figure to the native people. Wandering the bush far from Sydney, where few other whites ventured, McEntire shot birds, kangaroos, possums and an emu (some of which were used as models for illustrations), a pantheon of animals which were revered totem emblems to the native people. He shot and wounded one man and may have killed others or raped native women. Once, when McEntire was hunting, the natives set a dingo on him. For a short time the 'surly fellow' put up with the dog snapping at his heels, but then suddenly turned and 'shot poor Dingo dead on the spot'.[1] Surgeon George Worgan said the Eora were 'extremely terrified at this, and took to their Heels with the greatest Precipitation'.[2]

At some time, McEntire had mortally offended Bennelong, whose dread and hatred of him was well known. On the morning of the whale feast in early September 1790, when McEntire was told by Surgeon White to help him put on a shirt, Bennelong, said Watkin Tench, 'positively forbade him to approach, eyeing him ferociously, and with every mark of horror and resentment'.[3]

When Bennelong joyfully embraced his old companions on his return to Governor Phillip's house in October 1790, 'the gamekeeper McEntire', wrote Tench, 'he continued to hold in abhorrence and would not suffer his approach'. Tench added in a footnote: 'Look at the account of the governor being wounded, when his detestation of this man burst forth.'[4]

Bennelong also hated another man, one from his own race. This was Pemulwuy, described by Phillip as 'a native well known for having lost an eye, and who was supposed to be a leader of the tribe that reside about Botany-Bay'. Both Pemulwuy and Bennelong were about thirty years of age. In Collins and Phillip's language notebook, the entry *Pemul-why: Bediagal.Tugagal.tugara*, identifies Pemulwuy as being from a 'woods' or inland clan (from *tuga* meaning wood or vegetation).[5]

The time came for Bennelong to set one enemy against another. In the

Pimbloy [Pemulwuy]*: Native of New Holland in a canoe of that country*
Engraving by S.I. Neele, dated 10 January 1804.
James Grant, *The Narrative of a Voyage of Discovery, Performed in His Majesty's Vessel The Lady Nelson*, T. Egerton, Whitehall, London, 1803.

brawling and drama that followed Bennelong's abduction of Kurubarabulu from Botany Bay, the presence of a native at Bennelong's brick hut in Sydney Cove went almost unnoticed. Phillip thought it mysterious that 'a man belonging to the Botany-Bay tribe had for more than a fortnight slept at his hut, though he said the man was bad, and spoke of him as his enemy'.[6] This man might have been Bennelong's recent opponent Mety, come to talk to Bennelong about his daughter Kurubarabulu. However, David Collins called Mety an 'old man'.[7] Although he was not described as having a turned eye, it is more likely that Bennelong's visitor was the *bidjigal* warrior Pemulwuy, his old enemy from the Georges River, whom he had asked the soldiers to kill only one month earlier.

Had Bennelong and Pemulwuy reached an agreement to shelve their hostility while seeking revenge against their common foe McEntire? An alliance between the inland and coastal clans was unusual, but perhaps a council of elders had met to commission a payback. It is certain that Pemulwuy did visit Sydney, because a few weeks later he was seen clean-shaven and with short hair.

A small hut had been built at Rose Hill (Parramatta) for Governor Phillip, who would often stay there for a few days at a time. On 9 December 1790, Bennelong, Colby and two other men asked to go to Rose Hill with Phillip and got into his boat. First, the boat called at *Tubowgulee* for

Bennelong to fetch a cloak, but Barangaroo angrily forbade him to go. To pacify Barangaroo, Bennelong promised her that he would not stay away for more than one night. Despite her threats, he got into the boat as it was leaving the cove, but, wrote Phillip, 'the moment the boat pulled off she went to her canoe, which was a new one, and after driving her paddles through the bottom, she threw them into the water, and afterwards went off to their hut, probably to do more damage'. Bennelong fished the canoe paddles out of the water and got out of the boat, while the others went on to Rose Hill. Colby and his friends ate well at Rose Hill and slept the night at Phillip's hut, but they were anxious to return the next morning, so the governor sent them up to Sydney Cove by boat.[8]

That day, John McEntire, with a marine sergeant and two other convicts, went hunting, close to the north arm of Botany Bay near the Cooks River. This was the heartland of Pemulwuy's clan, the *bidjigal* (*bediagal*). Knowing from experience that kangaroos and wallabies kept under cover during the day, the shooters took shelter from the sun in a hut of branches and bushes, lit a fire and settled down to rest until sunset. At about one o'clock that afternoon, the sergeant heard a rustling noise, which he thought might be a kangaroo, and alerted the others. Looking out, they saw two Aboriginal warriors armed with spears crawling stealthily towards them, with three others close behind. Seeing one man clean-shaven and with short hair, McEntire knew that he must have recently been to Sydney. 'Don't be afraid, I know them,' said McEntire. He put down his gun and spoke to the warriors in their own language, but they jumped to their feet and slowly backed away. McEntire, still unarmed, followed them for about 100 metres. He called on them to stop, offered them bread, and asked one of his companions to put down his gun, saying they would not harm him.

Suddenly, the beardless man, less than 10 metres from McEntire, leapt onto a fallen tree, fixed his spear in a *womerra*, and launched it. 'I am a dead man,' cried McEntire, as the spear struck deep into his side. The spear, barbed with sharp stones, could not be removed without aggravating the injury. One hunter broke off the shaft and waited with McEntire while the others chased the attackers. McEntire begged not to be left to die alone in the woods. Though he had lost a great deal of blood, he still had enough strength left to drag himself slowly along, with the help of his comrades. In this way they staggered 10 kilometres through the bush, arriving at Sydney Cove at about two o'clock in the morning.

After examining McEntire, Surgeon White said he was unlikely to live. 'The poor wretch,' said Tench, 'now began to utter the most dreadful exclamations and to accuse himself of the commission of crimes of the deepest dye; accompanied with such expressions of his despair at God's mercy, as are too terrible to repeat.' McEntire asked the surgeon not to take out the spear until he had sought pardon from God, whom, he said, he had often offended. At the hospital, McEntire, a Catholic, asked to see the Anglican chaplain Richard Johnson. He confessed that he had led an evil life and asked Johnson to pray for him.

By his own testimony, this was not the first attack by natives against McEntire. He admitted, wrote Phillip, that 'once; when, having a spear thrown at him, he discharged his piece, which was loaded with small shot, and possibly wounded the man who threw the spear'. Due to the aversion shown by 'all the natives' to the game shooter, said Tench, McEntire had for a long time been suspected of having shot and injured some of them. Tench added: 'Notwithstanding this death-bed confession, most people doubted the [full] truth of his relation, from his general character, and other circumstances.'

McEntire was well known to the Eora in Sydney. Despite their aversion, Colby and some others went to see him at the hospital and 'expressed great marks of sorrow, all the women and several of the men shedding tears'. When one of the doctors suggested taking out the spearhead, Colby said that it should remain for some time and indicated by signs his belief that McEntire would die.

'The person who committed this wanton act,' Watkin Tench wrote later, 'was described as a young man, with a speck, or blemish, on his left eye.' The Eora in Sydney were quick to name McEntire's attacker as 'Pim-el-wi' (Pemulwuy), saying that he lived at Botany Bay. 'It appeared rather extraordinary,' thought Phillip, 'that the natives should immediately know the man who wounded the gamekeeper, and his tribe; they said his name was Pemullaway, of the tribe of Bejigal [bidjigal].'[9] In the Sydney language, pe-mall means earth or clay.

Still at Rose Hill, Phillip was surprised to see Bennelong and Barangaroo, who arrived in a boat on 10 December to visit him. Bennelong said he had not beaten Barangaroo after their last argument and they both dined with the governor 'in great good humour'. Phillip wrote: 'Every thing this couple wished for was given them, and they had both fish and baggaray [kangaroo]; but after dinner was over, the lady wanted to return, and Bannelong said she would cry if she was not permitted to go.' Late that afternoon, Bennelong and Barangaroo went to Sydney by boat.[10] Both Colby and Bennelong had firmly established their whereabouts and created cast-iron alibis for the period in which McEntire was attacked.

On 11 December, Governor Phillip came up from Rose Hill to Sydney, where he was told that his game shooter had been speared and could die. After making inquiries, the governor satisfied himself that McEntire had not been armed and was convinced that the attack was not provoked. Having reached this decision, Phillip was determined to punish Pemulwuy.

The following day, McEntire's wound started to discharge pus and was soft enough for the surgeons to extract the spearhead, which had a wooden barb at the point and was set with small, sharp, jagged-edged barbs of red stone stuck on with yellow gum. The spear had penetrated McEntire's left side under his arm to a depth of 18 centimetres, passing between two ribs and into the left lobe of the lungs. Most of the stone points were torn off and remained inside his body.[11] 'The spear with which the game-keeper was wounded, being shewn to one of the natives, he immediately named the tribe to whom it belonged; which shows that some of them arm their weapons differently from others,' Phillip remarked.[12]

Colby and Bennelong promised the governor that they would bring Pemulwuy into the settlement. Bennelong seemed prepared to allow Pemulwuy to take the blame for this crime, which it is possible that he organised and had been planning for some time.

Governor Phillip's reaction to the attack on McEntire was uncharacteristically harsh. He decided to make a 'signal example' of the *bidjigal*. He fixed on Watkin Tench to command an expedition to search for Pemulwuy and called him to his house for explicit instructions. Phillip told Tench he could choose the troops he needed from the Marine Corps and that the sergeant and two convicts who had been hunting with McEntire would act as guides. This squad was to march to the peninsula at the head of Botany Bay and, by surprise or force, capture two native men, kill ten others and destroy their weapons. They were to behead the slain and would be provided with hatchets and bags for this purpose. The marines were cautioned not to harm any women or children, or to burn any huts.

Tench must have been shocked to receive such an order from the normally compassionate Phillip, who attempted to explain his reasons for adopting such severe and cold-blooded measures. Tench was careful to record the details of their conversation. Since their arrival in the country, Phillip said, seventeen people had been either killed or wounded by the natives. He regarded the *bidjigal*, who lived around the north arm of Botany Bay, as the chief aggressors and was determined to strike a decisive blow against them to convince them of the superiority of the English forces and to promote 'universal terror' to prevent further mischief.

In every instance of hostility, said Phillip, the natives had acted either after being wronged or for some misunderstanding. 'To the latter of these causes,' he added, 'I attribute my own wound; but in this business of McEntire, I am fully persuaded that they were unprovoked, and the barbarity of their conduct admits of no extenuation.'

Phillip was disappointed in Bennelong and Colby who, he thought, had let him down in his resolve to punish Pemulwuy. 'I have in vain tried to stimulate Baneelon, Colbey, and other natives who live among us, to bring in the aggressor, yesterday, indeed, they promised me to do it, and actually went away, as if bent on such a design.' Instead of hunting for Pemulwuy, Bennelong took his canoe to the north shore, where he joined *cameragal* elders at an initiation ceremony in which he removed the front teeth of young men. Colby was seen 'loitering round the look out house' at South Head.

Providing an unheeded but significant clue to Pemulwuy's status as a *carradhy*, Colby said the fugitive could easily be recognised because the toes on his left foot had been bruised by a club. Anthropologists have noted that *kadaitja* (clever men) of Central Australia dislocate their small toes to travel swiftly and quietly in shoes made from blood and emu feathers when they set out to take vengeance against an enemy.[13]

Phillip continued to harangue Tench: 'I am resolved to execute the prisoners who may be brought in, in the most exemplary manner, in the presence of as many of their countrymen as can be collected, after having explained the cause of such punishment'. Pausing for breath, Phillip asked Tench if he could propose any alteration to his orders and promised to listen patiently. Tench suggested to Phillip that he should reduce his demands to the capture of six natives, some of whom could be 'set aside for retaliation' (executed, in short), while the rest would be allowed to go free 'after seeing the fate of their comrades'.

Phillip agreed with Tench's suggestion and accordingly amended the orders which appeared in his dispatches. 'If six cannot be taken, let this number be shot,' Phillip continued. 'Should you, however, find it practicable to take so many, I will hang two and send the rest to Norfolk Island for a certain period, which will cause their countrymen to believe, that we have dispatched them secretly.'

Phillip's final orders of the day for 13 December 1790 read:

> A party, consisting of two captains, two subalterns and forty privates, with a proper number of non-commissioned officers, from the garrison, with three days provisions, &c. are to be ready to march tomorrow morning at day-light, in order to bring in six of those natives who reside near the head of Botany Bay; or, if that should be found impracticable, to put that number to death.

The governor forbade any of the armed detachment to deceive the natives by holding up their hands, or to reply to this sign of friendship if it was made to them. 'This is the only departure from Phillip's normal humanitarian approach to the aborigines, and Tench's report of his explanation is of great interest,' commented historian L.P. Fitzhardinge (1961).[14]

Following Tench's terse interview with Governor Phillip, his friend and colleague Lieutenant William Dawes wrote a letter to his superior officer Captain James Campbell in which he refused to take part in the expedition. In so doing, he became, in the words of Professor G. Arnold Wood, 'the first conscientious objector in Australian history'.[15] Campbell could not persuade Dawes to change his mind and brought the letter to Phillip, who 'took great pains to point out the consequences of his [Dawes] being put under an arrest'. Phillip claimed that Dawes had used 'unofficerlike behaviour' to him in the presence of Lieutenant John Long and threatened Dawes with a court martial, but he would not submit to one, which was his right.

Dawes, who corresponded with William Wilberforce (1758-1833), leader of the campaign against slavery in England, evidently struggled with his conscience over Phillip's plan. After a talk with Chaplain Johnson late that evening, he told Campbell that he thought he might obey the order and was ready to go out with the party. Following a religious service held by Johnson, in which he had time for more reflection on the matter, Dawes changed his mind once more and told Phillip that he was 'sorry he had been persuaded to comply with the order' and would not obey a similar order in future.[16]

'At four o'clock, on the morning of the 14th, we marched,' wrote Tench, who strode out at the head of a 'terrific procession' which included Captain William Hill of the New South Wales Corps, Lieutenants Dawes and Poulden of the Marines, Surgeons Worgan and Lowe, three sergeants, three corporals and forty privates, including John Easty. By 9 a.m. the detachment had reached the peninsula at the head of Botany Bay, 'but having walked in various directions until four o'clock in the afternoon, without seeing a native, we halted for the night'.

In the morning, Colby came up to Sydney from South Head. He dined with Governor Phillip at midday, but left soon after, saying he was going to see his wife Daringa, who was at Botany Bay.

At daylight on 15 December, the English search party marched eastwards and found themselves on the coast at Botany Bay. As they approached, five native men ran quickly from the beach into the bush. As the redcoats marched rapidly towards the camp of five bark huts on the north shore of the bay, they saw three canoes 'filled with Indians' paddle across to the south shore. They searched the huts but found only fishing spears.

As they returned for their packs, Tench caught sight of a native spearing fish in water up to his waist about 300 metres from the shore. 'In such a situation it would not have been practicable either to shoot, or to seize him,' said Tench. He decided instead to pass 'without noticing him, as he seemed either from consciousness of his own security, or from some other cause, quite unintimidated at our appearance'. This man followed them and called to some of them by name. Tench ordered a halt so he could catch up, having decided, despite his orders, 'that he should be suffered to come to us and leave us uninjured'. It turned out to be Colby. Asked where Pemulwuy was, Colby said he had fled to the south and was by this time a long way off. 'When we arrived at our baggage, Colbee sat down, eat, drank and slept with us, from ten o'clock until past noon,' wrote Tench.

Colby had left Sydney the previous day after watching Surgeon White cut off a woman's leg at the hospital, an operation which he re-enacted. 'The agony and cries of the poor sufferer he depicted in a most lively manner.' Colby had gone to visit Phillip after Nanbarry had warned him about the search party. The governor offered him a blanket, a hatchet, a jacket, in fact anything he wanted, if he would not go to Botany Bay, but Colby rejected all these offers. He had obviously made up his mind to alert either Pemulwuy or his *damelian* (namesake) Botany Bay Kolbi about Phillip's headhunting expedition. In a droll footnote, Tench related Phillip's futile attempts to persuade Colby to remain in Sydney:

> At last it was determined to try to eat him down, by setting before him his favourite food, of which it was hoped he would feed so voraciously, as to render him incapable of executing his intention. A large dish of fish was accordingly set before him. But after devouring a light horseman [snapper fish], and at least five pounds of beef and bread, even until the sight of food became disgusting to him, he set out on his journey with such lightness and gaiety, as plainly showed him to be a stranger to the horrors of indigestion.

Colby, who had shed crocodile tears at McEntire's hospital bed, was not in the least inconvenienced by a full stomach, but walking swiftly, arrived at Botany Bay well before the English troops. There is a suspicion that Colby might have had a kinship obligation to Pemulwuy through his wife Daringa. David Collins, who adopted Daringa's brother Boneda (or Pundah), said the boy was related to 'Go-roo-bine, a grey-headed man, apparently upward of sixty years of age'.[17] The 'place of resort' of Steven Goorabun was given as Georges River when he was issued with government blankets at Parramatta in 1836 and 1837. He was therefore a member of the clan which succeeded Pemulwuy's *bidjigal*. Colby's claim that he was going to Botany Bay to see Daringa was true, as she was pregnant and had gone there for the birth of her child, which also suggests a kinship link in the area. Such a relationship would have made Colby an ally of Pemulwuy.[18]

The unlucky infantrymen passed a restless night camped by a swamp, kept awake and persecuted by swarms of mosquitoes and sandflies. After wading through two deep bays, the soldiers, their scarlet coats crusted with mud, got back to Sydney the following afternoon.[19] 'Thursday the 16th. Returned into Sidney again after a Troublesome Teadious March,' wrote Easty in his journal.[20]

David Collins characterised the expedition as a punitive party 'armed and detached purposely to punish the man [Pemulwuy] and his companions'. He also thought it was likely to have a good effect, 'as it was well known to several natives, who were at this time in the town of Sydney, that this was the intention with which they were sent out'. What effect, if any, would Tench's army blundering about in the Botany swamps have made on Bennelong, Colby and other 'town' natives?

In his account, Tench nowhere mentions using firearms. According to David Collins, however, the marines fired on the natives they saw 'at the head of Botany Bay, but without doing them an injury'.[21] It is possible that at least one of the fleeing men was wounded by musket shot, a fact we know only from the handwritten caption to a watercolour portrait of Bennelong (reproduced on the cover of this book) by the unknown Port Jackson Painter, which reads: 'Native named Ben-nel-Long. As painted when angry after Botany Bay Colebee was wounded.'[22] According to William Dawes, Warungin Wangubilye or Botany Bay Kolbi (or Colby), a member of the *gwea* clan from the south side of Botany Bay, was the elder brother of Bennelong's second wife Kurubarabulu.[23]

Phillip asked Tench to lead a second expedition to search for Pemulwuy. To 'deceive the natives' and stop them passing on information about his plans, Tench pretended that he was going to Broken Bay to punish Willemering for spearing Governor Phillip. If Bennelong believed this tale, he might have been somewhat dismayed.

As there was a full moon, Tench decided to set out for Botany Bay by night. Just before sunset on 22 December, he again marched south, accompanied this time by Lieutenant Abbot and Ensign Prentice of the New South Wales Corps, three sergeants, three corporals and thirty privates.

This expedition was just as farcical as the first. The troops were forced to cool their heels on the north arm of Botany Bay until 2.15 the next morning while waiting for the tide to go out before they could cross. To travel quickly, the soldiers took off their knapsacks, which were guarded by a sergeant and six men. The rest set out, carrying their firelocks and with powder boxes tied to the top of their heads to prevent them getting wet. The intention was to surprise the native 'village' at Botany Bay before dawn, but after crossing two 'rivers' the troops were soon up to their waists in thick, tenacious mud.

First the sergeant of grenadiers, then Prentice and Tench himself became stuck fast, unable to move. Cries of 'I am sinking' were heard on every side. Private John Easty said the mud was 'up to the armpits and had Like to have Smothred Sevaral of the men'.[24] One soldier called for tree branches to be cut and after half an hour they had all been pulled from the mud, using ropes which were intended to 'bind the captive Indians'. At sunset they separated into three units and rushed the camp, hoping to find the natives around their fires. 'To our astonishment, however,' wrote

Tench, 'we found not a single native at the huts; nor was a canoe to be seen on any part of the bay.'

Easty, however, provides some intriguing detail. 'The Morning of the 24 [December] ... we went Down the Beach for abought 3 miles whaare we Saw Several of the natives by thier fires,' he writes.[25] This seems to refer to another artwork by the Port Jackson Painter which provides a pictorial sequel to the wounding of Botany Bay Kolbi. The watercolour, captioned 'Mr White, Harris & Laing with a party of Soldiers visiting Botany Bay Colebee at that Place when wounded', shows the surgeons, natives reclining around their camp fire near the sea and a detachment of armed soldiers. A man sits apart on a log, holding a spear. Written under the log in pencil is the word 'Colebee'.[26]

The ignorant savages of Botany Bay had once more outwitted the English redcoats, who were happy to escape from the 'rotten spungy [spongy] bog' and return to Sydney.

McEntire had been walking about once more and seemed likely to recover when he died suddenly on the afternoon of 20 January 1791. In a post-mortem, Surgeon White found that the left lobe of his lung, where he had been wounded, was wasted away. 'Several of the small stones with which the spear had been armed, were found adhering to the side, and the rib against which the spear had broke, was splintered.'[27] 'This man [McEntire] had been suspected of having wantonly killed or wounded several of the natives in the course of his excursion after gain,' commented Collins; 'but he steadily denied, from the time he was brought in to his last moment of life, having ever fired at them but once.'[28]

1791

13

THE POTATO THIEVES

On 28 December 1790, some natives who had been visiting Sydney regularly for several weeks were caught digging up potatoes in a vegetable garden on the western point of Sydney Cove near William Dawes's hut, which they called *Tarra* (*Dara* or *Tdara*), meaning teeth. One man threw his fishing spear, which wounded the convict who was trying to drive them off. 'These people had lately made a practice of threatening any person whom they found in a hut alone,' wrote Phillip, 'unless bread was given to them; and one of those who were suspected in the present instance, had, on several occasions, shewn himself to be a daring fellow, who did not seem to dread any consequences.' This daring fellow was Bigon, a constant companion of Bennelong.

A sergeant and six privates were sent after the potato thieves with orders not to shoot unless they were attacked. Governor Phillip and some officers followed the redcoats, who found men and women gathered around a camp fire. The troops seized two men, but they struggled free and one threw his club.

As the men ran off, three soldiers opened fire with muskets, saying later that they had mistaken the club for a spear. The troops took away two women for questioning and seized their digging sticks.[1] The women said the spear which wounded the convict belonged to Bangai, another ally of Bennelong. The two women slept that night in a shed in the governor's yard and left the next morning after being given bread and fish to eat. One woman was Bangai's wife and the other was Noorooing (Gnoo-roo-in), who had been left by Yelloway at Phillip's house.[2]

The Eora in town, wrote Tench, suddenly became shy when asked about this incident. Meanwhile, on 29 December, a trail of blood was traced from the camp to the coast.[3]

Bennelong returned to Sydney with Barangaroo after an absence of ten days. He told Governor Phillip that he had been with many people at an initiation ceremony on the north shore, in which he had officiated by knocking out the front teeth of several young men and raising scars on their skin. He proudly showed Phillip a throwing stick which had been cut solely to remove teeth. Barangaroo's body was painted and she 'seemed to be sensible that she was finer than common'. Red ochre had been rubbed over her cheeks, nose, upper lip and the small of her back, while dots of white clay spotted the skin under her eyes. It is likely that Barangaroo, a *cameragalleon*, had taken a leading role in the women's business associated with the ritual. It seemed, wrote Phillip, that Bennelong was 'now on good terms with the Cameragals, as he said they were all good men; and being asked if he had seen the man who threw the spear at Governor Phillip (Willemering), he said yes, and had slept with him'.[4] Phillip realised that Bennelong had deceived him in claiming that he had beaten or even quarrelled with Willemering. Bennelong and Barangaroo left after eating, taking with them Kurubarabulu, who had been living with the governor's servants. The girl stripped off her European clothing, but kept her nightcap to sleep in as her head had been shaved.[5]

Bennelong had gained considerable status among his own people. As an elder or *kooringal* he could now extract teeth at initiation ceremonies of the *cameragal*, once his avowed enemies. This might have been in return for shielding Willemering from the intended punishment of the whites. Bennelong could also share the secret spiritual knowledge and influential power and authority of the *cameragal*.

The following Monday (3 January 1791) some Eora told the governor that Bangai had been wounded and would probably die. Yemmerrawanne, however, whispered that Bangai's life could still be saved. Ordered by Phillip to bring Bangai back to the hospital if there was any hope that he might recover, Surgeon White that afternoon took Yemmerrawanne, Nanbarry and one of the women in a boat to look for him. Some Eora they met said Bangai was dead and that his body was in a bay a further mile away. During this parley, Bigon, who had been with Bangai when he stole the potatoes, kept well away from the soldiers.[6]

White found Bangai's body lying next to a fire, still warm, and covered in green boughs, except for one leg. A musket ball had passed through Bangai's shoulder and cut the subclavian artery and the surgeon concluded that he had bled to death. His face was covered with a thick branch, interwoven with grass and ferns to make a screen. A strip of bark had been placed around his neck and a growing tree branch, stripped of bark, was bent to the ground to form an arch over the body. None of the Eora in the boat would touch Bangai or come near him for fear that the *mawm* or malicious spirit of the dead man would seize them. Phillip concluded that it was 'probable' that the Eora did not intend to either bury or burn the body, while Collins said it had been 'disposed of for burning'.[7]

Bangai's death was the cause of serious tension between Bennelong and Phillip. Bennelong 'at the head of several of his tribe' took revenge by threatening to spear the unarmed crew of a boat and robbing them of their fish. When he next saw Phillip, Bennelong at first denied any knowledge of this robbery and claimed he had been a long way from the scene, but he changed his tune when confronted with two people who had been in the boat. Attempting to justify his actions, Bennelong launched into a rambling, insolent speech, often mentioning Bangai and threatening revenge.

Bennelong was stirred to rage when Phillip refused to shake his hand as usual as a token of friendship. 'Who killed Bangai?' he demanded and 'seemed inclined to make use of his stick'. Phillip called for a sentry, but hoped to make Bennelong see reason without the use of force. An officer in the room diplomatically suggested that perhaps Bennelong might not be clearly understood. Phillip then asked Bennelong, who stood apart, to come closer, but he refused. Still angry, Bennelong snatched an iron hatchet as he passed the wheelwright's shop in the yard.[8] They chased him, but he got away. Bennelong might have promised a hatchet to one of his allies, although it is probable that he considered that he should be able to share property with Phillip, his classificatory father and namesake.

Phillip gave orders that no boat should leave Sydney Cove without arms and forbade the natives going to the scene of the crime, the western point of the cove. This order, if it was understood or enforced, would have prevented them visiting William Dawes at his observatory hut.

The English colony's colourful cloth signal pennants were usually left at the South Head flagstaff. About the middle of January 1791 some daring Eora raiders stole the flags and took them away. 'They were afterwards soon divided among them in their canoes, and used as coverings,' wrote David Collins.[9] The Eora, who watched the activities at the Look Out, would know that the pennants were used to send signals to the Flagstaff at Sydney. This sabotage was part of their resistance and was possibly motivated by the violation of their sacred burial grounds at South Head.

Bigon, who often stayed at Bennelong's hut and had been with Bangai when he was shot, was received in a friendly manner by Phillip when he came to see the governor at Rose Hill (Parramatta) in February 1791. Phillip decided to ignore his offence as he wanted 'a friendly intercourse to be kept up with the natives'.[10]

After his angry outburst and theft of the hatchet, Bennelong wisely kept away from Sydney, but other Eora continued to come in as usual. Several times Bennelong stopped fishing boats to ask those on board if Governor Phillip was still angry enough to shoot him. He went to the hospital and said he wanted to see Phillip and gave the name of a man, who, he said, had taken the hatchet. When Bennelong came to the governor's gate a few days later, Phillip was in the yard and ordered him away. Bennelong, who still denied taking the hatchet or seeking to revenge Bangai's death, was allowed into the yard (which was always open to the Eora) and given some bread and fish. Although still forbidden to enter

Phillip's house, he continued to go there frequently despite this humiliation, which the governor purposefully intended to put him on 'a level with the other natives'.[11]

In January 1791, after Bangai's death, David Collins expressed his regret that such cold-blooded reprisals were necessary. Collins was also sorry that 'we had not yet been able to reconcile the natives to the deprivation of those parts of this harbour which we occupied'. He added: 'While they entertained the idea of our having dispossessed them of their residences, they must always consider us as enemies; and upon this principle they make a point of attacking the white people whenever opportunity and safety concurred.'[12]

Not long after, on 28 February, Bennelong helped to save the infant colony's six-oared cutter, a swift boat with a deck, mast and bowsprit. While the Eora easily and skilfully handled their flimsy bark canoes, sudden squalls or rough weather could sometimes overturn the timber ships' boats manned by English sailors, many of whom could not swim or were afraid of the water.

Bennelong's sister, Carangarang, her two children and a little girl, went fishing in the cutter, which was skippered by William Bryant, a Cornish convict who had been the colony's fisherman for three years. The boat, filled with fish, was hit by a sudden gust of wind and swamped with water. She heeled over, but did not sink. 'The young woman [Carangarang] had the two children on her shoulders in a moment, and swam on shore with them,' wrote Phillip; 'the girl also swam on shore as did such of the boat's crew as could swim'. When Bennelong and his friends saw the boat heading for the rocks, they quickly paddled their canoes out and 'immediately plunged in, and saved all the people', according to Tench. They brought the victims ashore, undressed them, kindled a fire, and dried their clothes, gave them fish to eat, and then took them to Sydney. They also recovered the oars and mast, helped with repairs, refloated the cutter and towed her up to Sydney Cove.

The night before this incident, Bryant, a former convict whose sentence had expired, had been overheard plotting to steal the fishing boat.[13] The following month, Bryant and his wife Mary, their two children and seven convicts escaped in the cutter. In an epic voyage of sixty-eight days they sailed 4000 kilometres to Koepang in Timor, where they were detained.

As a reward for his bravery, Bennelong was rehabilitated and Governor Phillip received him 'in a more kindly manner' than before his fits of anger over Bangai's death. 'In consequence of this reconciliation,' wrote Phillip, 'the number of visitors greatly increased, the governor's yard being their headquarters.'[14]

14

RITES OF PASSAGE

Early in February 1791, about 100 Eora men, women and children gathered in a bay on the north shore of the harbour in *cameragal* territory for an initiation, the ceremonial ritual in which boys were made into men.

Among the initiates were Yemmerrawanne and another youth who lived at Governor Phillip's house (perhaps Ballooderry). They returned to Sydney wearing crowns of split rushes and reed bands bound around their upper arms. Each had a black streak painted on his chest, broad at one end and tapering to a point. According to anthropologist L.R. Hiatt, a totem design is often painted on a boy's chest at initiation.[1]

Their front teeth had been knocked out and Yemmerrawanne had also lost a piece of his jawbone. They were proud of their new status and defiantly wore the pain of their ordeal.[2] The practice of tooth evulsion in Australia is very ancient. Archaeologist Dr Alistair Campbell has examined skulls of male Aborigines, dated to 8000 years before the present, in which the right upper incisor teeth had been removed.[3] It is probable that many other Eora rituals were just as old.

The 'ceremony or operation of drawing the tooth' was translated from the Sydney language in the notebook attributed to Phillip and Collins as *Era-bad-djang*.[4] Referring to events in 1795, Collins speculated that *erah-ba-diahng* was derived from *erah*, part of the verb to throw, meaning that the young men were now allowed to throw spears.[5] An alternative derivation could be: (the ceremony in which) people are hurt, from *eora* (people) and *badiang* (to hurt).

Watkin Tench described the method used by the *kooringal* (elders) to extract the front teeth of initiates. 'The tooth intended to be taken out is loosened, by the gum being scarified on both sides with a sharp shell. The end of a stick is then applied to the tooth, which is struck gently, several times, with a stone, until it becomes easily movable, when the *coup de grace* is given, by a smart stroke.'

Teeth were seldom taken from boys under sixteen years of age. Yemmerrawanne, said Tench, suffered severe swelling and inflammation of his jaw, but still 'boasted [of] the firmness and hardihood, with which he had endured it'.[6] His name, given as Imeerawanyee by Tench, Imerawanga by Elizabeth Macarthur and as Yemmerrawanne by others, could be transliterated to *jam-ora wanne*, meaning 'I am in *wanne*' or 'my country [is] *wanne*', indicating that he was a *wangal*, like Bennelong, born in the district of *wann* to the west of Sydney. His full name was probably 'Yem-mer-ra-wan-ne. Ta-bong-en.Tan-ni', listed in the language notebook attributed to Phillip and Collins, but not translated.[7]

Yemmerrawanne was, wrote Tench in a footnote, a 'good-tempered lively lad' who soon became 'a favourite with us, and almost constantly lived at the governor's house'. Clothes were specially made for him and he was taught to wait at table. Conscious of his new status, Yemmerrawanne would not tolerate being ordered about by the cheeky uninitiated Nanbarry, as Tench relates in an anecdote about the day, in November 1790, when Elizabeth Macarthur dined at Phillip's house at the same time as Nanbarry.

> This latter [Nanbarry] anxious that his countryman [Yemmerrawanne] should appear to advantage in his new office, gave him many instructions, strictly charging him, among other things, to take away the lady's plate, whenever she should cross her knife and fork, and to give her a clean one. This Imeerawanyee executed, not only to Mrs. M'Arthur, but to several of the other guests. At last Nanbaree crossed his knife and fork with great gravity, casting a glance at the other, who looked for a moment with cool indifference at what he had done, and then turned his head another way. Stung at this supercilious treatment, he called in rage to know why he was not attended to, as well as the rest of the company. But Imeerawanyee only laughed; nor could all the anger and reproaches of the other prevail upon him to do for one of his countrymen, which he cheerefully continued to perform to every other person.[8]

Nanbarry must have been envious when Governor Phillip decided to take Yemmerrawanne with Bennelong to England when he left Sydney in 1792.

After his initiation, Yemmerrawanne proudly took the name of *kebarrah* which was given to a man whose tooth has been knocked out by a rock (from *kebba* or *kibba*, a rock or stone). This was revealed when he died in May 1794 and his name was entered in the burial register of St John's Church in the village of Eltham, Kent, as Yemmurawonyea Kebarrah, 'supposed to be 19 years of age'.[9]

BOOJERY CARRIBBERIE

> When asked to dance [Bennelong] does it with great readiness; his motions at first are very slow, and are regulated by a dismal tune, which grows quicker as the dance advances, till at length he throws himself into the most violent posture, shaking his arms, and striking the ground with great force, which gives him the appearance of madness. It is very probable that this part of the dance is used as a sort of defiance, as all the natives which were seen when we first arrived at Port Jackson, always joined this sort of dance to their vociferations of 'woroo, woroo,' go away.
> – Philip Gidley King, in John Hunter, *An Historical Journal...*, London, 1793

The word *corroboree*, which evolved from the Sydney language *carabbara* or *carribberie*, was translated merely as 'a dance' by the First Fleet eyewitnesses. It generally applies now to any assembly of indigenous Australians which involves singing and dancing. To Aborigines, however, a corroboree was, and is, the ritual acting out of stories and myths through a fusion of song, music and dance. It is usually held at night around camp fires during full moon.

'Like their songs,' wrote Tench, dances 'are conceived to represent the progress of the passions, and the occupations of life.' They consisted, he continued, of 'short parts, or acts, accompanied with frequent voiciferations, and a kind of hissing, or whizzing noise; they commonly end with a loud rapid shout, and after a short respite are renewed'.[10]

As early as 1790, the *gweagal* at Botany Bay had invented a 'contact corroboree' about Bennelong and the whites at Sydney which described the changed circumstances in which they found themselves. Acting out a story about the colonists at Sydney Cove with humour and mimicry might relieve some of the tension and anger that the Eora felt about the invasion of their country. Such a ritual could also be interpreted as an attempt to reduce or neutralise the superior power of the whites by transforming them into mythic creatures. At the same time, the corroboree expressed respect by the *gweagal* at Botany Bay for the new status Bennelong had gained through his dealings with Governor Phillip.

In March 1791, Bennelong invited Phillip and a group of officers, including Captain John Hunter and Lieutenant William Bradley, to attend a corroboree at night near his hut at *Tubowgulee*. It was the first time that the Eora had allowed the whites to witness this ceremony and the preparations for it.

The accounts left by Hunter and Bradley convey the picturesque spectacle of the sight and sound of the corroboree, but not the words of the songs, whose deeper meaning they could not comprehend or interpret. The foreign audience looked on this event merely as a 'show' to entertain and amuse them. A crowd of officers, marines and sailors arrived at the point soon after sunset. Each carried a weapon, for, said Hunter, 'experience had convinced us that these people have a good deal of treachery in their disposition'. Recalling the spearing of Governor Phillip, the officers looked about carefully to make sure there were no 'armed lurkers' in the bushes, then walked to the scene of the corroboree. First, the Eora prepared for the ceremony by painting their bodies. Hunter wrote:

> They were all Adams and Eves, without even a fig-leaf, but without their dignity. The young women were employed with all their art in painting the young men, who were chiefly ornamented with streaks of white, done with pipe-clay, and in different forms ... no fop preparing for an assembly was ever more desirous of making his person irresistibly beautiful.

The women spat the liquid white pipeclay over the faces of their male friends. Tench recorded some of the body painting designs for corroborees, which in Aboriginal society are associated with totems and particular songs or song cycles. 'Some are streaked with waving lines from head to foot; others marked by broad cross-bars, on the breast, back, and thighs; or encircled with spiral lines; or regularly striped like a zebra.' The dancer's eyes were sometimes outlined by large white circles, their hair was decorated with pieces of bone and they often carried clubs.[11]

Bennelong and Colby, who 'seemed to have the chief authority and direction' (as at Manly Cove), arranged the participants in a semicircle around several small fires. The spectacle began with a few small boys, followed by the men and then some women, until there were more than twenty-four people taking part. 'Their dance was truly wild and savage, yet in many parts, there appeared order and regularity,' Hunter commented. 'If any of the fires were in their way they danced through them,' wrote Bradley.

Frequently one man would separate himself and run around the others, singing loudly, 'using some expressions in one particular tone of voice which we could not understand', and afterwards merged again with the dancers. The songmen, who might have 'owned' specific songs, often started and sometimes ended the chanting. Men came forward to show their skill and agility at what, wrote Hunter, 'seemed to constitute the principal beauties of dancing'. They performed this by 'placing their feet very wide apart, and by an extraordinary exertion of the muscles of the thighs and legs, moving the knees in a trembling and very surprizing manner'. There was plenty of variety. The Eora danced in pairs facing each other, or back-to-back, they suddenly jumped up from the ground and advanced in rows, or circled around a solo dancer. Several times all those taking part held up green boughs, a symbol of peace.

The principal songman, a 'stout, strong voiced man', stood the whole time, singing continuously, rhythmically striking one hardwood stick against another held against his chest. Some women, who did not dance, and several young boys and girls, sat at his feet and beat time on their thighs with the hollow of their hands or sang along with him. Tench noted that the singer was 'usually a person of note and estimation'. In northern Australia, the songman, wrote anthropologist A.P. Elkin, 'is not simply a man with a good voice, but one who has been taught by, and inherited his position from, his father or uncle, and so on in lineal succession'.[12]

On the whole, Hunter thought the exhibition was worth seeing. The dancers were anxious to please their audience and asked their opinion at the end of each set, to which Phillip and his officers replied *boojery* (good) or *boojery carribberie* (good corroboree). After an hour, Bennelong asked his guests if they would like to stay for one more performance, which they did. Afterwards, the children returned to the settlement with the officers.[13]

TOTEM AND TABOO

The amateur ethnologists of the First Fleet witnessed many Eora rituals and ceremonies, including initiations, corroborees, body painting and burials. They frequently stumbled across stone engravings of ancestor heroes, weapons and sea and land animals. Bennelong told them that when a person died their spirit left the body and went into the sky and described the terrifying malevolent spirit called the *mawm*.

Despite this evidence and their curiosity about them, the officers concluded that the Eora had no religion. By the narrow European definition of the period, religion specifically meant belief in, or worship of, a single supreme god. David Collins could find no 'trace of religion',[14] but Philip Gidley King in his journal, was inclined to concede that the 'spirit' might mean the soul.

> No sign of any Religion has been observed among them, but they are not ignorant of a future state, as they say the bones are in the Grave and the Body in the Clouds. As those we have had with us, may be misunderstood it may be imagined that they mean the Soul is in the Clouds. Wolarewarre [Bennelong] once asked the Judge-Advocate [Collins] if the White men went to the Clouds also?[15]

Collins said that the Eora were afraid of thunder and lightning, which they regarded as a sign of danger, and when lightning struck they would chant and breathe heavily in an effort to dispel it.[16] To the north of Sydney, thunder was associated with the sky hero Baiami, whose voice in initiation ceremonies was represented by the loud roar of the bullroarer, a thin, narrow piece of wood which was whirled through the air by a string.

It is easy to be wise in hindsight. Possessing only a superficial understanding and appreciation of Aboriginal language and spirituality, the eyewitnesses were outsiders, unable to uncover or document their secret life, which was closely guarded by the elders or wise older men who were its custodians. They found no Dreaming, as it is understood today, but perhaps the entry *Gurugal — A long time before* was an expression for the period of creation heroes?[17] While collecting evidence which points to the existence of totemism, the English observers did not grasp its significance, nor, to be fair, were they seeking it.

A totem is an emblem or image from nature which indigenous people see as a part of their identity. In Aboriginal society, totems link the human, natural and supernatural worlds. Animals, birds, reptiles, fish, plants, the sun, stars and moon are all treated as totems. In most parts of Australia it is forbidden to kill, injure or eat your totem, that is, the animal or object with which you share your name, which is treated as a 'father' or an 'elder brother'. A.P. Elkin defined totemism as a view of nature and life and of the universe which colours and influences social groupings and mythologies, inspires rituals and unites humans with the natural species.[18] For insiders, those instructed in the mysteries, totems unite everyday life to the secret life of myth and ritual.[19]

The English explorer George Grey gave the first account of what is now termed a totem. 'Each family [clan] adopts an animal or vegetable as their crest and sign,' he wrote. 'A certain mysterious connection exists between a family and its *kobong*, so that a member of a family will never kill an animal of that species, to which his *kobong* belongs.' Grey related the *kobong* to the *totam* (totem) of the Ojibway, an Algonquian-speaking tribe of North American Indians.[20]

'The totem is a name first of all, and then ... an emblem,' observed Emile Durkheim.[21] Several examples of personal names which represented totemic emblems – birds, fish, kangaroos, other animals and plants – can be found among the Eora who lived in the Sydney area late in the eighteenth century. Two dominant sets of totems indicate the presence of bird and fish cults from the handful of names disclosed to the strangers, now preserved in journals, letters and language notebooks.

The journal keepers wrote down their own distinctive interpretations of the names and words they heard. Sounds that were not common to both languages presented difficulties in transcription. 'It is difficult to catch their exact pronunciation, more so to give you an idea of it by letters,' wrote Elizabeth Macarthur.[22] One way to compare names and words is by repeated pronunciation with varying inflections. For example all vowel sounds can often be interchanged, as can the consonants c, k and g, d and t, and p and b.

Caruey, who the whites called Carraway or Gurooee, is close to *garraway*, the Eora name for the white (or sulphur-crested) cockatoo. Another man, Yeranibi Goruey, had probably exchanged his name with Caruey. Carradah (Koorooda), the name of a *cameragal* (also called Mr Ball or Midger Bool), is similar to *carrate*, the glossy black cockatoo. Bennelong's daughter, Dilboong, who died in 1791, was named after a bird with a shrill note. Daniel Southwell referred to a young girl 'in the camp' called Worogan (also Worgan, Worgin, Wa'gan, Wagun), a crow. Botany Bay Kolbi's wife Muriang was named for the emu, *marong* or *muraong*, while Barring-an or Beringan, 'a handsome girl', the daughter of Mooroobera, is the inland dialect (Darug) word for the welcome swallow.

Bennelong said he was named after a fish 'but one that I never saw taken', remarked Collins.[23] Bennelong's friend Watewal (Waltewal or Wattewal Weeremurrah) was synonymous with *wattegal* (a large fish).

Ballooderry, said Collins, 'signified the fish named by us the leathern-jacket [leatherjacket]'. His father's name, Maugoran (*maugro, maugra, magra*) was the generic word for fish, while *maugerry* meant fishing. Mawberry (Mauberry), an older Eora woman, was 'the term by which they distinguish the gurnet [gurnard] from other fish', said Collins.

Arthur Phillip and his aides were puzzled by these names. At first, Phillip wrote, there was 'every reason to think that children are named after the fish they first catch'.[24] 'Each person has several names,' Watkin Tench surmised, 'one of which, there is reason to believe, is always derived from the first fish or animal, which the child, in accompanying its father to the chace [hunt], or a fishing, may chance to kill.'[25] According to Collins, it was the custom to name a child at one month to six weeks old. 'This is generally taken from the objects constantly before their eyes, such as a bird, a beast, or a fish, and is given without any ceremony.'[26]

Patyegarang, a young girl who was the principal informant of Lieutenant William Dawes about the native language, shared her name with the large grey kangaroo, while Burrowun (Burrowannie) was the burrawang palm (*Macrozamia*), a plant with poisonous nuts that were eaten by the Eora only after preparation. Boorong (or Birrong), according to Daniel Paine (1795), meant a star. Bennelong's sister, who married Yowarry, was called Carangarang, a word denoting both sea and pretty, while her daughter Kah-dier-rang is close to *kah-dien*, the shell of the Sydney cockle. Pemulwuy meant clay or earth.

Further evidence for Eora totems is provided by the hundreds of rock engravings of fish, whales, eels, kangaroos, emus, birds, echidnas and lizards which still survive in the sandstone art galleries of the Sydney area. In the opinion of anthropologist F.D. McCarthy: 'Most of the animal figures represent totems or emblems of clans, individuals, and of the men and women as separate groups.' Some of these were totemic sites, which marked clan territory and were the scene of sacred rituals. Some include lines or pathways of carved human, bird or animals footprints called *mundoes* or *mundowies*. 'During initiation ceremonies,' continued McCarthy, 'the novitiates were taken along the ritual paths to learn the myths, see the carvings and be taught how to make them.'[27]

Through fieldwork, inquiry and observation, particularly in central and northern Australia, anthropologists have found a consistent pattern in the deep spiritual and emotional relationship, through creation stories and totems, between indigenous people and their 'country', that is, the landscape they inhabit or were born in. Their stories tell of the wanderings of mythical ancestors. Moving through the landscape, these spirit beings sang songs and created, changed or named geological features such as hills, rocks and watercourses. What we call the Dreaming is the enmeshing of groups and individuals through totems, the landscape and stories about ancestor spirits which pervades Aboriginal culture. Dreaming embodies both law and lore.

Personal totems were symbols which unified the Eora with the animals and plants. To renew their world, they repeated myths and stories about them in rituals, song, dance, body painting and rock carvings. It is likely, for example, that Caruey imagined that he was *garraway* the white cockatoo and that he was descended from the white cockatoo in the sacred stories and songs he 'owned' or was entitled to relate.

THE CROW

One day Surgeon George Worgan of HMS *Sirius* was about to shoot a crow perched in a tree, but as he levelled his gun to fire, an Eora man ran forward and put his hand over the muzzle, crying out '*Bau Bau Bau Bau*' – 'meaning as I conjectured', wrote Worgan, 'that I was not to kill it (for they had seen the Effects of the Gun) I complied with his Request, and laughed off the Offence I had seemingly given, at which, he laughed likewise and seemed mightily pleased'.[28]

It is usual to interpret Worgan's anecdote as meaning that the bright-eyed Australian crow had a special significance to the man and was very likely his totem.[29] A deeper understanding is revealed if we reflect that the word for a crow was *worgan* or *worogan*. It follows that the Aborigine had bravely prevented the surgeon shooting what was, in his eyes, Worgan's own totem.

The Eora usually made it their business to find out the names of the whites. 'They are very fond of asking your names,' wrote Ralph Clark when he met Dourrawan and Tirriwan at Lane Cove in February 1790. 'I told them mine yesterday, which the[y] recollected and called me by it today.'[30]

How astonished the Eora must have been (on this or another occasion) when the surgeon shot and winged a crow which he then held in his hand and waved to try to entice them ashore from their canoes. William Bradley continues the story:

> Finding that they would not land the Surgeon threw the Bird towards them, which having recovered itself flew away & joined some others in a Tree close by, this uncommon circumstance which could not appear to them short of our having power to give & take life, astonished them so much, that they remained quite silent sometime & then all joined in a loud exclamation of wonder.[31]

Worgan obviously did not understand the significance of the crow as a spiritual emblem and continued to shoot and eat the birds. 'With famine staring us in the face,' he wrote later, 'happy is the man that can kill a rat or crow to make him a dainty meal.' Some years later, David Collins, who had read an English newspaper article about the man throwing himself in front of the surgeon's gun, ridiculed the inference drawn by the writer that 'the bird was an object of worship', while bearing out the bird's link with Worgan in particular by stating: 'I can with confidence affirm, that so far from dreading to see a crow killed, they [the natives] are very fond of eating it.'[32]

SHIPS

Although they usually found their totems in the natural world, the Eora were fascinated by the English sailing ships which moored in Sydney Cove. Two convict transports arrived in Port Jackson within a few days of each other in 1791 and went hunting for whales after discharging their passengers. Two native men adopted the names of these ships, which they perhaps regarded as their personal totems.

Willamannan, which David Collins said had been 'corrupted by their pronunciation', took his name from the whaler *William and Ann*.[33] He might have been one of two Aboriginal guides from the Sydney area who accompanied a hunting party from HMS *Gorgon* which came across the *William and Ann* at anchor in Broken Bay on 8 December 1791.[34] Willamannan, who was wounded in a punishment conflict in 1797, was mentioned in the *Sydney Gazette* in 1804 and 1805. Taking a ship's name did not make him a good sailor. In October 1805, the *Sydney Gazette* reported that 'Wilhamanan' had deserted the whaler *Raven* at Jervis Bay and returned to Sydney. He explained that 'the *ship* was very *little*, and the *sea* grew very big'.[35]

When the Russian voyagers under Captain Fabian Bellingshausen camped at Kirribilli on Sydney's north shore in 1820, they met a 'New Hollander' called Burra Burra who took them to his shelter where his family was gathered around a fire.[36] Willamannan is likely to be this man, whose name was written as *Burra burra vilam miny* when sketched by the Russian artist Pavel Mikhailov. He complained that Mikhailov's sketch did not show him in his 'full attire'. Picking up a small stick, he thrust it through the slit in his nose, so that it would be included in the portrait. After that, he asked the Russians for clothing.[37] By 1828 Willamannan, a member of the *walkeloa* or Brisbane Water clan, was known as William Munnan, who, according to the Reverend Lancelot Threlkeld, was named by the Broken Bay chief Bungaree as the brutal killer of a woman in the Government Domain in Sydney.[38] As William Manen, he collected blankets from government officials in Sydney in 1836. In the winter of 1844 William Menen met a tragic death, caused by exposure to the elements. According to the *Sydney Dispatch* of 8 June, the previous night police had turned Menen away from a Sydney hotel when he was 'helplessly drunk' and taken him to the racecourse at Hyde Park to sleep it off.[39]

Salamander, also sketched by Mikhailov at Kirribilli in 1820, took the name of the whaler *Salamander*. A member of the Brisbane Water or Broken Bay clan, he collected blankets at Sydney in 1833, 1835 and 1836, when he was said to be aged between thirty and forty.[40] In 1834, Salamander, with Toby and Bowen (sons of the Broken Bay chief Bungaree), lived at Camp Cove in Sydney Harbour and traded fish with the crews of visiting ships in return for rum.[41]

The son of Bennelong's sister Carangarang and her husband Yowarry might also have been named after a ship. His name, O-ring gnouey g'nouey, could be interpreted as *Warrane nowey nowey*, meaning 'many canoes in Warrane' (Sydney Cove), or, just possibly, as *Narrang nowey* or 'small canoe', the name the Eora gave to HMS *Supply*.[42]

SHARKS AND STINGRAYS

Sharks and stingrays were taboo and could not be eaten by the coastal Eora. 'These people last summer would neither eat shark nor stingray,' Arthur Phillip reported to Lord Sydney on 28 September 1788.[43] 'There are great numbers of the Sting Ray & shark, both which I have seen the Natives throw away when given to them & often refuse them when offered,' wrote William Bradley in October that year.[44] 'Sharks of an enormous size are found here,' wrote Tench. 'The Indians, probably from having felt the effects of their voracious fury, testify the utmost horror on seeing these terrible fish.'[45] Collins wrote: 'the sting-ray was (wee-re) bad; it was a fish of which they never ate'.[46]

Logically, these taboos imply that clan totems of the shark and stingray existed on the Sydney coastline. Perhaps, as in other parts of Australia, the Eora were divided into two groups or moieties – shark and stingray – in which a man could only marry a woman from the opposite half.

Eels, an important source of food, are common subjects of rock carvings. By implication, the eel was the clan totem of the *burramattagal*, who gave their name to Parramatta and the Parramatta River. *Burra* means eel, and *matta* a place associated with running water.

Around Sydney the taboo on the use of the name of a recently dead person was strictly enforced, while certain foods (possibly of totemic emblems) were forbidden to kin and other mourners during and after funerals. In 1792 a violent battle took place at Botany Bay when a man mentioned the name of someone in his clan who had died.[47]

15

EORA IN TOWN

Familiarity, and the contempt it tends to breed, was the consequence of the peaceful presence of the Eora in the 'camp', as the colonists called Sydney Town. In March 1791, as the *Waaksamheyd*, a Dutch ship purchased at Cape Town, prepared to depart, a flurry of letters was penned to friends, relatives and useful connections at home in England describing this peaceful invasion.

'The natives visit us every day, more or less, men, women, and children; they come with great confidence, without spears or other offensive weapon,' Elizabeth Macarthur informed her friend Bridget Kingdon. 'A great many have taken up their abode entirely amongst us, and Bannylong and Coleby, with their wives, come in frequently.'[1]

'Many More Men, Women & Children are Come Among Us, & Are Sometimes Quite familiar but other times are Shy, they would be Great thieves if they had ... pockets,' David Blackburn wrote to his sister Margaret at St Michael's, Norwich. Blackburn sent a box which contained 'some Drawings of Birds Plants & fishes of this Country'.[2]

'The Whole Tribe with their Visitors have plagued us ever since [coming in], nor can we now get rid of them they come and go at pleasure,' wrote Surgeon John Harris to an unknown correspondent. 'They are very fond of our Bread Beef &c. and are amazing fear'd of our Guns.' With unusual frankness, Harris added: 'We indeed have been obliged to shoot some of them but not lately.'[3]

On 22 March, Lieutenant William Bradley recorded the 'numbers of people in the Settlement':[4]

At Sydney and Rose Hill ... 1385
At Norfolk Island ... 627
Natives ... 6

Six of the Eora 'in town' therefore were regarded as 'honorary settlers', entitled to receive food rations. These were probably Nanbarry, who lived with Surgeon White; Boorong, who had been adopted by Chaplain Johnson and his wife; Yemmerrawanne, who stayed at the governor's house; and Bennelong, Barangaroo and Colby, who frequently took their meals with Governor Phillip.

'Since the Sailing of the last Ships, an Intercourse had been opened with the Natives of this Country, and many of them reside wholly amongst us,' David Collins wrote in a letter to his father on 23 March. If he did not return to England with the next ships, Collins advised, 'I mean to send for Publication, an Account of all our Transactions with them'.[5]

In a letter to Sir Joseph Banks on 24 March, Arthur Phillip referred to the spear wound he had received at Manly Cove. 'Many of these people [natives] are now much at home at Sydney as they are in their woods, but in bringing this about they treated me rather roughly, however I don't find any inconveniency from the hurt I received.'[6]

Captain John Hunter, in command of the *Waaksamheyd*, said the Eora had become 'exceedingly fond of bread', which at first they would not eat. Little children had all learnt the English words 'hungry, bread' and would draw in their stomachs to show they were empty.[7] 'Before I left Port Jackson [28 March],' Hunter wrote, 'the natives were become very familiar and intimate with every person in the settlement; many of them now took up their rest every night in some of the gentlemen's houses; their very unprovoked attack on the governor and his party being passed over and almost forgot.'[8]

However, by May 1791 the Eora 'most accustomed to live at the settlement' frequently went away, often for several days, to go fishing near the Heads.[9]

THE NATIVE INFORMANTS

In his second language notebook, begun in 1791, William Dawes continues to credit the informants who actively helped him compile his Vocabulary.[10] These Eora 'in town' included Bennelong (Benelang), Barangaroo, Boorong, Nanbarry, Colby, Daringa (Taringa), Warwiar or Warreweer, Worogan (Warrgan) and a little girl named Gonangoolie (Gonangulye). Some who did not provide words or phrases are mentioned in passing: Punangan, Tugear, Ngalgear, Bondel (Pandal), Daringa's brother Boneda (Poonda), and Boorong's little half-brother Bidya Bidya (Bidgy Bidgy).

This second notebook is filled with candid dialogues which show Dawes attempting to break down the language and cultural barriers between himself and the Eora. It is a rich historical, linguistic and ethnographic resource, full of clues about the kinship relationships between the native people who visited the settlement. At the same time it is a kind of diary of the flirtation and increasing intimacy throughout 1791 between Dawes and Patyegarang, a girl aged about fifteen, who was his principal language teacher, servant and very close companion, if not lover. Dawes wrote 'The names of Pateygarang' as *Tagaran Tuba Kanmangnal Patyegarang*, spelt her name phonetically as Badyegarang, and often called her Patye.[11] Some phrases (with comments by Dawes) indicate that Patyegarang stayed in Dawes's hut at night, for example:

Nangagolang – To go to sleep.
This Badyegarang said when the taptoo [tattoo] beat[12]

Matigarabangun naigaba – We shall sleep separate[13]

Tycrabarrbowaryaou – I shall not become white.
This was said to me by Patyegarang after I had told her, if she would wash herself often, she would become white at the same time throwing down the towel as in despair[14]

Tariadyaoie – I made a mistake in speaking.
This Patye said, after she had desired me to take away the blanket when she meant the candle[15]

P. Nyimang candle Mr. D.   Put out the candle Mr.D.[16]

D. Mlnyin bıal nangadyimi? Why dont you sleep?
P. Kandulin - - - Because of the candle[17]

Patyegarang praised Dawes for his accurate pronunciation of her language: 'Mr. Dawes budyeri karaga – Mr. D. pronounces well'.[18] Dawes was also teaching Patyegarang to read English and she told him that she was 'ashamed' when he could 'scarce prevail on her to read' to some strangers (possibly from HMS *Gorgon*) on 25 September 1791.[19]

Dawes referred to Patyegarang's companion Worogan (also Warrgan, Worgin, Wurrgan, meaning 'crow') as 'a great thief', inferring that Worogan had stolen from him.[20] In a few lines dealing with family relationships, Dawes includes 'Wurrgan' with Bennelong's sisters, which implies that she was closely related to him. She later married Boorong's brother, Yeranibe. Worogan, described as *'femme sauvage des environs de port Jackson'*, was sketched as *Oui-Ré-Kine* or *Oïe réquinè* (i.e., Warrekine or Weerekine) by French artist Nicolas-Martin Petit, who visited Sydney in 1802 with the Baudin expedition.[21]

There were two girls in the settlement called Warreweer. One was Bennelong's pretty younger sister, who married Gnunga Gnunga Murremurgan, nicknamed Collins because he had exchanged names with the judge advocate. Dawes called her Warreweer Biel-bool (two eyes). The other was Warreweer Wogul-Mi (one-eyed), who was probably the Wareweer mentioned in Dawes's notebook. She was a *burramattagalleon*, the daughter of Maugoran and Tadyera and therefore the sister of Bedia Bedia and half-sister of Ballooderry and Boorong.

THE SYDNEY LANGUAGES

'The Governor & those Gentlemen who attend to the getting of a Vocabulary of the Native language have made considerable progress in it, but many of the Customs of these Savages yet remain doubtful as to the cause,' wrote William Bradley in March 1791.[22]

There is no record of the name of the language spoken by the Eora, that is, the accumulated words and dialogues that Dawes, Phillip, Collins and others were collecting from native informants and attempting to write down in English letters. In September 1796, Collins called their language the 'Port Jackson dialect'.[23] Watkin Tench noted that 'the dialect of the sea coast' was spoken at Rose Hill (Parramatta) and drew attention to the differing inland dialect at the Hawkesbury River.[24] The consensus of scholars today is to use the term Sydney language.

The original manuscript notebooks compiled by William Dawes and the notebook attributed to Phillip and Collins are kept at the University of London and have not been published. 'Dictionary of the Coastal Darug (Eora) language' in *The Darug and their Neighbours* (Darug Link, 1993) by James Kohen and *The Sydney Language* (AIATSIS, 1993a) by Jakelin Troy provide the best insight into the Sydney languages.

Using the eighteenth-century notebooks and much later ethnographic information and word lists as evidence, various models have been constructed relating to the geographic boundaries of the language groups ('tribes') of the Sydney area, notably by Dr Kohen (1986), subsequently revised in 'Mapping Aboriginal Linguistic and Clan Boundaries in the Sydney Region' in *The Globe* (no. 41, 1995). Very broadly, the prevailing model identifies one language group, Darug, covering the Sydney coast and west to the Blue Mountains, while Kuringgai is said to be the language used on the north shore of Port Jackson, west to the Lane Cove River and north to Broken Bay, where people called themselves *koori* or *kuri*. The name Darug (Darook, Daruk, Dharug, etc.) was obtained by R.H. Matthews from Aboriginal people living on a reserve at Sackville on the Hawkesbury River about 1901. The name Kuringgai was coined as a 'convenient' term by the Reverend Arthur Capell as recently as 1970.[25]

Models should be challenged and questions must be asked. By looking at the pool of informants in Dawes a and b and the anonymous Sydney language notebooks, it is evident that the model is flawed, as in the period 1790-2 the same language was spoken and understood from Manly in the north to Sydney Cove, from Botany Bay in the south to Sydney Cove and west to Parramatta.

In the following dialogue recorded by Dawes, Patyegarang, his chief language informant, used the word *kamarigal* (*cameraigal* or *cameragal*) interchangeably with *eora* (people) and Dawes's 'black men'. This indicates that Patye was a *cameragalleon*, a woman from the powerful north shore *cameragal* (Cammeray clan). 'The tribe of Camerra,' wrote Philip Gidley King, 'inhabit the North part of Port Jackson which is somewhere named Camerra.'[26]

I then told her that a whiteman had been wounded some days ago in coming from Kadi to Warang [Sydney Cove] & asked her why the black men did it.

Ansr. Gulara   (Because they are) angry.

D. Minyin gulara eora?	Why are the b.m. angry?
P. Inyam ngalwi w.m.	Because the white men are settled here.
P. Tyerun kamarigal	The kamarigals are afraid.
D. Minyin tyerun k-gal?	Why are the k- afraid?
P. Gunin.	Because of the Guns.[27]

Bennelong's wife Barangaroo was a *cameragalleon*, as was the beautiful Goo-ree-dee-a-na, who Tench said 'belonged to the tribe of Cameragal'.[28]

The words given to Dawes and Phillip were provided by informants from a wide area of today's city of Sydney, including the North Shore (Patyegarang and Barangaroo), Eastern Suburbs (Colby), Botany Bay (Kurubarabulu), Parramatta River (Bennelong) and the Parramatta area (Maugoran's family). In short, the same language was spoken on both sides of Sydney Harbour.

The Sydney language notebooks merit more attention and will in the future provide authentic facts for analysis and interpretation by historians, anthropologists and linguists seeking the truth about the first contact period.

The origins of the informants must be taken into account in this research. For example, Capell (1970) concluded that three languages were spoken in the Sydney area at the time of European settlement in 1788. As we have seen, Capell allocated the Kuringgai (Guringai) language to the area starting immediately on Sydney's north shore and north along the coast through Broken Bay to Lake Macquarie, where the language was Awaba.[29]

Dr Kohen cites the sources for his 'Dictionary of the Kuringgai Language' (1993) as Long Dick, son of Bungaree and Gooseberry, who provided a word list to the explorer J.F. Mann (1819-1907) and a record of a dialect spoken at Carigal (West Head) just south of the mouth of the Hawkesbury River, mentioned by the Reverend Lancelot Threlkeld.[30] Both Long Dick (Boia) and Birabran (John McGill) were listed in blanket returns during the 1830s-40s as members of the *walkeloa* or Brisbane Water 'tribe'. In 1835-6, Long Dick was among a group from this clan who were imprisoned on Goat Island in Sydney Harbour and taught English by a catechist, George Langhorne.[31] Birabran or McGill came to Sydney in May 1836 to act as an interpreter for the prisoners. Threlkeld, the missionary at Lake Macquarie, put great faith in Birabran, whom he called 'my black tutor'. Birabran was brought up at the Barracks in Sydney as a child and spoke very good English.

Mann first met Long Dick at Brisbane Water in 1842.[32] 'Their territory was bounded on the south by the Hawkesbury River, which separated them from the Sydney or Cammeray tribe, with whom they were on terms of friendship,' he wrote later.[33]

As both informants came from north of the Hawkesbury River, it is unlikely that the vocabulary they provided represented a language spoken any further south than the Pittwater area, north of Sydney. The idea that the Kuringgai language extended south to Sydney's north shore therefore rests on shaky ground. It might better be termed the Broken Bay-Awaba language.

THE ITCH

> On asking Benelang: when the tyibul tyibul would go away, he answers Guago yura Bye & bye when the warm weather comes
>
> – William Dawes, Vocabulary, 1791

The Eora, including Bennelong, suffered from the t*yibul tyibul* or *djee-ball djee-ball*, a skin irritation which resembled scabies, a disease the English called 'the itch'.

David Collins blamed the predominantly fish diet of the sea coast natives for this malady, even though the itch seemed to be at its worst in winter, when fewer fish were caught. 'At one time, about the year 1791, there was not one of the natives, man, woman, nor child, that came near us, but was covered with it,' wrote Collins. 'It raged violently among them, and some became very loathsome objects.'[34] Bennelong told William Dawes that the *tyibul tyibul* would go away 'bye & bye', when warmer weather came.[35]

At the end of August 1791, the English doctors successfully treated several boys by rubbing brimstone (sulphur) into their skin. They persuaded Bennelong to come to the hospital and rub himself with sulphur. However, Phillip described him as 'a perfect Lazarus' when he refused to stay long enough to be cured.[36] Entries in Dawes's language notebook at this time refer to Patyegarang and Warreweer being dosed against the itch with sulphur and water. '*Nabaouwi ngalia naba eora widawara*,' said Warreweer, which Dawes translated as 'The eoras [people] shall see us drink [sulphur]'.[37]

This itchy skin condition might have been aggravated by the recent and abrupt change from the traditional native diet to different and unfamiliar foreign foods such as potatoes, pumpkins, melons, bread made from weevilly flour, tea, coffee, dried dhal and rancid salt beef and pork from Bengal (India). The itch lingered on among coastal Aborigines as late as 1845, when the Botany Bay fisherman Mahroot described 'Devil devil' as 'all over, smallpox like'.[38]

16

EXPEDITION TO THE WEST

An expedition commanded by Governor Phillip and accompanied by Colby and Ballooderry as guides left Rose Hill (Parramatta) on the morning of 11 April. Bennelong also wanted to go, but, wrote Watkin Tench, 'his wife would not permit it'.[1] While Colby was away, his wife Daringa and their child Panieboollong remained in Sydney, and were given provisions.

Phillip's plan was to walk inland to the west, cross the Hawkesbury River near Richmond Hill and then push on to the Blue Mountains. Tench, however, said the object of the journey was 'to ascertain whether or not the Hawkesbury and the Nepean, were the same river'. The explorers included Judge Advocate William Collins and his servant, Surgeon John White, Tench and Lieutenant William Dawes, two marine sergeants, eight soldiers and three convicts who were good shots. Each man (except the governor) carried his own knapsack with enough food for ten days and also a gun, a blanket, a water canteen, a cooking kettle and a hatchet. Colby and Ballooderry had small packs, but most of their provisions were distributed in the knapsacks of the soldiers and game shooters.

The course followed was determined by Dawes, who steered northwest by compass while 'counting the number of paces, of which two thousand two hundred on good ground, were allowed to be a mile'.[2] The two guides were intrigued by the compass, for which they coined the name *naa-moro*, meaning 'to see the way'.[3]

Only a short distance from Rose Hill, Colby and Ballooderry (who came from Parramatta) were already in unfamiliar country. Although they laughed 'to excess' when any of the party tripped or stumbled, 'the farther they went', said Tench, 'the more dependent on us they became, being absolute strangers inland'. The country immediately west of Rose Hill, the Eora men said, was 'inhabited by the *Bidjigals*, but ... most of the tribe were dead of the small-pox'. Further west was the territory of the *boorooberongal* (Hawkesbury River clan). Colby and Ballooderry wanted to destroy a hut belonging to these people, who they said were bad and were their enemies. After sunset the travellers made camp and met a young native man, about thirty years of age, carrying a lighted firestick and calling for his dog. The linguists among the whites (Collins, Phillip, Dawes and Tench) were able to follow some of the conversation during this encounter.

'I am Colby of the tribe of Cadigal.'

'I am Bereewan, of the tribe of Boorooberongal,' the man replied.[4]

Ballooderry also gave his name. Bereewan's hair was decorated with animal tails and he carried a *mogo* (stone hatchet), a spear and a spear-thrower. Although an initiated man, none of his teeth had been removed. The Eora guides introduced the English officers to Bereewan, repeating their names, and told him they were good and had come from the sea coast. Bereewan was given some food before he left.

Next day (12 April), the expedition followed the river, which was about 100 metres wide, with banks 6 metres high covered with straight trees. 'We saw many ducks, and killed one, which Colbee swam for,' Tench recorded. Colby and Ballooderry had never seen the Hawkesbury, which the *boorooberongal* called *Deerubin*. They had no idea where they were and when asked where Rose Hill was, pointed almost in the opposite direction.

Before he could be stopped, Ballooderry destroyed one of the *boorooberongal* bark huts. When the weary travellers made camp at night, cut and scratched all over by prickly bushes and frequent falls, the two guides ate their food and would then 'play ten thousand tricks and gambols', wrote Tench. 'They imitated the leaping of the kanguroo; sang; danced; poized the spear; and met in mock encounter. But their principal source of merriment was again derived from our misfortunes, in tumbling amidst nettles, and sliding down precipices, which they mimicked with inimitable drollery.'

Colby and Ballooderry thought Governor Phillip had organised the party to shoot ducks and *pategorang* (kangaroos). They soon grew weary of the prolonged journey and tried to persuade Phillip to turn back. When it rained they lost all patience, telling Phillip that there were 'good houses at Sydney and Rose-hill, but they had no house now, no fish, no melon (of which all natives are very fond)' and would have left the English party if they knew the country.[5] To Colby and Ballooderry, wrote Tench, Rose Hill or Sydney was *budyeree* (good) but the land they crossed was *weeree, weeree* (bad). 'At Rose Hill,' they said, 'are potatoes, cabbages, pumpkins, turnips, fish, and wine: here are nothing but rocks and water.' These comparisons always ended with the question: 'Where's Rose Hill; where?' When the foreigners rebuked them, Colby and Ballooderry called them *gonin patta*, meaning 'shit eaters'.[6]

The explorers came across several canoes hauled up on the sandy river bank, where they met an old man called Gomebeere known to Colby, whose body was marked by smallpox. He said he had come to find stones for hatchets from the river near Richmond Hill, still a long way off. After they had formally introduced Governor Phillip to him, Gomebeere gave the governor two stone hatchets, two spears and a *womerra* and in return received some bread, metal fishhooks and a couple of small English hatchets. He then walked ahead of the party, pointing out the pathway. Gomebeere and his family group ate some pork and biscuits and drank from the English canteens, but kept their wives and children well away on the other side of the river. Gomebeere and his son Yarramundi (Yellomundee) each had two wives and were hereditary 'doctors of renown' or *carradigan*. Yarramundi's son, Jim-bah (Deeimba) would succeed him.

'Although our natives and the strangers conversed on a par, and understood each other perfectly, yet they spoke different dialects of the same language,' Tench noted. He was baffled by this, as the coastal dialect was spoken at Rose Hill, only 30 kilometres away. The linguists recorded a few words which differed between the two dialects.

By sucking his chest, Yarramundi treated Colby for an old wound below his left breast caused by a short two-pronged spear, for which Colby gave him some of his supper and a knitted woollen nightcap. In the 'Vocabulary' most likely compiled by Phillip and Collins, *doo-ul* is given as 'Colebe's word for the two barbs' (a spear) and *car-rah-dy* as 'a person skilled in treating wounds'.[7] The *boorooberongal* told Tench that the river yielded only mullet and they lived on small animals and roots, mainly yams, which they dug from the ground. Neither of the adult men had 'suffered the extraction of a front tooth'. Colby and Ballooderry (whose front teeth had been knocked out at initiation) would not ask why and quickly dropped the subject. They slept the night before the camp fire, Yarramundi cradling his son in his arms and always moving him first whenever he wanted to turn over.

After breakfast on 15 April, in return for a biscuit, Gomebeere gave his visitors a demonstration of how the inland people climbed trees in search of small game. Using a *mogo* or stone hatchet, he cut a small notch in the tree trunk about 45 centimetres from the ground, where he placed the big toe of his left foot as he wrapped his left arm around the tree. Tench continued:

> In an instant, he had cut a second notch for his right toe on the other side of the tree, into which he sprung; and thus alternately cutting on each side, he mounted to the height of twenty feet, in nearly as short a space as if he had ascended by a ladder, although the bark of the tree was quite smooth and slippery; and the trunk four feet in diameter, and perfectly straight.

While climbing, Gomebeeree kept his hands free by holding the hatchet between his teeth, which did not stop him constantly talking and laughing with his friends below. The watercolour *Method of Climbing Trees* by the Port Jackson Painter seems to be based on this incident.[8] If so, the unknown artist could have been one of the Hawkesbury explorers, perhaps Collins's servant. On the second day of the journey, Colby and Ballooderry had described the *boorooberongal* as 'climbers of trees'. 'In this manner,' noted

Phillip, 'do these people climb trees, whose circumference is ten or fifteen feet, or upwards, after an opossum or a squirrel, though they rise to the height of sixty or eighty feet before there is a single branch.'[9]

Colby spoke of his wife Daringa in Sydney and said his child would cry without him. Both men kept up their chant of 'Where's Rose Hill; where?' and were delighted when the expedition was cut short the following day. On the return journey the explorers shot some ducks, but Ballooderry refused to swim after them. 'He told us, in a surly tone, that they swam for what was killed, and had the trouble of fetching it ashore, only for the white man to eat it,' Tench wrote, admitting the truth of the accusation. When they reached the Rose Hill settlement, Colby and Ballooderry immediately jumped into a boat leaving for Sydney 'to communicate to Baneelon, and the rest of their countrymen, the novelties they had seen'.

After this trip, contact between the inland and coastal clans increased. Some people from the west came to visit or live in Sydney, including Bereewan (also Burrowun or Burruwannie), who became an ally of Colby.[10] Another *boorooberongal* called Yowarry made an alliance with Bennelong, who, in return, would give him his sister Carangarang. 'Bur-ro-wun, Gom-bee-re, Yello-mundy or Yellah-munde, DJimba or Jimbah' are the first entries in 'Names of Native Men' in 'Vocabulary of the language of N.S. Wales in the neighbourhood of Sydney', evidence which links this notebook to the expedition to the west and confirms its date as 1791.[11]

'In my last little journey, I found on the banks of the Hawkesbury, people who made use of several words we could not understand, and it soon appear'd that they had a language different from that used by those natives we had hitherto been acquainted with,' Phillip wrote to Sir Joseph Banks on 3 December 1791. He added that the language was different from that of 'two of those natives who have lived amongst us [Ballooderry and Colby]'. They 'appeared to have some knowledge of it', but did not know it well.[12]

In Collins's opinion, 'our companions conversed with the river natives without any apparent difficulty, each understanding or comprehending the other'.[13]

Bennelong and Colby caused a stir at night when they tried to abduct Kurubarabulu from Governor Phillip's house on 8 May. Earlier that day, the two men, with Barangaroo and Daringa, had eaten with Phillip and 'came in as usual to have a glass of wine and a dish of coffee; after which they left the house to go and sleep at Bennelong's hut on the point'. In the middle of the night, Phillip heard cries from a backyard shed where Kurubarabulu was sleeping. Bennelong and Colby and two other men were prevented from dragging her away by the sentries, who allowed the culprits to jump over the paling fence and escape. It appeared that they had left their wives at their fires at *Tubogowlee* and come back to the governor's yard to sleep before the gates were closed.

Bennelong and Colby were not seen for the next week. Colby came in first and, when accused, said he was asleep at the time and laid the blame on Bennelong. Bennelong, who arrived soon after, listened sullenly to the charges but could not make any excuse or deny he was in the yard. Governor Phillip told Bennelong he was angry and said the soldiers would shoot him if he ever again tried to take any woman away at night. Bennelong, however, 'very coolly replied that he would spear the soldier' and said that he was very hungry. Phillip could see little advantage in punishing Bennelong, so he gave him some food, but afterwards ordered the sentries to fire on any natives who climbed the fence.

Asked whether Bennelong and Colby were going to take her away to beat her, Kurubarabulu replied – No, it was to force her to sleep with them.[14]

In October 1791 a sailor from one of the convict transports deliberately scuttled the canoe of an Eora man who had been paddling around the ship before going on board. The seaman was confined to his ship and ordered to give the native a complete suit of clothing in the hope that he would not seek further revenge. Convicts, sailors and marines now had more opportunities to obtain spears and fishing tackle legitimately from the Eora by exchange, but they continued to steal them.

VOYAGERS

Bondel, a native boy about 10 years of age, was an orphan. His mother had been bitten in half by a shark and his father had been killed in a battle with spears and clubs. So Bondel (also called Pandel and later Bundle or Bundell)[15] attached himself to Captain William Hill of the New South Wales Corps and went to live in what Hill called his 'miserable thatched hut, without kitchen, without a garden'. When Hill was ordered with his detachment to the Pacific Ocean settlement at Norfolk Island, Bondel was keen to go with him, saying he liked the idea of a sea voyage. They left Port Jackson on board the brig *Supply* on 22 March 1791.[16] 'He is the first [native] who has had confidence & Courage enough to go to Sea,' wrote William Bradley.[17] When the *Supply* returned to Sydney without Bondel, his friends 'inquired eagerly for him', said Watkin Tench. Many of them wanted to go to Norfolk Island when told that there were plenty of birds and other game there.[18]

In September, Bondel came home aboard the 298 ton transport ship *Mary Ann*. The master, Mark Monroe, said the boy had left the island reluctantly. During his five-month visit he seemed, wrote David Collins, 'to have gained some smattering of our language, certain words of which he occasionally blended with our own'.[19]

On 27 November 1791, Patyegarang told William Dawes that she and her two young male companions, Boneda (Poondah) and Bondel (Pundal) had been beaten by a white man.[20] If Bondel was well enough he could have sailed again on HMS *Supply*, which left Sydney Cove the following day. If so, he became the first indigenous Australian to reach England. When the ship arrived at Plymouth on 21 April 1792, the *British Journal* reported: 'The Supply has brought home several live Congaroos [kangaroos], a Native that has been civilised, and a very singular plant, of a lively green.'[21] The ship's commander, Lieutenant Henry Lidgbird Ball, took back a kangaroo, but did not mention any New South Wales native on board.

Bondel did continue as a sailor. He is next mentioned in 1811, when, as Bundell, he was included among those natives who, about 1806, were said to have 'made themselves extremely useful on board colonial vessels employed in the fishing and sealing trade'.[22] Years later, in May 1821, when he was about forty years old, Bundell joined Captain Phillip Parker King on the exploration ship HMS *Bathurst*.

Captain Hill sailed for England on the *Shah Hormuzear* on 24 April 1793 but was killed on Timor.

Bennelong wished to follow in Bondel's wake. On the morning of 16 October, he came into the settlement, carrying a bundle of spears, a *mooting* or fizgig, bones for spear points, a stone hatchet and his basket, ready to be packed up. In a letter that day to his mother in England, William Neate Chapman (soon to be storeman at Norfolk Island) said Bennelong 'has taken a fancy to go with us to Norfolk Island. The Governor is to give him two Nankeen Dresses, 6 white shirts & a Trunk to keep them in, which pleased him very much.' That night, Bennelong drank tea and ate supper with Governor Phillip and his officers. Chapman described him as 'a very well behaved man'.[23]

'The Natives are now on the most sociable terms with us, and Bannelong the native who was so long in the Governors Family goes with me to Norfolk,' Philip Gidley King advised Sir Joseph Banks on 25 October, adding, 'as it is a voluntary offer of his own I hope we will be able to instruct him in English.'[24] King, the newly appointed lieutenant governor of Norfolk Island, with his wife, Captain William Paterson and his wife, the Reverend Mr Johnson and Surgeon William Balmain, sailed from Sydney Cove on 26 October, aboard HMS *Atlantic*, bound for Norfolk Island and then Calcutta to obtain food and supplies.

Bennelong might have gone to Norfolk Island, but King does not mention him in his journal. Bennelong's wife Barangaroo was very ill and could have died about this time, which is a possible reason he might have postponed the voyage. If he did go, Bennelong's stay was brief, because he was back in Sydney by at least 14 December 1791, when

Ballooderry became ill. He could have returned on the *Queen* convict transport, which reached Sydney from Norfolk Island on 5 December, bringing Major Robert Ross. The normal time for the voyage was about ten days each way. Johnson had earlier advised a friend that he expected to return to Sydney 'about Christmas'.[25]

While the storeship HMS *Gorgon* was in port at Sydney Cove, from 21 September to 18 December 1791, Bennelong went 'up the country' with Captain John Parker, as the captain's wife, Mary Ann Parker, recalled in her book *A Voyage Around the World*.[26] The ship's officers went on several hunting trips. On an excursion to Broken Bay from about 8 to 12 December 1791 they were 'accompanied by two of the Natives best acquainted' with the place, noted first lieutenant John Gardiner.[27] If Bennelong was one of these guides, the date of his return from Norfolk Island can be brought forward even further.

'I think my old acquaintance Bennillon will accompany me when ever I return to England,' Phillip wrote in a letter to Sir Joseph Banks on 3 December 1791, '& from him when he understands English, much information may be attained for he is very intelligent.'[28]

> We learn that the Captain of the Pitt has brought from Botany Bay a curious beast called a "Congaroo". He is about the size of a large monkey ... Five female natives of Botany Bay are likewise on board the Pitt as they are entirely a different race of people, they will no doubt excite the observation of the curious.

> – *Calcutta Gazette*, 18 October 1792

The idea that five Eora women stowed away on the *Pitt* at Sydney Cove in 1792 and were seen on the ship in the Bengali port of Calcutta is astonishing, and raises questions about their fate, which is not known. As they were probably smuggled on the ship by sailors for sexual purposes, these women were not mentioned in any official reports. They could have disembarked in Calcutta, sailed on to England, or returned to Sydney. 'Several girls, who were protected in the settlement, had not any objection to passing the night on board of ships,' wrote David Collins. The rewards they received, which some concealed on coming ashore, might be 'a loaf of bread, a blanket, or a shirt ... when either was offered by a white man, and many white men were found who held out the temptation'.[29]

The *Pitt*, a 775 ton East Indiaman from Calcutta, sailed from Sydney to Norfolk Island on 7 April 1792. On 3 April a convict stowaway, Sarah Brennan, who had been hidden by the fourth mate, Mr Tate, was discovered and taken from the ship. More convicts were found hidden on board. It seems that the *eoragalleon* stowaways escaped detection. Two convicts who had served their time were allowed to join the *Pitt*, which left for Bengal via Batavia (Jakarta) on 7 May 1791. It is risky, however, to take the *Calcutta Gazette* report at absolute face value. It might be an example of eighteenth-century facetiousness, with white convict women characterised as 'female natives of Botany Bay'. They were certainly a different race of people! The *Pitt* went on to England and was to make more voyages under charter to the East India Company.

HMS *Gorgon*, 44 guns, a frigate converted to a storeship loaded with cows, sheep, hogs, fruit trees, seeds and six months' provisions, arrived in Sydney from Cape Town on 21 September 1791. Mary Ann Parker admired the green vegetation on each side of Sydney Cove. Although it was very rocky, she wrote, 'the little habitations on shore, together with the canoes around us, and the uncommon manners of the natives in them were more than sufficient amusement for that day'.

The urge to collect artefacts, that 'rage for curiosity' identified by Daniel Southwell, had been given new impetus by the arrival in Sydney of the convict transports of the Second and Third Fleets. After a native funeral at Manly about 12 December 1792, John Gardiner, first lieutenant on HMS *Gorgon*, and some friends tried to persuade some natives to exchange their spears for 'their dinners', but 'they satisfied their hunger & none could be got afterwards'. Due to the increased demand, the Aborigines had craftily begun to make second-rate implements specifically for the 'tourist trade'. 'They now find that we wish to get their articles & frequently make a much inferior sort for sale,' Gardiner noted. To obtain the best weapons, Gardiner suggested bartering bread, but it was necessary to 'keep the hungry Fit on as long as possible for the moment their craving ceases you need not expect the most trivial article'.[30]

The departure of the *Gorgon* from Port Jackson with a fair wind on 18 December marked the end of a period of friendly inquiry between the curious observers and the Eora. On board were William Dawes, Watkin Tench, Sergeant James Scott and John Easty, who would write no more in their notebooks and journals about New South Wales or its inhabitants. With the *Gorgon* also went the marines of the First Fleet. The ship was crowded with live kangaroos, dingos and possums, skins of animals, shrubs and plants in tubs on the main deck and a greenhouse on the quarterdeck, samples of timber and, wrote Mary Ann Parker, 'every curiosity which that country produced'. A convict woman attempting to escape on the ship was found 'disguised in men's apparel' in Bennelong's hut.[31]

17

BALLOODERRY

By June 1791, the Eora who lived among the colonists in Sydney had developed a taste for English bread, salt meat, rice and vegetables. As they sometimes caught more fish than they needed, the officers of the garrison at Parramatta persuaded some of them to bring them surplus mullet, bream and other fish caught near the Heads at Port Jackson to exchange for food.

One of these fishermen was Ballooderry, who had a new *nowey* or canoe and was very proud of it. He had probably cut out the tree bark to make it using one of the sharp-edged iron hatchets that his sister Boorong had made sure he was given. Ballooderry, who David Collins described as 'a fine young man', had lived for some months at the governor's house in Sydney and Phillip planned to take him to England.

The fish trade had only been going on for a few days when Ballooderry appeared at Phillip's hut at Parramatta in a violent rage. His hair and body were painted with red ochre and he carried a spear-thrower and several spears. White men, declared Ballooderry, had broken his canoe and he intended to kill them. 'His rage at finding his canoe destroyed was inconceivable; and he threatened to take his own revenge, and in his own way, upon all white people,' wrote Collins.[1]

Eventually, Ballooderry promised not to spear anyone, but only after Phillip promised to hang those who had destroyed his canoe, which he had left in the river some distance from Parramatta while he took fish to the huts. The governor had previously issued strict orders that canoes belonging to the natives should not be interfered with. Not long after, six convicts who had been seen sinking the canoe were caught. Ballooderry was taken to witness their punishment by flogging. This did not satisfy him, so he was told the convenient lie that one of the offenders had been hanged. Phillip also gave Ballooderry 'several little articles'.

Three weeks later, Ballooderry took his revenge by spearing the first white person he saw. A convict had strayed along the Parramatta River from Parramatta to The Flats near Kissing Point (Meadowbank), where he passed two young Eora men, a woman and two children. Suddenly, the convict was struck in the back by a spear. Several more spears were thrown and he was wounded in the side, but escaped with his life.

Governor Phillip asked some natives gathered around a camp fire who had wounded the white man as he returned to Sydney from Parramatta that evening. 'It was Ballooderry,' they told him. They also disclosed the names of a man who was with Ballooderry and of the women and children. Phillip issued an order to capture or shoot Ballooderry, who was not seen for a long time afterwards. No native people came to Parramatta, no canoes were seen in the creek and fish bartering came to an end. 'How much greater claim to the appellation of savages,' asked David Collins, 'had the wretches who were the cause of this, than the native who was the sufferer?'

After lying low for a while, Ballooderry began to ask his friends if Governor Phillip was still angry. They said he would be put to death for wounding the convict. This did not prevent Ballooderry paddling into Sydney Cove in a canoe during August. Phillip, who was in the garden, ordered his soldiers to seize him, but Bennelong shouted a warning and Ballooderry paddled across to the far side of the cove where he defiantly threatened to spear his pursuers.

Six men, many women and some children stopped at Governor Phillip's house on 23 August 1791, on their way to a corroboree at Botany Bay. They were sharing out some bread they had been given when Phillip was informed that Ballooderry and a group of men, some armed with spears, were on the other side of the cove. Phillip waited until his visitors had finished eating and gave them some metal fishhooks. He then ordered his soldiers to go after Ballooderry.

Meanwhile, Nanbarry heard what was going on and ran to warn Ballooderry. A sergeant and some marines clashed with a group of Eora, who had seemed friendly until one suddenly tried to snatch a musket. A spear was hurled, some said by Ballooderry, and two musket shots were fired in return. One man was shot in the leg, but Ballooderry escaped.

Reports came in that the Eora were gathering at the Brick Fields (present Haymarket), about 1.5 kilometres south of Sydney Cove. Phillip sent an officer and troops to 'disperse' them and to 'make a severe example of them' if they attacked with spears, but no natives could be found. As the marines lined up on the parade ground, Nanbarry again stripped off his clothes and ran into the bush to warn his people. The boy was hiding in the undergrowth when Phillip passed by with some officers. Nanbarry laughed when an officer's servant told him where the troops were going. They were too late, said Nanbarry, because the natives were all gone. In these events, Nanbarry, who was a close friend of Ballooderry and had exchanged names with him, showed again that his first loyalty was to the Eora, for whom he remained a valued spy in the white camp.

When Bennelong and Barangaroo came to Phillip's house not long after they were told that the soldiers had gone to punish Ballooderry. This news did not stop them eating a hearty meal. Bennelong left a bundle of spears and fish spears in the governor's care.

Next day (24 August) more than twenty Eora who had been to the Botany Bay corroboree called at the governor's house on their way home to the north shore. They said the man who had been wounded in the leg by a musket shot had gone back to his clan. Some stayed in Sydney overnight.

Phillip again issued orders to capture Ballooderry and declared that any native throwing a spear in his defence would be punished. 'Those who knew Ballooderry,' wrote Collins, 'regretted that it had been necessary to treat him with this harshness, as among his countrymen we had no where seen a finer young man.' The wounded convict had still not recovered. Bennelong constantly pressed Governor Phillip to forgive Ballooderry, but Phillip continued to refuse.

More than three months later (13 December), Bennelong came to see Phillip and told him that Ballooderry was very ill. Bennelong took Surgeon White to see Ballooderry, who lay in a fever. Early the next morning Ballooderry, ill and trembling with fear, was brought into the settlement. Phillip took his hand to comfort him and promised that when he recovered he could come to live in his house again. 'From being one day in apparent perfect health [Ballooderry] was brought in the next extremely ill,' wrote Collins. They found Bennelong acting out the role of a *carradhy* or healer, singing over Ballooderry, who lay on the ground in pain. Bennelong treated Ballooderry 'with much attention and friendship'. He breathed heavily on the parts of Ballooderry's body that might be affected and fanned him with branches dipped in water, perhaps to cool his fever.

On the morning of 15 December, a *carradhy* 'who came express from the north shore' (probably Willemering) visited Ballooderry at the hospital. The native doctor put his mouth to Ballooderry's body, writhed and seemed to be in great pain and, as a finale, spat out a piece of bone about 4 centimetres long. Despite this treatment, Ballooderry's fever increased during the night. The nature of Ballooderry's illness is not known, but it might have been a common cold, measles or influenza.

Those Eora who died of old age, or a disease such as smallpox, were usually cremated and their ashes buried, according to John Gardiner, first lieutenant of HMS *Gorgon*, who had witnessed such a ceremony at Manly Cove a few days before.[2]

Ballooderry's friends put him in a canoe to take him over to the north shore, but he died while crossing the harbour. The reason for doing this was to avoid having to abandon or burn the camp, to drive away his spirit or traces of his presence if he died there. The same custom was followed in 1830 on the death of the Broken Bay elder Bungaree, who was taken in a canoe to Garden Island, where he died.[3]

THE FUNERAL

> When Ba-loo-der-rey, a very fine lad who died among us, was buried, I saw
> the tears streaming silently down the sable cheek of his father Mau-go-ran;
> but in a little time they were dried, and the old man's countenance indicated
> nothing but the lapse of many years which, had passed over his head.
>
> – David Collins, *An Account of the English Colony in New South Wales*,
> London, 1798

Ballooderry was buried in Governor Arthur Phillip's garden at the edge
of Sydney Cove on 17 December 1791 in the first cross-cultural funeral in
Australia. The ceremony closely followed the traditional customs of the
indigenous people of southeastern Australia, but also included some
elements borrowed from English culture. His coffin was a canoe, but
Ballooderry was wrapped in an English jacket and blanket instead of
sheets of paperbark, while marines in their red jackets beat a drum tattoo
as he was interred. Some white spectators helped fill in the grave with
earth. The ceremony was organised and directed by Bennelong, who used
the occasion to cement old alliances and to make some new ones.

David Collins, who could not imagine that the Sydney Aborigines
had any religion, nevertheless recorded a detailed description of the
ceremony. Watercolour portraits of some of the funeral party, showing
their body decorations, were made by the Port Jackson Painter.[4]

The mourners included Ballooderry's family from Parramatta: his father
Maugoran, his mother Goorooberra, his sister Boorong and his little half-
brother Bedia Bedia (afterwards Bidgy Bidgy). The *moobies* or chief
mourners were Colby, Watewal (a close friend of Bennelong) and Boorong,
whose chests and shoulders were painted with red ochre and white pipeclay.
The principal corpse-bearers were Gnunga Gnunga Murremurgan
('Collins'), husband of Bennelong's sister Warreweer, and Yowarry, a
boorooberongal from the Hawkesbury River area, far to the west, now
Bennelong's brother-in-law. Also present were Bennelong's infant child
Dilboong and Colby's nephew Nanbarry and Yalowe or Yelloway, a
35-year-old *gweagal* from Botany Bay. There is no mention of Barangaroo
attending the funeral.

At the moment of Ballooderry's death, the assembled women and
children gave a loud shriek of grief. Soon after, Bennelong came into the
settlement and conferred with Governor Phillip, who agreed that
Ballooderry could be buried in the grounds of his garden.

That afternoon Ballooderry's body was brought across Sydney Cove
and placed in a hut by the water's edge near the fishermen's huts, where
a group of women and children were crying and howling dismally.
Ballooderry was wrapped in the English jacket he usually wore and some
pieces of cloth or blanket were tied around it.

At this stage, two Eora men fought each other with clubs. A few of the women also traded blows, during which Boorong's head was gashed by her mother Goorooberra. This blood-letting was a customary part of mourning. A few spears were thrown, evidently as part of the ceremony. Bennelong asked for a woollen blanket, which he laid over the corpse. Colby sat by the body through the night and refused to leave.

All was quiet until about one o'clock in the morning of 17 December, when the women again began to cry. At daylight, Bennelong brought Ballooderry's canoe and began to cut it 'to the proper length'.

The body was laid in the canoe, and with it a spear, a throwing stick, a pronged fishing spear or fizgig and the line (probably a band of woven hair received at initiation) that Ballooderry usually wore around his waist. The men went about their tasks in silence, but the women, boys and children continued to weep and cry. Maugoran stood apart alone, 'a silent observer of all that was doing about his deceased son and a perfect picture of deep and unaffected sorrow', according to Collins.

A grave had already been dug in Governor Phillip's garden close by the shore of *Warrane* (Sydney Cove). When everything was ready, the men and boys picked up the corpse in the bark canoe and placed it on the heads of Gnunga Gnunga and Yowarry. Some of the men carried bunches of grass in their hands, which they waved underneath the canoe, 'as if', wrote Collins, 'they were exorcising some evil spirit' by brushing it away.

The funeral procession set off, led by Bennelong and Watewal, followed by Maugoran, who carried spears and a throwing stick. They walked briskly towards *Tubowgulee*, the eastern point of the cove where Bennelong's hut stood. The two leaders continued to wave tufts of grass, sometimes through the bushes, to drive away spirits. This practice is followed by the Central Desert Warlpiri, according to anthropologist Mervyn Meggitt, 'to confuse the spirit'.[5] Whenever they turned to face the body, the corpse-bearers shook their heads from side to side. Watewal left the path and went to a bush which he examined closely, waving a grass switch, as if looking for Ballooderry's spirit or seeking clues about the cause of his death. The funeral party returned to the track and walked on more quickly than before. When they came to the women and children who were sitting with the other men, Maugoran threw two spears towards them, which fell short, 'evidently intentionally', Collins commented. This was a warning that Ballooderry's death would be avenged.

Bennelong now held up his baby Dilboong in front of the corpse, but the bearers tried to avoid her. 'Bedia Bedia the reputed brother of the deceased, a very fine boy of about five years of age, was then called for but came forward very reluctantly, and was presented in the same manner as the other child,' wrote Collins. After this, they continued on to the grave. Collins noticed that the front bearer (originally Yowarry) was changed twice, but Gnunga Gnunga carried the corpse all the way. The ceremony came to a halt when it was found that the prepared grave was not long enough. When the cavity had been enlarged, Yelloway levelled the bottom with his hands and feet and spread some grass in it. He jumped into the grave and stretched himself out full length, first on his back and then on his right side.

Bennelong had requested some military drummers to attend the funeral. 'Two or three marches were beat while the grave was being prepared,' wrote Collins. Bennelong highly approved of the drummers' performance. He pointed to the corpse and then to the sky as if to say 'now his spirit has begun its journey'.

Five or six Eora men got into the grave with the body, but the hole was still not long enough, so they trimmed off the ends of the canoe. This loosened the bindings and revealed the body, which by this time seemed to be in 'a very putrid state'. At last, Ballooderry's corpse was placed in the grave with his head pointing to the northwest. Great care was taken to position the body so that 'the sun might look at it as he passed'. To ensure this, Bennelong and Colby made observations and cut down any bushes that would obstruct the view.

Working together, the Eora and their white friends filled in the grave. When it was covered and the earth mounded up around it, Yowarry collected several shrubby branches and placed them in a semicircle on the south side of the grave. He laid grass and boughs over the mound, which he topped with a large log. He then spread some grass over the log and stretched himself out on top for several minutes, looking at the sky.

Ballooderry's funeral rites were complete.

*   *   *

The Eora observed the tradition, still common throughout Australia, that the name of a recently dead person must not be spoken. Ballooderry became a 'nameless one'. The mourners warned the whites about this taboo – 'a custom they rigidly attended to themselves whenever anyone died', said Collins.

Nanbarry, who had exchanged names with Ballooderry, gave up his own name and took the name *Bo-rahng* (possibly meaning a shadow).[6] When Barangaroo Daringa died, Colby's wife Daringa Barangaroo, with whom she had exchanged names, lost both names and was called *Bo-rahng-a-leon*; so did a little girl who lived in the settlement who Barangaroo used to call by her own name.[7]

Close family and friends of the dead person were also expected to obey various food taboos. As *moobies* at Ballooderry's funeral, Colby and Watewal told Collins, they must eat sparingly. Before they left, the men spoke to the women 'in a menacing tone' and warned Boorong that she must not eat fish or meat that day.[8]

18

WOMEN'S BUSINESS

Bark *bangalle* or baskets, shaped like tiny canoes, appear in the detail of watercolour paintings made in Sydney between 1788 and 1792 by the naive artist known as the Port Jackson Painter.[1] They were formed from a single piece of brown fibrous bark, gathered and folded at each end and bound with string, which was used as a carrying handle. In the folk memory of Aboriginal elders, one of three men who landed at Botany Bay from a boat wore on his head 'something like a bang-alle'.[2] Inverted, a bark basket would resemble a cocked hat like the one worn by Lieutenant James Cook at Botany Bay in 1770. Bark water troughs or buckets were made in the same way as baskets and patched with waterproof gum tree resin. The bark used for baskets might have come from either the southern mahogany (*Eucalyptus botroides*) or swamp mahogany (*E. robusta*), both called *bangalay* (pronounced *bang alley*) by Port Jackson Aborigines.[3]

Women made wooden containers called *goo-lime*, by hollowing out protruding rounded knots or gnarls cut from eucalyptus trees.[4] This word, given phonetically as *gulima* by linguist Jakelin Troy (1993a), is the probable origin of coolamon, which is usually said to be derived from the Kamilaroi *gulaman*.[5]

The wildflowers of the Sydney coastal heath surpassed in 'beauty, fragrance, and number, all I ever saw in an uncultivated state', wrote

A Basket of the Bark of a Tree – Detail from 'Axe, Basket, and Sword', *The Voyage of Governor Phillip to Botany Bay*, John Stockdale, Piccadilly, 1789.

Watkin Tench.[6] Many of these spectacular blossoms produce nectar, a sweet, honey-like solution of sugars, which the Eora sucked as they passed, or collected to soak in water to make drinks. William Dawes recorded the names of 'flowers bearing honey in sufficient quantity to render them notorious to the natives'.[7] They included *watanggre* or *wattangurry*, the saw or old man banksia (*Banksia serrata*), warata or waratah (*Telopea* species) and *weereagan*, described as 'a low tree bearing a fruit like the Wa-tang-gre' – perhaps a prostrate banksia or a melaleuca.[8] William Bradley described the banksia as the 'Honeysuckle tree, called so because it bears a flower which contains a great deal of Honey'.[9] When the flower spikes of *ingera*, the hairpin banksia (*Banksia spinulosa*), were abundant the inland natives gathered 'purposely to drink it, which may be truly called a native feast', wrote botanist George Caley in 1807.[10] Other nectar-producing plants included callistemon, grevillea, mountain devil and hakea.

The Eora were adept at tracing the small, stingless Australian native bees (*Trigona* species) to their hives of rounded wax in hollow trees and cut out the honey (*noaga*) with their hatchets. This 'sugarbag' was added to water and sucked from pieces of shredded bark soaked in the sweet liquid.[11]

Some wild fruit-bearing trees were called *wigi*, which Dawes thought might be berries 'as I know most of the bushes, all of which bear berries which the natives eat'.[12] Berry fruits included geebung, appleberry, sour currant and lilly pilly.

Manmagun tyibung wellan madwara – 'We will gather tyibungs [geebungs] as we come back'. These words, spoken by the young girl called Patyegarang who was Lieutenant William Dawes's chief informant about her people's language, resonate across space and time between the two cultures on the shores of Sydney Cove.[13] They tell us that the Eora ate the astringent and succulent fruits of the *tyibung* or geebung as a snack and thirst quencher as they walked through the bush. Other snacks were the fruits of the pretty five corners (*Styphelia* species) or *gadegal badieree*, translated as the 'Scarlet & Yellow bell flower'[14] and appleberries (*bomula* or *bo-murra cammeral*) or 'Potatoe apple' (*Billardiera* species)[15] and the liquorice-flavoured leaves and raw berries of the *warraburra* or sweet tea.

The spreading *tammun* or Port Jackson fig (*Ficus rubignosa*) was distributed freely by birds and seedlings grew in the crevices of bare sandstone cliffs like the Tarpeian Rock at Bennelong Point.[16] One man showed John White some wild figs growing at what is now Walsh Bay.[17] The small, seed-filled yellow fruits were eaten raw when they were soft and ripe and preserved by pressing into 'cakes' which were left to dry. 'In one of the Coves we found a piece of a Cake which appear'd to be made of a wild fig,' wrote Bradley in February 1788.[18]

The starchy rhizomes or roots of *gurgy* or bracken fern (*Pteridium esculentum*) and the bungwall fern (*Blechnum indicum*) were eaten only after being roasted in hot fire ashes.[19] On his first expedition along the Parramatta River in May 1788, Phillip found 'the root of a fern ... that had been chewed by one of the natives; he could only have left the spot a few minutes; but we never saw any of them'.[20] Young fern fronds were also roasted and eaten. A native man suffering from diarrhoea was seen to chew fern root and made a speedy recovery.[21]

The fleshy edible roots and tubers of a wide range of plants, including orchids and lilies, were staples of the inland clans to the west of Sydney. An expedition to the Hawkesbury in July 1789 found wild yams growing on both sides of the river. The underground stems or rhizomes of *baraba*, the broad-leafed cumbungi bulrush (*Typha* species) which grew in swamps, were roasted to provide starch and sugar. Young green-white cumbungi shoots were relished and cumbungi fibres were also used to make string.

Collins described the *wiggoon*, a spear-thrower made of heavy wood, rounded at the end, but with no adze shell like the *womerra*. 'With this they dig the fern-root and yam out of the earth,' he wrote.[22] A similar tool was used to dig up potatoes from a convict garden at *Tarra* (Dawes Point) in December 1790.

As they foraged for bushfruits, women and children collected many kinds of bird eggs, as well as lizards, snakes, grubs, ants and ant eggs. Large lizards and snakes were roasted in the fire, but in some clans they were reserved for male elders.

• Daringa

In November 1790, Colby brought his wife Daringa, 'big with child', to visit Governor Phillip. Though she 'appeared to be within a very few days of her time', wrote Phillip, 'there were several wounds on her head, which she said he had lately given her: he seemed to be pleased that she could shew her marks, and took some pains to inform the governor that he had beat her with a wooden sword'.[23] Colby, said Tench, 'who was certainly, in other respects, a good tempered merry fellow', was known to beat and club Daringa 'who was a gentle creature'.[24]

Daringa's mother Tadyera had died of dysentery, according to William Dawes. Her name was also written as Daringha, Daringe, Dorringa, Gnaringa and Taringa. Daringa's young brother Boneda (also Poonda or Pundah) was adopted by Judge Advocate William Collins. Daringa's older brother Mooroobera (or Mooro-baroh) had two wives, named by Daniel Southwell as Tunnal Bar-an-goo-noo and Kie-marlie-ty (or Kei-marte Riumah-le) and three children, Barangan (Barring-an or Beringan) and Caroo, both girls, and Cabieary (Co-ro-by), a boy.[25] Daringa often went to Botany Bay and probably had relatives in that area among the *gweagal* or *bidjigal*.

Daringa gave birth to a baby girl at Botany Bay and returned to Sydney on 23 November, carrying the child, who was only two or three days old. 'Both the parents appeared to treat it with great tenderness,' wrote Phillip. All three stayed that night at Governor Phillip's house. They were accompanied by Yelloway or Yalowe (died 1792), a *gweagal* ally of Botany Bay Kolbi, Noorooing, who Yelloway had abducted from Watewal, and a child about three years old.

'Mawberry, his [Yelloway's] first wife, happened to be at the governor's house when he came in, and did not seem pleased at the meeting.' However, after two days at the governor's house, Yelloway left, taking Mawberry (who he had recently rejected after beating her and breaking her arm) and leaving behind Noorooing, who was crying and distraught. She asked to stay with the governor's servants, as did Kurubarabulu and a boy about fourteen years of age.[26] Phillip interpreted Noorooing's cries of '*yalloway*' as meaning 'go away', rather than as her husband's name. The 'Ioras' (Eora), wrote Captain James Campbell in a letter to Dr Farr at the Royal Naval Hospital in Plymouth in March 1792, were 'often known to turn off one woman and take up with another'. Referring to Yelloway's action, Campbell continued: 'Very lately, one of them made the Govr [Governor Phillip] a gift of his Din [gin or wife] and carried off with him another woman that was there.'[27] The deserted woman left Phillip's house on 5 January 1791 but soon after was reconciled to Yelloway. Mawberry, wrote Phillip, then lived with another man, but frequently visited Sydney and was 'said to have granted favours to several of the convicts'.[28] Collins, however, described 'Mauberry' as 'an elderly woman who occasionally visited us'.[29]

In June 1790, John Macarthur, an officer in the newly raised New South Wales Corps, with his wife Elizabeth, settled in a hut made from cabbage tree posts framed with wattle and daub beside the stream at Sydney Cove. About 24 January 1791, Elizabeth. Macarthur had a visitor, as she told her friend Bridget Kingdon in a letter dated 7 March 1791:

> Mrs. Coleby, whose name is Daringa, brought in a new born female infant of hers, for me to see ... it was wrapp'd up in the soft bark of a Tree, a Specimen of which I have preserved, it is a kind of Mantle not much known in England, I fancy. I order'd something for the poor Woman to Eat, and had her taken proper care of for some little while, when she first presented herself to me she appear'd feeble and faint, she has since been regular in her visits. The Child thrives remarkably well and I discover a softness and gentleness of Manners in Daringa truly interesting.[30]

One night while they slept, Daringa's child Panieboollong (Pin-niee-bool-long) rolled out of her mother's arms and into the fire. Two of her toes were burnt off and the sinews of her leg shrank.[31]

MAL-GUN

The little finger of the left
hand of the woman when $\Big\}$ Mal-gun[32]
the two joints are cut off

The majority of women and girls in the Sydney area had lost the little finger of their left hand above the first joint, a practice which mystified the English observers. Their finger stumps, said Surgeon John White in August 1788, were 'as well covered as if the operation had been performed by a surgeon'.[33] Governor Phillip thought that the explanation given by the Eora (as he understood it) – 'to enable the women to fish the better, and to wind the line around the remaining three fingers' – was 'too trivial to be the real cause'.[34]

'Before we knew them, we took it to be their marriage ceremony,' wrote Collins, 'but on seeing their mutilated children we were convinced of our mistake.' The Eora called this practice *mal-gun* and said it was very good. Collins, who was told the same story about fishing lines, was on the right track in his first supposition.[35] In this instance, the Eora women were able to conceal the real reason for this 'women's business' and keep it a secret from the whites. It is likely that the *mal-gun* amputation, which took place when a female child was still being carried on her mother's shoulders, was a sign that she had been promised in marriage by the tradition of *nanarree*, sometimes contracted before the child was born.[36]

Colby and Daringa were often told that if Panieboollong's finger was to be cut off, Governor Phillip wanted to see the operation.

A thread was tied around the second joint of the child's little finger when she was two months old. When Daringa brought her in again, two or three days afterwards, the binding had been broken or removed. 'This being mentioned to the mother, she took several hairs from the head of an officer who was present, and bound them very tight round the child's finger,' wrote Collins. In time the cut became gangrenous.[37] Other officers took an interest in the process. 'The little wretch seemed in pain, and her hand was greatly swelled,' Tench wrote dispassionately, 'but as it hung by a bit of skin, they begged Mr. White, the surgeon, to take it off, which he did with a pair of scissars, and which the child did not seem to feel'.[38] Hunter thought Panieboollong was three or four months old.

The Eora customarily removed the finger from the child's left hand, yet Panieboollong's right-hand finger had been cut. 'I never saw but one instance where the finger was taken off from the right hand, and that was occasioned by the mistake of the mother,' wrote Collins.[39] Daringa was well aware of this, as Hunter commented: 'The mother ... frequently pointed out that it should have been the left hand.'[40] Phillip had brought such pressure to bear on Colby and Daringa that to oblige his curiosity they put themselves and their child through the ordeal of needlessly cutting off her finger. It is obvious that Panieboollong was not yet promised in marriage.

In May 1791, a convict was caught while stealing fishing tackle from Daringa. Governor Phillip gave orders for the man to be severely flogged in front of as many natives as could be assembled, so that the reason for the punishment could be explained to them. Several Eora men and women were brought to witness the flogging. All showed their sympathy for the offender and were horrified at the punishment. Daringa cried and Barangaroo was so angry that she threatened the flogger with a stick. In Tench's view, each of the women reacted according to their different characters: Daringa meek and feminine and Barangaroo fierce and unsubmissive.[41]

David Collins, or more likely his editors in London, made an error in stating that 'Cole-be's wife, the namesake of Ba-rang-a-roo ... did not survive [Barangaroo] many months. She died of consumption brought on by suckling a little girl who was at her breast when she died.'[42] Bennelong's wife Barangaroo is believed to have died towards the end of 1791.[43] However, Daringa, as 'Dorringa, his [Colby's] Wife' was painted by the Port Jackson Painter as a mourner at the funeral ceremony of Ballooderry in December 1791 and later as 'Da-ring-ha, Cole-bee's Wife' (with her small child) by the convict artist Thomas Watling, who did not arrive in Sydney until October 1792.[44] At Collins's request, Daringa obtained teeth taken from three boys at the *erah-ba-diang* (initiation ceremonies) at *yoo-lahng* or *yu-ron* (Farm Cove) which took place in January and February 1795.[45]

• **Barangaroo**

Barangaroo, Bennelong's wife, was a member of the *cameragal* (Cammeray clan) who dominated Sydney's north shore and whom Bennelong often urged the whites to attack.

Bennelong's assertion, on the morning of the whale feast (7 September 1790) that Barangaroo had 'become the new wife' of Colby and that he had replaced her with two large women, was treated as a joke by Surgeon White and those with him.[46] It might have been the truth, as several instances show that whenever men were away others would appropriate their wives. It looks as if Colby took up with Barangaroo after his escape from Governor Phillip's house, where Bennelong was kept for a further four months. When Bennelong, in a boat with Phillip, met Barangaroo at Rose Bay on 3 February 1790, she told them that Colby was fishing on the other side of the hill and still had the shackle on his leg.[47]

Discussing the attitude of Eora men to the 'Fair Sex', Daniel Southwell wrote in a letter to his uncle:

> I have heard this Youngster [Nanbarry] once at the Govrs Table ... signified that Colby – then present ... had formerly had his Mother (by them esteemed mightily handsome) several hours in his possession, this the arch Warrior so far from denying, laugh'd at very humorously and it fail'd not to make those that were present do so too.[48]

The woman Colby had abducted was his sister in law. This text was omitted from the version of Southwell's letter printed in the *Historical Records of New South Wales*.[49] There is no record of a battle between Bennelong and Colby over Barangaroo, which was usual, but, whatever happened, Bennelong was reunited with her early in September 1790.

When he first met Barangaroo, Governor Phillip thought she looked older than Bennelong. Her two children by a previous husband had died, possibly of smallpox. 'She is very straight and exceeding well made,' Phillip declared, 'her features are good, and she goes entirely naked, yet there is such an air of innocence about her that cloathing scarcely appears necessary.'[50] Barangaroo had two scars from spear wounds, one of which had passed through her thigh.[51] The septum of her nose was pierced and she sometimes pushed a small bone or piece of stick through it, a common practice with initiated men, but not usual among the women.

Bennelong treated Barangaroo roughly and often bashed her with his club. In October 1790, after he had severely beaten Barangaroo twice within a few days, Phillip said that she still seemed very fond of Bennelong, while he 'professed great affection for her, but laughed when he was told that it was wrong to beat a woman'.[52] Some days later, at Phillip's house, Barangaroo complained of a pain in the stomach and went to sit by the fire with Bennelong, who 'seemed to express great sorrow on seeing her ill'. Bennelong blew on her hand, warmed it and placed it on her stomach and began to sing a healing song. A bystander warmed a piece of flannel and put it on Barangaroo's stomach, but Bennelong kept up his chant, 'keeping his mouth very near to the part affected and frequently stopping to blow on it'. Whenever he stopped blowing, Bennelong made a noise like a dog barking, to which Barangaroo made 'short responses'.

Phillip sent for a doctor and Barangaroo 'was persuaded to take a little tincture of rhubarb which gave her relief'.[53] It is possible that Barangaroo's stomach pains were the result of a beating, although she might have had pregnancy pains or suffered a recent miscarriage.

Although they frequently quarrelled, Bennelong and Barangaroo just as often seemed to be very happy together. That Bennelong 'was certainly attached' to her had been shown in 'many instances of which we had at different times been witness', said Collins.[54] On 13 November 1790 Bennelong and Barangaroo returned to Sydney from Botany Bay. Bennelong had cut Barangaroo on the head after she had broken a spear and *womerra*, probably during an argument over his abduction of Kurubarabulu.[55] However, it was about this time that William Dawes jotted an entry in his notebook which described Barangaroo 'laughing & playing with Bennelong, while I was shaving him'. '*Kotbarabang* (he will cut),' she teased him.[56]

Some nine months later, in August 1791, when she was close to giving birth, Barangaroo came to Governor Phillip's house with two net dilly bags hanging from her neck. Phillip asked for one bag, which was new, and she gave it to him after first taking out a large piece of neatly folded paperbark, which 'she intended to lay her infant upon'. Bennelong requested an English blanket for the child, which was supplied. The following day Barangaroo was given 'a net made in the English manner' and seemed pleased with the exchange.

Bennelong told Phillip that Barangaroo intended 'doing him the honour of being brought to bed in his house', in other words giving birth to her baby there. Phillip argued with Bennelong about this and 'at length persuaded him that she would be better accommodated at the hospital'. In Phillip's opinion the native women 'all seem best pleased with having boys' and Bennelong often said his child would be a son.[57] Bennelong's initiative in seeking to have his child born at the governor's house can be seen as a further attempt to bring Phillip into his family kinship circle and to classify him literally as his *beanga* or father.

Analysing these events, Ann McGrath pointed to the importance in Aboriginal society of a person's birthplace, 'for it allowed the child special association with a site'. She further commented: 'In moving into Cadigal clan territory [Governor Phillip's house], Bennelong's clan was forging new land associations, and a prime way of deepening and perpetuating them was through their children's birthplaces.'[58]

The colony's hospital, as McGrath suggests, would be repellent to Barangaroo, who would believe it was 'contaminated by spirits of the recently deceased'.[59] Bennelong might have taken the opportunity to claim some of the territory of Colby's clan, the *cadigal*, which included the site of the Sydney settlement, possibly on Colby's behalf. The *cadigal* had been severely depleted by deaths from smallpox and only Colby, Nanbarry and one other man (possibly Caruey) remained. In any case, Barangaroo was neither at the hospital nor at the governor's house in late August 1791 when her daughter Dilboong (named after 'a bird with a shrill note') was born. Her birthplace might have been at Bennelong's hut at *Tubowgulle* or somewhere close to Phillip's house, because David Collins was surprised to see Barangaroo, a few hours after the child was born, walking about alone, picking up sticks to make a fire. The newborn child, who had reddish coloured skin, lay on a soft piece of paperbark on the earth – not on a blanket or a strip of English net. For their first few days, Eora babies were wrapped in this soft bark and were later carried on their mother's shoulders.[60]

Mystery surrounds Barangaroo's death, which took place towards the end of 1791. Phillip, whose published journal ends on 16 December 1791, did not report it, while David Collins, who described her funeral, gives neither a date nor cause for her death.

William Dawes made an entry in his language notebook on 23 August 1791, but did not, as normally, record the English equivalent:

> Berangaroo to me
> Benelong gulara ngari Mr. D.
> badyul tdara. Ngia tungi.[61]

Roughly translated, Barangaroo told Dawes ('Mr. D.') that Bennelong was angry when she was sick at Tdara (Tarra, the site of Dawes's Observatory) and had made her cry. According to Phillip, Barangaroo and Bennelong had come to his house as usual that day and enjoyed a 'hearty dinner'.[62] In a footnote, Collins recalled that Bennelong had severely beaten Barangaroo 'a short time before she was delivered' on the morning of the day she gave birth to Dilboong, one or two days after 24 August.

Another possibility is that Barangaroo became seriously ill about the end of October 1791, when Bennelong appears to have cancelled a planned voyage to Norfolk Island. There is no record of Barangaroo attending Ballooderry's funeral, arranged by Bennelong, which took place on 17 December 1791.

> I then told her that a whiteman had been wounded some days ago in coming from Kadi to Wárán. I asked her why the black men did it. ans.ʳ Gúlara .. (Because they are) angry. D. Minyin gúlara eora? Why are the b. m. angry? P. Inyám galawí w. m. Because the white men are settled here.
>
> P. Tyérun kamarigál The kamarigals are afraid. D. Minyin tyérun k-gál? Why are the k— afraid? P. Gúnin . — Because of the Guns. —

Extract from William Dawes second notebook, 1791. *Vocabulary of the language of N.S.Wales in the neighbourhood of Sydney (Native and English).* MS 4165 (b), School of Oriental and African Studies, University of London, London (Dawes b.34.7).

There will always be a suspicion that Bennelong caused or contributed to Barangaroo's death by his frequent beatings, which, although provoked by her fiery temper, might have resulted in a fractured skull. The English officers felt sorry for Daringa when Colby assaulted her. However, while Bennelong often beat Barangaroo, said Tench, 'she was a scold, and a vixen, and nobody pitied her'.[63] George Howe, the Government Printer, gave currency to rumours of this crime in his 'Chronology of local occurrences' in the New South Wales Pocket Almanac (Sydney, 1818), with the statement: 'He [Bennelong] was naturally barbarous in his manner; and to him is imputed the murder of one of his wives ...'

Barangaroo, who Collins judged to be aged about fifty when she died, was prone to illness and might have suffered complications after the birth of her child. McGrath comments: 'Possibly the estimates of her age were wrong and she was much younger. It seems rather strange for a woman near fifty to be giving birth, and also unusual that the British men found her physique so attractive, as their descriptions of other women emphasise the attractions of youth.'[64]

Bennelong asked Governor Phillip, Surgeon White and Lieutenant David Collins to witness Barangaroo's cremation. The mourners included Bennelong's sister Carangarang, Caruey (Carraway), Yemmerrawanne and one or two women. Gnunga Gnunga Murremurgan or 'Collins', husband of Bennelong's pretty sister Warreweer, cleared the ground where the funeral pyre was to be built by digging out the earth about 10 centimetres below the surface. Over this, the men arranged small sticks and bushes, with bigger pieces at the sides, to form a mound about a metre high. The ends and sides were built from big pieces of dry wood, packed around broken twigs and branches. Some grass was spread over the wood. Barangaroo's body, wrapped in an old English blanket (perhaps the one Governor Phillip had given Bennelong), was laid on top of the pyre with her head facing north. By Barangaroo's side they placed a basket containing her fishing gear and other personal belongings. Bennelong stacked some logs over the body and lit the fire. The dry wood was quickly engulfed and Bennelong pointed to the black smoke which rose as the flames licked her body. The English spectators left before the last piece of timber was burnt.

After the ceremony, Bennelong seemed cheerful and talked about finding a nurse among the white women for his daughter, who was being breastfed.[65] Bennelong told Governor Phillip that he was now the *beanga* or father of the child (and so responsible for her care).[66] It is likely that Phillip did arrange a wet nurse for Dilboong, as Daniel Southwell wrote in a letter to his mother that 'some of the [Eora] dames, like too many of ours, gladly forgo the d'r [dear] pleasure of nurturing their own bratts, and leave them in perfect security to the care of sever'l of the convict women, who are suitably rewarded by the Governor'.[67]

The day following the cremation, Bennelong invited Phillip, White and Collins to attend while he scraped up Barangaroo's ashes and powdery bones. No other Eora were present. Bennelong's rake was a spear, which he said he would use to punish the *carradhy* Willemering, who had not come when Bennelong sent for him as Barangaroo lay dying. Bennelong took a piece of bark to smooth the ashes into a mound, around which he placed some wooden logs, then put the bark on top. He asked the English officers if the burial ceremony was *budgeree* (good) and was happy when they agreed that it was. Collins described Bennelong's bearing throughout as 'solemn and manly'. At the end, Bennelong stood for a few minutes with his hands folded across his chest and his eye 'fixed upon his labours in the attitude of a man in profound thought'.[68] He repeatedly said that he would not be satisfied until he had taken vengeance for Barangaroo's spirit.

Several warriors were wounded in the ritual spear-throwing which followed her death. Bennelong had a fierce battle with Willemering and speared him in the thigh. These 'funeral games', said Collins, coincided with a whale feast which had attracted several people 'from the northward, who spoke a dialect very different to that with which we were acquainted'.

Not long after, little Dilboong died and 'several spears were thrown'.[69] Bennelong and two or three others kept a vigil through the night close to her grave in Governor Phillip's garden.[70] The remains of Barangaroo and her little daughter lie buried beneath the city of Sydney, close to Circular Quay.

- **Boorong**

A young girl called Boorong was brought into Sydney suffering from smallpox in 1789. Estimates of her age varied between ten and fifteen years, but she was probably about twelve or thirteen years old at the time. When she had recovered, Boorong was placed in the care of the colony's chaplain, Reverend Mr Richard Johnson and his wife Mary and went to live in their 'miserable hut' built of soft cabbage tree slabs at the head of Sydney Cove.[71]

On 31 July 1789, Boorong went down the harbour to Manly by boat with Chaplain Johnson, and met a group of Aborigines, some of whom said they were her relations. As instructed, she told them that she had been well cared for and was very happy and used 'every persuasion to get one or more of them to return with her', wrote William Bradley, 'but to no purpose'.[72]

Boorong, whose name meant a star, may have possessed the gift of prophecy. One night she saw a falling star and went into violent convulsions, exclaiming that she and her people would be destroyed. When questioned about the cause of her agitation, she went to the door, pointed to the skies, and said that whenever the stars looked that way, misfortune always followed. 'The night was cloudy and disturbed by meteors,' wrote Watkin Tench.[73] It was true that little but misfortune was to follow for the indigenous people of the Sydney area. 'Some say she particularly alluded to the Murry Nowey or Sirius,' Philip Gidley King wrote in the margin of his journal.[74] HMS *Sirius*, flagship of the First Fleet, was holed and later sank when she hit a reef at Norfolk Island on 19 March 1790.

Chaplain Johnson took great pains to teach Boorong to read and after almost one year said he had no reason to complain of her improvement. He taught her to recite prayers, including the Lord's Prayer. 'She can likewise begin to speak a little English, and is useful in several things About our little Hutt,' Johnson wrote in a letter to his friend Henry Fricker.[75]

Boorong had a fiery temper. 'The Girl at times is very angry & cannot bear to be thwarted,' wrote King in his journal in April 1790.[76] David Blackburn, master of the *Supply*, said Boorong was 'a fine Girl about 15 Year Old', adding that little had been learned from her 'tho she is Very fond of Mrs. Johnston [sic]'.[77] William Dawes also tried to teach Boorong about the Christian religion in the hope that she would give him some information about her own beliefs, but, wrote Tench, 'her levity and love of play, in a great measure, defeated his efforts'.[78] Dawes noted this 'love of play' as Boorong and Nanbarry swam together and played with a blanket in November 1790.[79]

Boorong was not an orphan. Her father Maugoran was an elder of the *burramattagal*. Her mother was Gooroobera, which means 'firestick' in the Sydney language, and her brothers were Ballooderry (died 1791) and Yerinibe Goruey. She was the half sister of Warreweer Wogul-Mi ('Warreweer One Eye', died 1798) and Bedia Bedia, later Bidgy Bidgy, who was appointed chief of the Kissing Point 'tribe' by Governor Lachlan Macquarie.[80]

Yeranibe (Yerinibe) was mentioned as Boorong's brother in William Dawes's first language notebook, begun about November 1790, after the peaceful 'coming-in' of Bennelong and the Eora to Sydney:

> Naboangoong Boorong We will see, or shall we see Boorong?
> These words were spoken to me by Yirinibe, Boorong's Brother, and he was
> evidently anxious in enquiring after Boorong.[81]

Ballooderry (Baluderri) first met Dawes on 15 November 1790 when he came with Nanbarry to ask for a plaster for a sore.[82]

All members of Maugoran's family, apart from Yeranibe, were mourners at Ballooderry's funeral in Sydney in December 1790. Boorong was a *moobee* (official mourner) at the funeral, in which her mother cut her head with a club.

Boorong had reached puberty and much of what was recorded about her concerned her love life. About 15 September 1790, she asked Chaplain Johnson if she could go away, saying that she wanted to be married. Johnson said she would be allowed to leave and could take new clothing with her and return to see her friends in town. When Yemmerrawanne tried to woo her, she 'disclaimed his advances, repeating the name of another person, who we knew was her favourite'.[83] Boorong's beloved might have been a young man described by David Collins as a 'native of the tribe of Cammerray, a very fine fellow named Carradah'. Their names were linked in the following exchange in William Dawes's notebook: 'Yenma kaoul Walk come, or in plain english come here or walk this way. Said by Boorong on — 1790 to Koorooda'.[84]

Carradah (also spelt Goorooda, Karrada and Koorooda) had exchanged names with Lieutenant Henry Ball, commander of HMS *Supply*, and, wrote Collins, was afterwards known as Mr Ball 'which they [the natives] had corrupted into Midjer Bool'.[85] Ball had a hut next to Dawes's observatory at what is now Dawes Point. Carradah's portrait was painted (as Goo-roo-da) by the Port Jackson Painter, who noted: 'We suppose this Man is a chief among the Thommarragals [*cameragal*].'[86] Carradah died in April 1794.[87]

In October 1790, after Boorong had been away for one week, she returned to the Johnsons, but only stayed a further week.[88] After another week away, Boorong returned to Sydney with some officers who were visiting the north harbour. 'By her own account,' wrote Phillip 'she had joined the young man she wished to marry, and had lived with him three days, but he had another wife, who the girl said was jealous, and had beat her.' The girl's head wounds and bruises were serious enough to require treatment by one of the surgeons. Her young man had beaten his wife because she had attacked Boorong.[89]

Once after a visit to the north shore Boorong was very sick. She blamed this on the *camerragalleon* (Cammeray women, probably including her husband's wife) who had intentionally urinated in the path she would cross. When she complained about being sick, the women told her triumphantly what they had done.[90] Surgeon White bled Boorong in the arm, but she did not recover. She chose instead to undergo a ritual called *be-anny*, which was only performed by women and in which, said Collins, 'the operator suffers more than the patient'. A woman healer cut Boorong's forehead with an oyster shell, deep enough to draw blood. One end of a string line was then knotted at the wound and tied around her head, while the other end was held in the mouth of the woman, who sat at a distance and began to sing. The woman rubbed her own gums with the string until they bled freely and spat the blood into a vessel beside her half filled with water, into which she sometimes dipped the string. Boorong believed that the blood flowed from her head and along the cord until it reached the woman's mouth. Tench wrote: 'Boorong became well; and firmly believed that she owed her cure to the treatment she received.' Surgeon White took note of this woman's healing rite and the caption 'A Woman of New South Wales curing the head ache ...', written under a watercolour by the Port Jackson Painter which probably depicts Boorong's treatment, is in White's handwriting.[91]

'We are now on a pretty friendly intercourse with the Natives. – Numbers of them are coming into the Camp daily, or rather are in Night and day,' the Reverend Johnson wrote to Henry Fricker in Hampshire in March 1791. 'This intercourse was principally brought about by means of a little girl [Boorong]. For some time,' Johnson continued, 'this girl made good improvement in her Book, and [I] began to be very partial to her.' However, after the Eora had come into the settlement 'in common', Boorong no longer behaved 'so well or so complyingly' and had been 'off in the woods' several times. Significantly, Johnson sent Fricker a *barrin*, the kangaroo or possum fur tassel apron worn by young girls but discarded when they took a partner. Johnson also included, in a box sent by William Dawes to his father at Portsmouth, a small kangaroo skin and fishing lines and shell hooks, presumably obtained from Boorong.[92]

When Bennelong's sister Warreweer gave birth to her child some time in 1791, Boorong helped by pouring water over her stomach, while another woman tied a string around Warreweer's neck and rubbed her own lips with the string until they bled. A convict woman cut the umbilical cord and, despite objections by Boorong and some others, washed the child. After the birth, Warreweer squatted over a small hole and waited for the afterbirth.[93]

Boorong was mentioned, indirectly, by Johnson in March 1792 when he wrote of 'two Native Girls I have under my roof', whom he considered 'ignorant and benighted heathens'. The second girl, who disappointed the Johnsons because of her 'want of attachment', might have been Boorong's half-sister Warreeweer Wogul-Mi or perhaps Patyegarang, who asked Dawes on 19 September 1791, 'When will domine (that is Mr Johnson) read in the book?'[94]

1792

19

AMITY ... AND REVENGE

Peace and amity, as King George had decreed, prevailed between the native people and the white settlers, at least in the Sydney coastal area, through most of 1792. 'The natives had not lately given us any interruption by acts of hostility,' noted David Collins in April that year.[1]

Bennelong and his friends continued to take their midday meal with Phillip and his officers. 'There are three or four of the chiefs who attend the Governor's house every day for their dinner and a glass of wine,' wrote George Thompson in his journal in May 1792. Many bold and curious young Eora men and women came to live in different huts in Sydney Town and were often visited by their relations. Others came into the town each day 'for the sake of what they can get to eat' and returned to their bush camps at night. 'Several of the officers have both boys and girls as servants, but they are so lazy that it is with difficulty you can persuade them to get themselves a drink of water,' Thompson continued. 'If you attempt to strike them, they will immediately set out for the woods, and stay four or five days ... If they were shy at first settling in the colony, that is not the case now, for the people [settlers] can scarcely keep them out of their houses in daytime,' Thompson complained.

Outside the European settlements, the pattern of life continued as before. The Eora went fishing, made a fire, ate, and went to sleep, but there were a few cultural changes. 'When in their canoes, they keep constantly singing while they paddle along,' wrote Thompson. 'They have the French tune of Malbrook very perfect; I have heard a dozen or twenty singing it together.'[2] At Botany Bay in January 1788, Surgeon John White had whistled the old French song, *Malbrooke s'en va-t-en guerre* to calm a group of natives who reacted with shock when he shot a hole through a bark shield with his pistol. They appeared highly charmed with the tune, wrote Tench 'and imitated him with equal pleasure and readiness'.[3]

In April 1792, a violent battle broke out between 'the Natives of Botany Bay and this place [Sydney], in which many were wounded on both sides'. According to Richard Atkins, the dispute was caused by a man at Botany Bay who mentioned the name of someone in his clan who had died. 'For so trifling a cause do men murder each other,' he wrote.[4]

Atkins was presumably referring to the clash in which Beerewan (Beriwani or Burrowannie), the *boorooberongal* befriended by Colby in

April 1791 during the expedition to Richmond, had been beaten by two *gweagal* from the south shore of Botany Bay. Subsequently, one of these men had to face Beerewan in a payback combat. That warrior could have been Punangan, who William Dawes said had been beaten by 'Kolbi & Beriwani' (Colby and Beerewan) for 'seaming' (wounding) Beerewan.[5]

A corroboree was held at night 'at the head of the stream' (present day Hyde Park), during which the *gweagal* danced with the rest and then lay down to sleep. Early the next morning, while still sleeping, he was suddenly attacked by Colby and Beerewan. Colby thrust his spear at the man and Beerewan struck two severe blows with his club to the back of his head. Wounded and bleeding, the unarmed man sprang to his feet and hung his head while Colby and Beerewan spoke to him. Bennelong wiped the blood from his wounds with grass and no more blows were traded. Satisfied with this punishment, Beerewan walked about the town with his victim, whose chest and back were still covered with dried blood. On being asked, the man said Beerewan was good. 'In the evening I saw him with a ligature fastened very tight round his head,' wrote David Collins, 'which certainly required something to alleviate the pain it must have endured.'[6]

Yelloway (Yalowe or Yalloway), a *gweagal*, had abducted Noorooing (Gnoorooin) the wife of Watewal, who, in revenge, killed Yelloway one night as he slept. Noorooing, 'a dismal, sorrowing figure', came into town on 27 May to tell the whites of Yelloway's death. She covered herself in ashes and while in mourning refused all kinds of food and was termed *go-lahng*.[7] Atkins thought Yelloway had been 'Kill'd and burnt' because of his attachment to the whites.[8] In Collins's opinion, Yelloway 'seemed endowed with more urbanity than the rest of our friends' (the Eora in town). Five months earlier, Watewal and Yelloway had been prominent members of Ballooderry's funeral party.

In the ritual battle that ensued Watewal faced a hail of spears thrown by Colby, Bennelong (usually his ally) and several others, but escaped unhurt. For some time he resumed living with Noorooing and seemed to be on good terms with both Colby and Bennelong. However, a few months later, Colby, who had been a friend of Yelloway, crept up on Watewal at night as he slept and killed him with a spear, after first gently removing an infant he held in his arms. Colby later brought the child into town. 'Yelloway was so much esteemed among us, that no one was sorry he had been so revenged,' Collins commented.[9]

On 8 June, the grieving Noorooing met Gonangoolie, a little girl related to Watewal.[10] Seeking revenge, Noorooing picked up a large stone and bashed the child until her skull was fractured in several places. Gonangoolie died a few days later. 'It appears to be a great determination that the friends of the murdered person revenge his death by the murder of the Guilty person or upon any relation they may have an opportunity of doing it on,' wrote Atkins. When Noorooing realised that the foreigners did not approve of the payback killing, she denied beating Gonangoolie and blamed her death on two other girls who had beaten her with a club. Eora men questioned by Collins blamed Noorooing, but said she had done 'no more than what custom obliged her to'.

Gonangoolie had been a quiet child, 'much beloved in the town'. She lived at the hut of an officer and every day since Yelloway's death had asked that Noorooing could eat there. This was possibly William Dawes's hut at Tarra (Dawes Point). 'Gonangulye' is mentioned several times in Dawes's second language notebook. In one entry, she wished to wear Patyegarang's petticoat but it was too long for her; in another she asked Dawes to speak to someone on HMS *Gorgon*, and in a third she wanted a biscuit.[11]

Watewal, wrote Collins, 'was in great union' with Bennelong, who twice confidently assured the whites that it was not Watewal who had killed Yelloway, but Weremurrah, another of Watewal's names. 'By giving us the second [name], he saved his friend and knew that at all times he could boldly maintain that he had not concealed his name from us,' wrote Collins. 'On apprising [Bennelong] some time afterwards, that we had discovered his artifice, and that it was a meanness we did not expect from him, he only laughed and went away.'[12]

To protect themselves from sudden attacks with spears or clubs at night, the friendly Eora asked the English settlers for spaniel and terrier puppies, which they fed with fish. 'Not a family was without one or more of these little-watch-dogs,' wrote Collins.[13] Governor Phillip himself kept a native dog or dingo which he intended to send to England on one of the returning transport ships. At first the 'Tingo' would eat nothing but fish, 'that being its constant food', noted Newton Fowell.[14]

Captain John Hunter tried to train a dingo puppy, but found that 'it took every opportunity ... to snap off the head of a fowl, or worry a pig, and would do it in defiance of correction'.[15]

THE WESTERN FRONTIER

By 1792, the frontier of white settlement had moved inland from Sydney Cove to the west and was focused on Parramatta with its governor's house, military garrison, government farm and cornfields and convict village of huts and gardens. Transported prisoners who had served their time were given 25 acre (10 hectare) land grants in new settlements at the Northern Boundary (near the present Kings School), Toongabbie (Seven Hills) and to the south west at the base of Prospect Hill (Prospect).

The establishment of the township of Parramatta and the Northern Boundary farms disrupted the *burramattagal*, forcing them into areas owned by other clans, while Toongabbie and Prospect were located in the territory of the *bidjigal* (*bediagal*) or 'woods tribes', identified by William Dawes as the *bediagal-tugagal-tugara*. These people probably spoke the inland dialect of the Sydney language.[16] Bennelong, despite his negotiating skills, had no influence any further west than Parramatta.

Trouble between the indigenous people and the new settlers began on 18 May 1792, when seven men and two women stole clothing and corn from a hut at Prospect. They ran off when a convict fired at a man preparing to throw a spear, leaving behind nets containing corn, some blankets and spears. 'One man it is imagined was wounded,' wrote Atkins.[17] The natives took their revenge by brutally killing a convict walking from Parramatta to Prospect. The man's head was cut in several places, his teeth were knocked out and his body was punctured by at least thirty spear wounds. The blame for this murder was placed on the 'woods tribes', which were believed to be led by Pemulwuy.[18] There were very few reports or information about the native people for the remainder of 1792, which reflects the fact that Atkins and Collins were the only remaining journal keepers in Sydney.

The provision of basic rations seems to have been a part of the Eora peace agreement. On 8 December, Commissary John Palmer reported that there were five 'Natives victualled from the stores' at Sydney.[19]

20

THE SKILFUL GAME

Traditional kinship and gift exchange systems have given today's Australian Aborigines a unique group identity, a sense that each individual belongs to a vast extended family. In Aboriginal society, people and kinship relationships are far more important than material things. This window into Aboriginal culture is revealing, but is not readily understood by outsiders.

Exchanging gifts between relatives, within clans and wider connected groups, was common among indigenous hunter-gatherers. When large groups came together, stone tools, axe heads, spear barbs, spears, spear-throwers, ochre and possum skin cloaks were exchanged. This often coincided with rituals and ceremonies, such as initiations, corroborees or feasts, when sacred and cultural knowledge, for example, songs, stories, dances and body painting designs, were passed on by hereditary custodians.

Goods also moved out along networks of exchange, so that in northern Australia, baler shells from the coast might be traded for ochre from the inland desert. Gifts were reciprocal and, after a certain period, had to be repaid, either in kind or with a mutually agreed equivalent. Gift exchange created a bond between giver and receiver which became an underlying factor of social life.

Anthropologists have been fascinated by the notion and practice of gift exchange, which was not simply a system of barter. 'It is the act of giving rather than what is given that is valued,' stressed W.E.H. Stanner (1933). According to anthropologist Donald Thomson, every man had a special trade partner, related by kinship, to whom he was obliged to send gifts, which circulated over a wide area. 'It is primarily a matter of prestige,' wrote Thomson after a field trip through Arnhem Land (Northern Territory) in the 1930s. 'And failure to repay gifts quickly involves a loss of prestige.'[1]

The cycle of gift exchange is infinite. No gift can be refused and each gift must be passed on. Conflict follows if a person or a group of people refuses to take part in the exchange system. In his pioneering fieldwork in the Trobriand Islands, pioneer anthropologist Bronislaw Malinowski noted that these economic obligations were 'kept very scrupulously' and failure to comply would place a person outside both the social and economic order.[2] As John Lechte contends: 'Those societies whose social structure is entirely based on the gift ... have no space which is not subject to exchange.'[3]

On a one-to-one level, gift exchange necessarily involves direct personal communication. Giver and receiver must meet, look each other in the eye and talk together before they agree on an exchange. In his famous *Essai sur le don* (Essay on the Gift, 1924), the French savant Marcel Mauss called gift exchange 'a total social fact', one that ties individuals and groups together, through the agency of 'things' (the goods exchanged) in social relationships. Mauss implied that objects exchanged, for example, a stone axe, become symbols which create a sense of mutual obligation, mediate relationships and cement alliances. He concluded that similar systems of reciprocal gift exchange existed in all oral (non-literate) societies.[4]

Europeans had a basic, practical approach to gift exchange. British navigators quickly realised the value of trade goods to barter for wood, water, fresh meat, fruit and fish. During his three voyages in the Pacific Ocean (1768-79), navigator and explorer James Cook set the precedents for the Royal Navy by taking with him quantities of iron nails, hatchets and adzes to give to Maori, Hawaiian and Tahitian leaders. After Cook's first voyage, the hatchets he left behind contributed to a change in the power structure of Tahiti. With a fleet consisting of hundreds of huge, double-hulled war canoes, built with iron hatchets, Tu, chief of three villages near Matavai Bay, soon gained absolute sea power and became high chief of Tahiti and neighbouring islands.

In 1774, Cook advised voyagers who would follow him:

> Who ever comes to this isle [Tahiti] will do well to provide himself with red feathers, the finest and smallest that are to be got, he must also have a good stock of Axes and Hatchets, Spike Nails, Knives, Looking Glasses, Beads &c. Sheets and shirts are much sought after.[5]

Cook ordered his blacksmiths to make *toi*, small adzes preferred by the Tahitians, from damaged anchors and scrap iron. 'We generally gave three or four for a Hog of 100 lb weight or more & there was nothing went so well as these Tois,' wrote David Samwell, surgeon on HMS *Discovery*.[6] Sailors were happy to exchange nails, hatchets and adzes for sexual favours from native women. 'So long as he got his toi,' wrote Samwell, an islander 'would as soon let you lie with his Wife as with his Daughter or Sister.'[7]

In England, at a time when there was twelve pence (12d) in one shilling (1s) and twenty shillings in one pound sterling (£1), iron hatchets could be purchased for as little as nine pence or one shilling each. Arthur Bowes Smyth, surgeon of the convict transport *Lady Penrhyn*, referred to this in his log book on 24 July 1788, when he exchanged two goats for 'Each a 9d Hatchett' in Tahiti on the return voyage from Sydney Cove. The

Polynesians placed a high value on the English hatchets. When one was stolen from the ship's steward, Bowes Smyth remarked: 'This I should deem a temptation equal to an Otehetian [Tahitian] wt. that of a Diamond to an Englishman.'[8]

On his final visit to Tahiti in 1779, Cook realised with regret that by the time the iron tools he had given them were worn out, the natives would have almost forgotten their traditional artefacts. 'A stone hatchet is, at present, as rare a thing amongst them, as an iron one was eight years ago, and a chisel of bone or stone is not to be seen,' he wrote. By that time, red bird feathers, regarded as sacred objects, were eagerly sought by the Tahitians.

Meanwhile in New Zealand, iron hatchets had become common and were not so highly valued. On the same voyage, John Gore, lieutenant on HMS *Resolution*, complained of the ingratitude of Maoris at Queen Charlotte Sound: 'Give one of them a Hatchet, afterwards Ask the same person for the Claw of a Crawfish he'll not Part with it without being paid,' Gore wrote.

Linguistic evidence points to the existence of reciprocal gift giving among the indigenous people of Port Jackson in the late eighteenth century. In the language spoken by the Eora, as understood by those who compiled the word lists and language notebooks, *wea-je-minga* and *weeang* meant 'relating to giving anything', a word very close to *wyanga* or mother. *Damuna* meant exchange and *damoly* or *tamooly* was the act of exchanging a name with a friend. The person with whom you exchanged your name (and in some Aboriginal societies therefore became your trading partner) was your *damelian* (*damelabillia*) or namesake. On the other hand, the perjorative term *damunalung*, someone who refused to give, was translated into English by William Dawes as 'a churl'.

The *mogo*, a hatchet with a head made of hard, durable stone, sharpened at one end, was an important tool, used to strip sheets of stringybark from trees to make canoes or bark shelters, to carve battle shields, to cut toeholds for climbing and to enlarge holes in trees to catch possums and obtain edible grubs and honey. A hatchet is usually smaller than an axe, has a shorter handle, and is easy to use with one hand. Hatchet heads could not be made from the soft, flaky sandstone of the coastal ridges around the Sydney area, so chip-resistant stones, like the waterworn basalt pebbles found in the bed of the Hawkesbury-Nepean River, some 50 kilometres from Sydney Cove, had to be 'imported'. This implies the existence of gift exchange between coastal and inland river clans.

A TRAIL OF HATCHETS

With Cook's experience in mind, Captain Arthur Phillip planned to trade English goods with the native inhabitants as he organised the details of

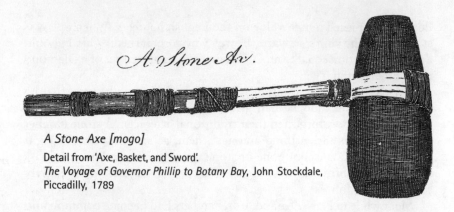

A Stone Axe [mogo]
Detail from 'Axe, Basket, and Sword'.
The Voyage of Governor Phillip to Botany Bay, John Stockdale,
Piccadilly, 1789

the voyage to the penal colony at Botany Bay at Portsmouth in April 1787. 'By what I am informed,' wrote Phillip, 'Hatchets & Beads are the Articles for Barter.'[9] Among iron tools loaded on board the ships of the First Fleet were 700 hatchets, 700 felling axes, 747 000 nails, 50 pick axes and 700 clamp knives.[10]

In April 1770, despite their offers of trade goods, Cook and Joseph Banks had failed to establish friendly negotiations when HMS *Endeavour* dropped anchor at Botany Bay. Rather, the landing party fired on two men who shouted and defiantly shook their spears and fled when riddled with buckshot. Cook and Banks took away a collection of spears and in return left some beads in the bark shelters. Although they offered the natives mirrors, hair combs, beads and cloth, 'all they seem'd to want was for us to be gone', wrote Cook.[11]

By contrast, the diplomatic role of gift exchange is tangible in the first meeting at Botany Bay between the indigenous people and the English expedition on Friday 18 January 1788. To avoid a crowd of some forty natives on the south shore of the bay, 'shouting and making many uncouth signs and gestures', Phillip beached his boat on the north shore, in order, wrote Watkin Tench, 'to take possession of his new territory and bring about an intercourse between its old and new masters'.[12] As the boat approached, a group of natives 'got up & called to us in a Menacing tone, & at the same time brandish[ed] their spears or lances. However, the Governor shewed them some beads and ordered a man to fasten them to the stern of the canoe.'[13] By dipping his hat into the sea and pretending to drink from it, an officer indicated that they wanted to land to get fresh water. The 'Indians' pointed to a spot where there was running water. Governor Phillip, according to Philip Gidley King, advanced 'alone & unarmed'. One man came towards him, 'but would not come near enough to receive the beads which the Governor held out for him, but seemed very desirous of having them & made signs for them to be lain on ye ground, which was done, he (ye native) came on with fear and trembling

& took them up, & by degrees came so near as to receive Looking Glasses &c. & seemed quite astonished at the figure we cut in being cloathed'.[14] An 'interview' then took place, wrote Tench, in which:

> the conduct of both parties pleased each other so much, that the strangers returned to their ship with a much better opinion of the natives that they had landed with; and the latter seemed highly entertained with their new acquaintances, from whom they condescended to accept of a looking glass, some beads, and other toys.[15]

By their established laws of exchange, the Botany Bay natives could not refuse the proffered trinkets, which they 'condescended to accept'. Exchange had led to cross-cultural communication and interaction in which each race had been able to size up the other. Another encounter between the two races was extraordinary because it is recorded both by Philip Gidley King and in the oral tradition of the Botany Bay people through a story told about 1833 to Father J. McEncroe, a Catholic priest later attached to St Patrick's in Sydney, who had asked about the landing of James Cook. McEncroe's informant (possibly Mahroot or one of the brothers Blewitt and Potter) said his father had told him that two natives had gone to meet the people from the ship. One took a jacket and put it on, but threw it off when he found himself cramped. However, the Botany Bay men were most attracted by an iron tomahawk (hatchet) which they realised would help them cut wood 'to make gunyahs and spears'. Earlier the women had warned the two men not to eat or drink anything the strangers might give them for fear of poisoning. When offered a tomahawk if they would drink wine, they took some after seeing the sailors drink it without ill effects. One of them took some of the drink, McEncroe continued, 'and he had hardly done so when he thought he was burning alive, and cried out to his companions in his own language: "Fire in eyes, fire in nose, and fire all over", and ran off to throw himself in the water to quench the fire.'[16] Recollections of the landing of sailors from HM Bark *Endeavour* in 1770 and the First Fleet ships eighteen years later were obviously mingled in the folk memory of the Botany Bay clan, as Cook had no friendly meetings with the natives there. King, who was accompanied by Lieutenant William Dawes, does not mention any hatchets being given at Botany Bay, but wrote in his journal for 20 January 1788:

> I gave two of them a glass of Wine which they had no sooner tasted than they spit it out, we asked them the name of a number of articles, which they told us & repeated our words & had already learnt so much English, as to express their want for any thing by putting their finger on it gently looking me in the face & saying 'No'?[17]

On 8 February, less than two weeks after the colonists had moved to the shores of Sydney Cove, two elders from Botany Bay strolled into the new camp. Phillip tied some red bunting and yellow tinfoil around their heads and gave each of them an iron hatchet. They sat cross-legged under a tree for about one hour, while one man, wrote David Collins, 'curiously shewed us his knowledge by turning up his foot, and sharpening a piece of wood on the sole with the hatchet'.[18] If they had come to spy out the land and see whether the foreigners planned to stay permanently, the elders seemed remarkably detached and took no notice of Phillip's portable canvas house, which had just been assembled. 'The Objects which must have been entirely new to them did not excite their Curiosity or Astonishment so much as one might have expected,' noted Surgeon George Worgan. 'They just looked at them with a kind of vague indifference.'[19]

Looking Glass Point on the Parramatta River, near the present suburb of Gladesville, got its name on 15 February 1788, when Phillip, Captain John Hunter and some others in three boats stopped there for breakfast. They were joined by an intelligent native man, who put down his spear and curiously examined the boats. Phillip gave the man a hatchet and a mirror. 'When he looked into it,' William Bradley wrote in his journal, 'he looked immediately behind the Glass to see if any person was there & then pointed to the Glass & the shadows which he saw in the water signifying they were similar.'[20]

There must have been many unofficial transactions, but few were recorded. For example, Lieutenant Ralph Clark and his two convict servants went up the Lane Cove River on Sunday 14 February 1790 where they exchanged an iron hatchet for two spears when they met two men named Dourrawan and Tirriwan. Clark returned the next day with some red cloth for their children.[21]

In the weeks leading up to his return to the Sydney settlement, Bennelong became a player in what Claude Lévi-Strauss (1957) has called 'the skilful game of exchange'.[22] Bennelong demanded iron hatchets at the whale feast at Manly Cove on 7 September 1790, when he met Governor Phillip for the first time since his escape. After Phillip's arrival, wrote Watkin Tench:

> Hatchets still continued to be called for with redoubled eagerness, which rather surprized us, as formerly they had always been accepted with indifference. But Baneelon had probably demonstrated to them their superiority over those of their own manufacturing.[23]

From that day, iron hatchets were on the agenda at every meeting with Bennelong. Surgeon White and Commissary John Palmer gave Bennelong a hatchet and some fish on 15 September 1790 and two days later Bennelong received another hatchet and some English fishing lines. On her harbour boat trips as an interpreter, Boorong ensured that her father Maugoran and her brothers, Ballooderry and Yeranibe Goruey, also received hatchets. It is likely that Ballooderry used one of the sharp new hatchets to cut out the bark for the canoe he later used in the fishing trade. Similarly,

Nanbarry's uncle Colby was given a hatchet by Phillip at Farm Cove on 18 October 1790.

It can be argued that Phillip, unwittingly or by design, had created an elite group of initiated men who possessed hatchets, which might be termed the *mogogal* or 'hatchet people'. Gifts of iron hatchets had become part of a political process which disturbed whatever natural balance of power had survived the destruction of the Sydney clans by the smallpox epidemic of 1789.

The formal offering of hatchets on the morning of 8 October 1790 – the day that Bennelong came peacefully to Sydney – would have been seen by the Eora as cementing an agreement between the two peoples. They immediately took out spears, fishing lines and fizgigs to make reciprocal exchanges. Caught up in the excitement, Watkin Tench rowed back to Sydney to get a hatchet, which he exchanged for a spear and spear-thrower. Bennelong and his friends were given more hatchets that afternoon at Governor Phillip's house and continued to demand and receive iron hatchets after they began to frequent the Sydney settlement.

Boorong again obtained hatchets for her two brothers, when they came with Bennelong on 10 October 1790 to pick up his metal shield. 'Hatchets,' wrote Phillip, 'appeared to be the most valuable articles that could be given them.'[24]

If the Dutch settler Peter Minuit bought the island of Manhattan from its Indian owners in a treaty for goods worth the equivalent of $US24, it could be said that, although he did not buy any land, Governor Arthur Phillip had purchased 'peace' from the Eora at the bargain price of perhaps one dozen iron hatchets, worth less than £1 Sterling.

Accepting the new cross-cultural reality at Sydney Cove, the Eora had found ways to accommodate their traditional practice of reciprocity. In each transaction, they sought to bring the white settlers into their gift exchange network. Sadly, this was probably not realised by the English negotiators at the time. The incidental jokes and laughter, singing and dancing involved in these encounters indicate exchanges far more subtle than the received colonial history of racial interaction. To Nicholas Thomas (1996), such relationships imply 'that colonisers and colonised, travellers and natives, are socially bound through exchange relations, when we have always posited a lack of sociality and a clash of cultures'.[25] Indeed, the First Fleet accounts bristle with descriptions of exhilarating meetings and a spirit of play – overlaying the latent fear and suspicion – which involved giving, receiving, gesturing, mimicking, joking and exchanging words and ideas.

A report in *The Gentlemen's Magazine* in March 1789 gave London readers a good account of the innocent humour at Botany Bay: 'It was a practice with the seamen, in these intercourses, to dress up the inhabitants with shreds of cloth, and tags of coloured paper; and, when they surveyed each other, they would burst in loud laughter, and run hollowing to the woods.'[26]

Thomas (1991) aptly applied the word 'entanglements' to describe such contacts and exchanges, however uneven.[27] This picture of the Eora, enmeshed in a complex web of negotiations and social obligations, does not sit easily with colonial notions of brute savages in the wilds, hunting their food and possessing no capacity for reflective thought. The later clashes, misunderstandings and thefts on both sides were inevitable complications of dispossession and subjugation by the English colonists.

In traditional Aboriginal society, gifts given or received were symbols which signified the passing of war into peace (or of hostility into amity). In the exchange system, gifts create relationships of debt and dependency between giver and receiver. It was to Bennelong's advantage (and very much in his nature) to play the skilful game on both sides, by trading on the hatchets he received from the English to influential men in other Sydney clans. Such gifts, associated with the powerful figure of Phillip, his soldiers and their firesticks, enhanced Bennelong's status among his people, strengthened old alliances and initiated new ones.

While the focus might have been on weapons, clothing and artefacts, gift exchange clearly involved political dynamics and entangled relationships between specific individuals, particularly Bennelong and Phillip. The Eora made a distinction between useful implements and mere trinkets, such as beads, coloured cloth, tinfoil and handkerchiefs, which they soon discarded as fleeting fancies. While they 'greedily' took necklaces, scraps of cloth and handkerchiefs, 'they scarce ever kept the gift beyond a day, and all their finery was found from time to time scattered about the woods and unregarded', wrote a correspondent in *The London Chronicle*.[28] 'They accept of presents as Children do play things, just to amuse them for a moment and then throw them away, disregarded,' Elizabeth Macarthur noted.[29] The Eora did not discard artefacts which were useful to them, like hatchets, knives or fishhooks.

In a flash of insight in February 1791, Lieutenant David Collins realised that the settlers were being manipulated by Bennelong and the Eora elite, who had 'cornered the market' and were preventing others from trading with them.

> It was conceived by some among us, that those natives who came occasionally into the town did not desire that any of the other tribes should participate in the enjoyment of the few trifles they procured from us. If this were true, it would for a long time retard the general understanding of our friendly intentions towards them; and it was not improbable they might for the same reason represent us in every unfavourable light they could imagine.[30]

ADOPTING HATCHETS

For many years to come, the usefulness of iron hatchets to the native Australians would continue to be exploited by the settlers. Writing to his employer Sir Joseph Banks in June 1802, botanist George Caley said he would 'always strive to be upon good terms' with the natives around Parramatta 'by giving them small axes ... and filling their bellys'.[31]

While his ship was moored at Kirribilli on Sydney's north shore in 1820, the Russian astronomer Ivan Mikhaylovich Siminov watched the native people using 'small iron axes' as well as stone ones for fashioning fishing implements, which were then smoothed down with glass.[32] Judge Barron Field told the members of the Philosophical Society of Australia on 2 January 1822 that, thirty years after white settlement, the Aborigines had not adopted any European arts of life apart from 'exchanging their stone hatchets and shell-fish hooks for our iron ones'.

By 1836, there was 'scarcely a black to be seen who is not possessed of the common English tomahawk with an iron blade', wrote surveyor William Romaine Govett, who illustrated an adze-like iron hatchet which, he said, was sharpened in the same way as the stone axes it had replaced.[33]

Moving along the trade routes which crisscrossed Australia, iron hatchets preceded settlers and even explorers like Major Thomas Mitchell, who in 1846 met Aborigines with iron tomahawks far inland in central Queensland.[34] 'In a very few years the stone weapons of these central tribes will be a thing of the past and I am afraid we shall contribute to their extinction by distributing iron tomahawks and knives,' F.J. Gillen in Tennant Creek wrote to Baldwin Spencer in July 1901.[35]

21

A HEAD FOR SIR JOSEPH

Something snapped in Governor Arthur Phillip's normally cool, deliberate mind after Pemulwuy's attack in December 1790 against his convict game shooter John McEntire, which was to prove fatal.

However, the pressure brought to bear on Phillip by Sir Joseph Banks to send him an Aboriginal skull could explain, in part, the governor's uncharacterisically violent reaction. There is no record of a request from Banks for a native skull or skulls, but Phillip's strong sense of obligation to his influential patron in London can be traced through a series of apologies which run through his letters from Port Jackson to the great man of science in London.

In March 1790 Banks had promised 'exotic skulls' to his German colleague, the anatomist Johann Fredrich Blumenbach, professor of medicine at the University of Göttingen. In January 1791, Banks specifically promised to provide Blumenbach with 'South Sea' skulls.[1]

After some time in New South Wales, Phillip was frustrated to find that the bodies of natives who died were usually cremated. In 1788 he ordered a burial mound to be opened, but it contained only ashes. Another grave, in which part of a jawbone was found, was opened by Captain John Hunter. Phillip noted that no graves were found 'near their Huts'.[2] 'I shall send Skulls by the Gorgon,' Phillip advised Banks by letter on 26 July 1790, some five months before the unsuccessful headhunting expedition to Botany Bay.[3] 'I am sorry I cannot send you a head,' Phillip told Banks on 26 March 1791, 'after the ravages of the small pox, numbers [of bodies] were seen in every part, but the natives burn the bodies, some may be found hereafter.'[4]

It is likely that further pressure was exerted on Phillip through Philip Gidley King, who returned to Sydney on HMS *Gorgon* in 21 September 1791. While in London, King had met Sir Joseph Banks, who showed him some of his curio collection and recruited him as a natural history collector.

On 17 November 1791, Phillip wrote to Banks: 'The natives burn their dead, but when skulls can be got they will be sent.'[5] On 3 December, it was: 'You shall have heads when I can get any, but the Natives burn their dead: no European has yet seen the ceremony.'[6] This letter was sent by HMS *Gorgon*, which left Sydney on 18 December 1791.

As a young man, Banks first came across exotic human skulls in the *marae* or stone terrace temples of the Pacific Ocean island of Tahiti in June 1769 on his voyage around the world aboard HMS *Endeavour* with James Cook. In New Zealand, at Queen Charlotte Sound early in 1790, Banks was fascinated by the decapitated heads of Maori warriors who had been killed in battle, which, he wrote in his journal, 'were somehow preserved so as not to stink at all'. Banks obtained the head of a boy of about fifteen or sixteen years of age from an elderly Maori in exchange for a pair of white linen drawers.

After resigning his post as governor of New South Wales, Arthur Phillip, sailed from Sydney Cove in HMS *Atlantic*, arriving in England on 21 May 1793. Shortly afterwards, Banks, who corresponded from his home in Soho Square with scientists around the world, passed on the skull of a New South Wales native to Blumenbach. 'The New Hollander's scull is happily arrived,' wrote Blumenbach to Banks from Göttingen in November. He noted that the skull was missing the upper front tooth which had been pulled out during initiation 'according to the custom of these savages'.[7]

Blumenbach was a pioneer in the now discredited science of physical anthropology. Just as botanists collect plants, Blumenbach classified the 'varieties of mankind'. His museum at Göttingen became the grisly laboratory in which he measured and compared human skulls, skeletons, mummies and samples of skin and hair. The term 'Caucasian' was coined by Blumenbach, who believed that the white races had originated in the Caucasus Mountains and that other races had 'degenerated' from this 'primary type' due to climatic variations. In the third edition of *De Generis Humani Varietate Nativa* (On the Natural Varieties of Mankind), 1795, Blumenbach classified the Australian Aborigines amongst the 'Malay race'.

By 1856 Blumenbach's collection, housed in the Department of Anatomy at Georg-August University, Göttingen, included 245 complete skulls and fragments, one Egyptian and one *Guanche* mummy and the preserved head of a New Zealand Maori (perhaps one obtained by Banks). While there was no suggestion in Blumenbach's work that the skulls were intended to support a racist view of humanity, wrote Jacob Bronowski in *The Ascent of Man* (1973), they 'became a core of racist, pan-Germanic theory, which was officially sanctioned by the National Socialist [Nazi] Party when it came into power'.[8]

This skull and a second skull of an initiated man from the Sydney area supplied by Banks and received by Blumenbach by 12 June 1799 survive today at Göttingen. The university has not replied to letters asking about the New Holland skulls. A colleague in Germany was told the old chestnut that the skulls were destroyed by bombing during World War II. There is a good photo of the Blumenbach Skull Collection in Bronowski's book (Plate 182).

22

SAILING

On 10 December 1792, Bennelong and his young kinsman Yemmer-rawanne boarded the storeship HMS *Atlantic*, moored at the Governor's Wharf on the eastern side of Sydney Cove. The two men, who were 'much attached' to Governor Phillip, embarked 'voluntarily and cheerfully', wrote David Collins, 'and withstood at the moment of their departure the united distress of their wives, and the dismal lamentations of their friends, to accompany him to England, a place they well knew was at a great distance from them'.[1]

Spears, shields and fishing tackle, specimens of timber, plants, animals and birds, four live kangaroos and several dingos had been loaded aboard. Arthur Phillip, returning home after five years of solitary leadership, took with him a portfolio of watercolour drawings of plants, animals and portraits of native people. The returning marine detachment, commanded by Lieutenant John Poulden, had marched on board one week earlier as fires swept the heights of The Rocks on the western side of the cove.

Officers and oarsmen in small boats accompanying the departing ship shouted 'Huzza' as she slipped her ropes from the jetty. Soon she passed Bennelong's brick house at *Tubowgulle* and had left *Weerong* behind. By English reckoning, *Atlantic* cleared the Heads of Port Jackson at nine o'clock on the morning of 11 December 1792. The officers in the boats gave three cheers for Governor Phillip and turned back, but the Reverend Mr Johnson's boat was staved in when it accidentally rammed the side of the ship.

Wind filled the sails. From the Look Out Post, high on South Head, the burial ground of *Woolara*, the ship was visible at midday. Gazing far out to sea, the Eora could still detect a white speck on the horizon well into the afternoon.

Bennelong and Yemmerrawanne had sailed out of the Eora world and into a new Dreaming.

> *Wau be-rong orah*
> *Where is a better country*
> – Anon., 1791

APPENDIX

THE NAMES OF BENNELONG

BA-NA-LANG P.G. King in Hunter 1793

BA-NA-LANG, VOGLE-TROOYE, VO-LA-RA-VERY John Hunter 1793

BANALANG Mary Ann Parker 1795

BANALONG James Scott 1790

BAN-EE-LON WO-LAR-A-WAR-EE Watkin Tench, 1789

BANEELON Watkin Tench 1790

BANELONG John Shortland 1795

BANILONG John Hunter 1795

BANNELON, WOLLEWARRE, BOINBA, BUNDE-BUNDA, WOGETROWEY
P.G. King in Hunter 1790

BANNELONG Arthur Phillip in Hunter 1790

BANNOLONG Letter dictated by Bennelong 1796

BANNYLONG Elizabeth Macarthur 1791

BENALLON William Bradley 1789; Henry Waterhouse 1791

BENALONG Henry Waterhouse 1790, 1795, 1799

BENELONG William Dawes 1790; David Blackburn 1791; William Neate
Chapman 1791

BENNELONG Joseph Holt 1800; *Sydney Gazette* 1805, 1806, 1813, 1817 etc.;
Samuel Marsden 1826

BENNILONG Port Jackson Painter c. 1791; Samuel Bennett 1865; Richard
Sadlier 1883

BEN-NIL-LONG Samuel Leigh 1821

BENNILLONG David Collins 1798

BEN-NIL-LONG, WO-LAR-RA-BAR-RAY, WO-GUL-TROW-E, BOIN BA,
and BUN-DE-BUN-DA David Collins 1789[1]

BENNYLONGS George Caley 1809

O-GUL-TROYEE or BENELONG Rev. Richard Johnson 1790

VOLAHOAVERRY Elizabeth Macarthur 1791

VUL-AL-A-VARRY WOGLETROWEY BENALONG Newton Fowell 1790

WALLERBIO George Caley (1809)[2]

WE-LAR-RE-BARRE, WO-GUL-TROWE, BAN-NEL-LON, BO-IN-BAR, BUNDLE-BUNDA William Dawes 1790

WOGLETROWEY, WOLARRABARREY, BAUNELLON, BOINBA, BUNDEBUNDA Arthur Phillip 1790

WOOLARAWERY OCULTROWAY BENALLON Daniel Southwell 1790

WOLAREWARRE; WOLLEREWARRE P.G. King Journal 1790

WOLARE-WARRE P.G. King in Hunter 1793

WOOLARAVERAY BENNALON Daniel Southwell, July 1790

WOLLE-WARRE P.G. King, vocabulary in Hunter 1793

According to John Hunter (1793), Vogle-troo-ye and Vo-la-ra-very 'were names by which some of his [Bennelong's] particular connections were distinguished, and which he had, upon their death, taken up'.[3]

'Bennillong told me his name was that of a large fish, but one that I never saw taken,' wrote Collins.[4]

NOTES

ABBREVIATIONS

ADB *Australian Dictionary of Biography*

BL British Library, London

BT Bonwick Transcripts (ML)

DL Dixson Library, Sydney

HRA *Historical Records of Australia*

HRNSW *Historical Records of New South Wales*

JRAHS *Journal of the Royal Australian Historical Society*

ML Mitchell Library, Sydney

PRO Public Record Office, London

SG *Sydney Gazette*

SMH *Sydney Morning Herald*

1 BENNELONG POINT

1. 'Kah-dier-rang', Collins 1798:592 (1975:493); Cadimanga – Elizabeth Macarthur to Kingdon 7 March 1791 [*HRNSW* 11:505].
2. David Collins 1798:592-3 (1975:492-3). *An Account of the English Colony in New South Wales*, London. Notes hereafter refer to the more generally available edition issued by A.H. & A.W. Reed (Sydney 1975).
3. Phillip to Lord Sydney, 28 September 1788 [*HRNSW* 11:191-2].

2 SALTWATER ECONOMY

1. Flood 1990:281.
2. 'Goomun – The Fir Tree', King 1790:400; Anon. 20.17; Worgan 1978:17. If not specifically cited, words from the Sydney language are drawn from Anon. (1790-1), Dawes (a) and (b), or printed First Fleet word lists and vocabularies. See 'The Sydney Languages' in the Bibliography.
3. Hunter 1793:63.
4. Bradley 1969:68-9.
5. Worgan 1978:16.
6. Gardiner 1791:67.

7. Bradley 1969:131.
8. Waterhouse to his father, 11 July 1788 [MS 262/52, ML].
9. Tench 1793:18.
10. 'Na-re-wang, A paddle', Hunter 1793:410; 'Ghar-awang A Paddle', Blackburn, Vocabulary 1791.
11. Waterhouse op. cit.
12. Banks Journal, August 1770 [Beaglehole 1963 11:134].
13. Tench 1793:187.
14. Bradley 1969:188.
15. Collins 1975:461; Bradley 1969:131.
16. 'Car-re-jun – a fishing line', Anon. 18.14; 'a deal of Currijon [trees]', Caley Journal, 5 November 1804 [NHM London].
17. Tench 1793:191.
18. 'Dtuuraduralang – The bark to make fish lines', Dawes 1790b:5.24.
19. White 1790:200.
20. Banks op. cit. 131. Elsewhere Banks described the technique as 'between netting and Knitting' (i.e., like crochet).
21. Collins 1975:461.
22. Bradley 1969:92.
23. Lampert and Megaw in P. Stanbury (ed.) 1979. *10 000 Years of Sydney Life* (Sydney).

24. Collins 1975:499.
25. Tench 1793:199.
26. Collins 1975:461.
27. Worgan 1978:16.
28. Bradley 1969:69.
29. Tench 1793:195.
30. Bradley 1969:112.
31. Harris to unknown correspondent, 21 March 1791 [A1597:858, p. 6. ML].
32. Blackburn to Margaret Blackburn, 17 March 1791 [Reel 133/3, Norwich Record Office UK].
33. Bradley 1969:103.
34. V.J. Attenbrow 1991 and subsequently. The Port Jackson Archaeological Project. See Australian Museum, Sydney, Internet website.
35. Phillip 1979 (1793):70; Tench 1789:132.
36. Worgan 1978:11.
37. Phillip to Sydney, 15 May 1788 [PRO CO 201/3].
38. Threlkeld (1825) in Gunson 1974:55.
39. Phillip 1970:75.
40. Threlkeld op. cit.
41. Collins 1975:457.
42. Gardiner 1791:69.
43. Tench 1793:176.
44. Gardiner op. cit.
45. Collins 1975:462-3.

3 A LINE IN THE SAND

1. Nagle 1988:93-4.
2. Phillip 1970 (1789:75).
3. 'North Head – Car-rang-gel; South Do. – Tar-ral-be', Anon. 36.10-11. Later carrangle was used to mean an English jacket – Anon. 36.10, 11.
4. 'Manly Bay – Kay-ye-my', Anon. 38.13.
5. Phillip to Sydney, 15 May 1788 [PRO CO 201/3].
6. Ibid.
7. Clark 1981:93.
8. Robert Brown Journal, 26 January 1788 [HRNSW 11:407 et seq.].
9. King in Hunter 1793:406; 'Worra Woora Wea', Fowell 1988:67; 'whurra which signifies, begone', Tench 1789:56.

10. Sydney Parkinson 1784:134. A Journal of a Voyage to the South Seas, in his Majesty's Ship The Endeavour ... (London).
11. Easty 1965:94.
12. Clark op. cit.
13. Bowes Smyth 1979:64.
14. Worgan 1973:33.

4 MEN'S BUSINESS

1. Tench 1793:190.
2. Southwell to Butler, 12 July 1788 [HRNSW 11:689].
3. Collins 1975:455.
4. Ibid.
5. 'A Shield made of bark – E-le-mong', Anon. 27.11; 'E-li-mang, A small shield, made of bark', Hunter 1793:408; 'E-lee-mong', Collins 1975:487.
6. Banks Journal, August 1770 [Beaglehole 1963 11:133-4].
7. 'a Shield made of wood – Ar-ra-gong', Anon. 27.10; 'Ar-rah-gong', Collins 1975:487; 'A-ra-goon, A war shield', Hunter 1793:478.
8. 'Fire – Guyon (or) Gwee-yong', Anon. 26.3; 'Gwee-ung Fire', Southwell 1787-93:58; Gwee-ang Fire', Hunter 1793:409; 'Gweè-un (fire)', Arabanoo to Tench 1793:12.
9. Bennelong to King, Journal, April 1790 [C115 ML].
10. King's description, edited from his journal, was printed in Hunter (1793:414) and repeated verbatim by Collins (1975:493), who remarked: 'Bennillong, or some other native, shewed me the process of procuring it [fire]'.
11. Tench 1793:192.
12. 'what gives fire – Ger-rub-ber (or) Ge-re-bar', Anon 29.11; 'Goòroobeera. that is a stick of fire', Tench 1793:292.
13. Phillip 1789:25.
14. Hunter 1793:61-2.
15. Jones 1968:205-10.
16. See: James L. Kohen 1995. Aboriginal Environmental Impacts (Sydney: University of New South Wales Press).

17. Banks Journal, August 1770
[Beaglehole 1963 11:127].
18. Barrallier 1802 [*HRNSW* V:751].
19. Caley Journal, 15 February 1804 [MS
C112:20-21 ML].
20. Phillip to Sydney, 13 February 1790
[*HRNSW* 11:310].
21. Phillip in Hunter 1793:507.
22. Tench 1793:28; Collins 1975:462.
23. Worgan 1978:11.
24. Waterhouse to his father, 11 July
1788 [ML 262/52].
25. Anon 17.13.
26. Threlkeld (1825) in Gunson 1974:33.
27. Phillip in Hunter 1793:544-5.
28. Tench 1793:28.
29. Banks Journal, August 1770
[Beaglehole 1963 11:127].

5 RESISTANCE

1. Bradley 1969:68-9.
2. Hunter 1793:52-3.
3. Collins 1975:16.
4. Worgan 1978:28-9.
5. White 1790:118.
6. Anon 29.11; 'Dje-ra-bar or Je-erab-ber
– the name given to the Musquet. The
Natives frequently called us by the name
they give the Musquet.', Anon. 16.22.
7. This derivation was first suggested by
Irene Smith.
8. Bowes Smyth 1979:66.
9. Bradley 1969:84.
10. Bradley 1969:84-5.
11. Southwell to Butler, 27 May 1790
[Southwell Papers, Reel M1538:712
BL]. This theme is explored by art
curator Richard Neville 1997. *A Rage
for Curiosity* (Sydney: State Library of
NSW Press).
12. Bowes Smyth 1979:57, 75.
13. Collins 1975:13.
14. Bradley op. cit.
15. Clark 1981:100 [MS C219 ML].
16. Collins op. cit.
17. Clark op. cit.
18. Sinclair Journal, 9 March 1788
[*HRNSW* 11:401].
19. Worgan 1978:14.
20. Phillip to Sydney, 15 May 1788
[*HRNSW* 11:131].

21. Bowes Smyth 1979:77.
22. Bradley 1969:96-8.
23. Bradley 1969:100.
24. Bradley 1969:109; *HRA* 1:62.
25. Worgan 1978:46; Collins 1975:24;
Bradley 1969:107-8.
26. Bradley 1969:111.
27. Fowell 1988:83.
28. White 1790:30.
29. Bradley 1969:110.
30. Collins deposition of 2 June 1788
[quoted in Cobley 1963:157].
31. Worgan 1978:46; 51.
32. Richard Williams, Extract of a Journal
from England to Botany Bay,
Broadside, 1789, ML.
33. Hunter 1793:79.
34. Bradley 1969:111.
35. Phillip to the Marquess of Lansdowne,
3 July 1788 [*HRNSW* 11:411].
36. Phillip to Sydney, 9 July 1788 [HRA
1:49].
37. Phillip to Sydney, 10 July 1788 [PRO
CO 201/3 BL].
38. Bradley 1969:100.
39. Phillip to Sydney, 18 July 1788
[*HRNSW* 11:133].
40. Hunter 1793:8.
41. Collins 1975:34.
42. Collins 1975:32-3.
43. Clark to William Collins, 1 October
1788 [Clark 1981:271].
44. Easty 1965:106.
45. Collins 1975:35-6.
46. Collins 1975:37.
47. Fowell 1988:115.
48. Blackburn, 15 November 1788 [AB
163 ML].
49. Phillip to Sydney, 18 November 1788
[*HRNSW* 1.ii].
50. Tench 1793:7.

6 ARABANOO

1. Tench 1793:9.
2. Hunter 1793:133.
3. Tench 1793:12.
4. Ibid.
5. Bennett 1865:279.
6. The Guardhouse was built near the
present corner of George and
Grosvenor streets, Sydney.

7. Hunter 1793:133.
8. Fowell 1988:114.
9. Tench op. cit.
10. Fowell op. cit.
11. Collins 1975:43.
12. Nagle 1988:104-5.
13. Tench 1793:14-15.
14. Tench 1793:16-17.
15. Collins 1975:47-8.
16. Tench 1793:17.
17. Fowell to his father, Batavia, 31 July 1790 [*Sirius Letters* 1988:113].
18. Hunter 1793:133.
19. Fowell op. cit.
20. Bradley 1969:162.
21. Tench 1793:18.
22. Scott 1963:47.
23. 'Cud-dur – the man who died', Anon. 41.2. He follows Nanbarry in a list of 'Names of Native Men'.
24. Tench 1793:19-20.
25. Tench 1793:20-1.
26. Collins 1975:496.
27. 'Bàdo, bàdo (water)', Tench 1793:20.
28. Collins 1975:54.
29. Collins 1975:496.
30. Collins 1975:496-7.
31. Arabanoo to Collins 1975:53; 'Galgalla – the small pox', Anon. 17.22. Lieutenant Ralph Clark, writing in February 1790, was told at the Lane Cove River that mittayon or smallpox had killed the wife of his informant Tirriwan [Clark 1981:109].
32. Fowell to his father, Batavia, 31 July 1790 [*HRNSW* 11:373 et seq.].
33. Hunter 1793:134.
34. Phillip to Sydney, 12 February 1790 [*HRNSW* 11:299].
35. Gillen 1989:4.
36. Bradley 1969:108.
37. Clark to B. Hartwell, 12 July 1788 [Clark 1981:267].
38. Mahroot (1845:3). 'Report from the Select Committee on the Condition of Aborigines.' NSW Legislative Council Votes and Proceedings, Sydney (1845:3).
39. Phillip 1979 (1789):65; White 1790:142-3.
40. Bradley 1969:118.
41. Phillip to Banks, 2 July 1788 [BP CY3005/26].
42. Bradley 1969:117.
43. Collins 1975:29.
44. Obed West *SMH* 1882.
45. Hunter 1793:132.
46. Fowell op. cit.
47. Collins 1975:54.
48. Tench 1793:23.
49. Fowell op. cit.
50. Bradley 1969:164.
51. Collins 1975:496.
52. Bradley 1969:178.
53. Bradley 1969:118.
54. Bradley 1969:124.
55. Collins 1975:34.
56. Collins 1975:66-7.

7 TAKING A NATIVE

1. Bradley 1969:181.
2. King Journal, 9 April 1790 [MS C115 ML].
3. Bradley 1969:182-3. Hunter 1793:166-8 seems to rely on Bradley's account.
4. Tench 1793:34.
5. Hunter 1793:168.
6. King op. cit.
7. Tench 1793:34.
8. Hunter 1793:168.
9. Fowell, Batavia, 31 July 1790 [*HRNSW* 11:373 et seq.].
10. Southwell, 14 April 1790 [*HRNSW* 11:709].
11. Collins 1975:482.
12. Elizabeth Macarthur to Bridget Kingdon, 7 March 1791 [*HRNSW* 11:502].
13. Hunter 1793:168-9.
14. Bradley 1969:185.
15. Banks, 12 July 1769 in J.C. Beaglehole (ed.) 1963:312-13. Tupia later died in Batavia.
16. George R. 25 April 1787 [*HRNSW* 11:89-90].
17. Bradley 1969:185.
18. Tench 1793:35.
19. Fowell op. cit.
20. Hunter 1793:169.
21. Phillip to Sydney, 13 February 1790 [*HRNSW* 11:309].

22. George Brummell, arbiter of fashion and manners in Regency England.
23. King op. cit.
24. Blackburn to his sister Margaret, Batavia, 19 August 1790 (Blackburn was not aware that Bennelong had escaped on 3 May 1790).
25. King op. cit.
26. Tench 1793:35.
27. King op. cit.
28. Tench 1793:36.
29. Ibid.
30. Bennelong to King, op. cit.
31. Tench op. cit.
32. Blackburn op. cit.
33. King op. cit.
34. Elizabeth Macarthur to Bridget Kingdon, 7 March 1791 [*HRNSW* 11:594].
35. Tench 1793:35.
36. King op. cit.
37. Langton 1997:79.
38. Langton 1997:85.
39. Tench 1793:35.
40. Southwell to Butler, 14 April 1790 [*HRNSW* 11:709].
41. Southwell to Butler [BT Box 57:63] – omitted from Southwell's Vocabulary as printed in *HRNSW* 11:697 et seq.
42. Bradley 1969:187-8.
43. Bradley 1969:163.
44. Tench 1793:14.
45. Tench 1793:12.
46. Hunter 1793:93.
47. Tench 1793:10.
48. Troy 1993b:35.
49. Tench 1793:14, 24.
50. Tench 1793:36.
51. Elizabeth Macarthur [*HRNSW* 11:503].
52. Bennelong, quoted in Phillip to Sydney, 13 February 1790 [*HRNSW* 11:308].
53. Phillip in Hunter 1793:531; Collins 1975:137. Phillip later also officially adopted the native name of Toongabbie for the New Grounds farms.
54. Bennelong to Collins 1975:497.
55. Collins 1975:490.
56. Phillip to Sydney, op. cit.
57. King op.cit.
58. Bennelong to King, Journal, 9 April 1790, op. cit.
59. Anon. 34.
60. Tench 1793:40-4.

8 PAYBACK

1. Southwell Journal, c. June 1790 [BL Add. MSS 16381-5].
2. Hunter 1793:204.
3. Phillip to Banks, 26 July 1790 [PRO Reel CY300 2/89-94].
4. Southwell op. cit. and Southwell to Rev. W. Butler, 27 July 1790.
5. Hill to Wathen, 26 July 1790 [*HRNSW* 11:370].
6. Southwell Papers [Box 57:357-61].
7. Tench 1793:52.
8. Scott 1787:53.
9. Harris to unknown correspondent, 21 March 1791 [A1597:858 ML].
10. Collins 1975:109.
11. Tench 1793:54.
12. Surgeon's log, Britannia, 1793 [MS Q36 DL].
13. Tench 1793:55.
14. Waterhouse in Bradley 1969:228.
15. Tench 1793:58.
16. Waterhouse in Bradley 1969:228.
17. Tench 1793:58.
18. Phillip in Hunter 1793:462.
19. Phillip in Hunter 1793:463.
20. Bennelong to Phillip, according to the *British Journal*, London, 23 June 1792.
21. 'Wil-le-me-ring – the man who threw ye spear', Anon. 41.3; 'It was Willa-mi-ring speared Govr. Ph.', Southwell 1787-93:63.
22. Tench 1793:60.
23. Waterhouse in Bradley 1969:225-30; Waterhouse in Hunter 1793:206-10; Phillip in Hunter 1793:459-65; Collins 1975:110-11.
24. Brodsky 1973:53.
25. Collins 1975:111.
26. McBryde 1989:15
27. Hunter 1793:463-4, 46.
28. Bradley 1969:230.
29. Collins op. cit.
30. Stanner 1979:184.

9 COMING IN

1. Tench 1793:62.
2. Maugoran to Tench 1793:61.
3. Hunter 1793:468-9.
4. Tench 1793:62-7.
5. Collins 1975:112.
6. Bennelong to Tench 1793:67.
7. Scott 1963:57.
8. Smith and Wheeler 1988: Plate 66.
9. Collins op. cit.
10. Hunter 1793:469.
11. Hunter 1793:470-1.
12. Bennelong to Collins 1975:497.
13. Tench 1793:67-8.
14. Scott 1963:58.
15. Hunter 1793:471.
16. Tench 1793:71.
17. Collins 1975:111-12.
18. Hunter 1793:473.
19. Hunter 1793:476.
20. Tench 1793:83.
21. Collins 1975:113. See McCormick 1987: Plates 16, 20, 21, 27, 28; Smith and Wheeler 1988: Plates 136, 139.
22. Blackburn to his sister Margaret, 17 March 1791 [Norfolk Record Office, Norwich, UK].
23. Hunter 1793:476.
24. Bennelong to Phillip in Hunter 1793:493. Not 'As the First Fleet's Surgeon-General remarked' nor 'his' tribe, as given in Carter (1992:167), a misquotation of the accurate text in Willey (1985:121).
25. Bennelong to Hunter 1793:493.
26. *SMH* 23 February 1901.
27. Thompson [*HRNSW* 11:797].
28. Smith and Wheeler 1988: Plate 142.
29. Collins 1975:355.
30. *SG* 21 October 1804 3c.
31. Christies, London. Exploration and Travel. Wednesday 8 April 1998. Lots 130-5.
32. Harris, 21 March 1791 [A1597:858 ML].
33. Hunter 1793:467.
34. Harris op. cit.
35. Tench 1793:83.
36. Hunter 1793:487.
37. Hunter 1793:471.
38. Hunter 1793:471-2.
39. Hunter 1793:472.
40. Bennelong to Phillip in Hunter 1793:474.
41. Tench 1793:83.
42. Collins 1975:498.

10 GETTING WORDS

1. MS 4165 (a), School of Oriental and African Studies, London. The notebook, titled in another hand, Grammatical forms of the Language of N.S. Wales, in the neighbourhood of Sydney, is referred to in this work as Dawes 1790a.
2. Bennelong to Dawes 1790a:22.2.
3. Bennelong to Dawes 1790a:22.7.
4. Bennelong to Dawes 1790a:20.6.
5. Phillip to Sydney, 13 February 1790 [*HRNSW* 11:309].
6. Tench 1979:189.
7. Tench 1979:293.
8. King Journal, 9 April 1790 [MS C115 ML].
9. King in Hunter 1793:406 et seq.
10. MS 4165 (b) Anon. n.d. [1790-1]. Vocabulary of the language of N.S. Wales in the neighbourhood of Sydney (Native and English, but not alphabetical. School of Oriental and African Studies, London. Here called Anon.
11. Troy 1993a:14-15.
12. C. Lévi-Strauss 1978 (1955):511. Tristes Tropiques (Harmondsworth: Penguin).
13. King 1790:408.
14. Anon 22:16.
15. Dawes 1790a:44.5 (giving lines from the bottom of the page, as text is upside down).
16. Hunter 1793:411.
17. Collins 1975:508.
18. Collins 1975:454.
19. James Kohen 1988:240. 'The Dharug of the Western Cumberland Plain: Ethnography and Demography', in R. Jones and B. Meehan (eds). *Archaeology With Ethnography: An Australian Perspective* (Canberra: ANU). 'People – E-o-rah', Southwell 1787-93:58; 'Yes E-e. Ee.', Southwell 1787-93:63.

11 ABDUCTING A WIFE

1. Collins 1975:463-4.
2. Dawes 1790b:43.6; Phillip in Hunter 1793:486.
3. Elkin 1966 (1938):157.
4. 'Karangarany', Dawes 1790b:43.2; 'Punangan', Dawes 1790b:32.2.
5. Tench 1793:73-4.
6. Tench 1793:83.
7. Probably Sergeant James Scott.
8. Bennelong to Tench 1793:85.
9. Phillip in Hunter 1793:482.
10. Phillip in Hunter 1793:487, Collins 1975:116.
11. Phillip in Hunter 1793:485.
12. Ballooderry and Nanbarry to Dawes.a:10.2-10.
13. Phillip in Hunter 1793:486.
14. Tench 1793:87.
15. Phillip in Hunter 1793:487-8.
16. Barangaroo to Dawes 1790 b.23.13.
17. Anon. 14.13-16.
18. 'His native names were Gnung-a gnung-a, Mur-re-murgan', Collins 1975:250.

12 DEATH OF A GAME SHOOTER

1. Tench 1789:83. Collins (1975:469-71) intimates that 'power over the dog' (dingo) and the power to kill kangaroos was the domain of initiated men.
2. Worgan 1978:20.
3. Tench 1793:55.
4. Tench 1793:70.
5. Anon. 5.2. However, Anon. 45.17, 19 lists tooga-gal and bediagal as separate tribes.
6. Hunter 1793:487.
7. Collins 1975:464.
8. Hunter 1793:489-90.
9. Not unlikely if Colby and Bennelong had known about Pemulwuy's intentions beforehand, Hunter 1793:493. This account of the attack on McEntire is based on Tench 1793:89-101, Phillip in Hunter 1793:491-6 and Collins 1975:117-19, 122.
10. Hunter 1793:490.
11. Hunter 1793:493-5.
12. Hunter 1793:496. Dr James Kohen (1988:242-3) suggests that 'the

Sydney natives identified [Pemulwuy's] band because of the red stone barbs on the spear ... almost certainly the red silcrete found to the west across the Cumberland Plain'.
13. Spencer and Gillen 1938 [1896]:478.
14. See Fitzhardinge, Chapter XII, note 7 in Tench (1961:319). *Sydney's First Four Years* (Sydney: Angus & Robertson).
15. G. Arnold Wood 1924. 'Lieutenant William Dawes and Captain Watkin Tench', *JRAHS*, vol. 10, pt 1, p. 7.
16. Phillip to Grenville, 7 November 1791 [*HRA* 1:292].
17. Collins 1975:490.
18. Return of Aboriginal Natives, 1834-43, NSW Archives.
19. Tench 1793:94-7.
20. Easty 1965:121.
21. Collins 1975:119.
22. Watling 41, NHM London. Also Smith and Wheeler 1988: Plate 7.
23. Dawes 1790b:9.2; b.43.4.
24. Easty 1965:122.
25. Ibid.
26. Watling 25, NHM London; Smith and Wheeler 1988: Plate 237.
27. Hunter 1793:504.
28. Collins 1975:122.

13 THE POTATO THIEVES

1. A rare mention of women's yam digging sticks in the First Fleet records.
2. 'Gnoo-roo-in', Anon 43.7. Possibly a version of gnar-rang or narrong, meaning small; also a species of lizard.
3. Tench 1793:101.
4. That is, he slept by the same camp fire as Willemerring, indicating that the two men were on friendly terms.
5. Hunter 1793:498-500.
6. Tench 1793:102.
7. Collins 1975:121.
8. Tench 1793:103-4; Hunter 1793:502-3.
9. Collins 1975:122.
10. Hunter 1793:509.
11. Hunter 1793:508-9.
12. Collins 1975:122.
13. Hunter 1793:509-10; Tench 1793:132.
14. Hunter 1793:511.

14 RITES OF PASSAGE

1. Hiatt 1965:54.
2. Hunter 1793:506-7.
3. Noel Wallace in R. Charlesworth et al. 1990:79. *Ancient Spirits: Aspects of Aboriginal Life and Spirituality* (Geelong: Deakin University Press).
4. Anon. 17.7.
5. Collins 1975:485.
6. Bennelong told Collins (1975:503) that the tooth knocked out at his initiation was bour-bil-liey pe-mal, that is, 'buried in the earth' and that other teeth were thrown into the sea.
7. Anon. 4.11.
8. Tench 1793:86.
9. Entry in Parish register, Eltham, cited in McBryde 1989:23, 55.
10. Tench 1793:198.
11. Ibid.
12. Elkin 1966:294.
13. Based on Hunter 1793:210-13 and Bradley 1969:231.
14. Collins 1975:454.
15. King, April 1790.
16. Collins 1975:495.
17. Anon. 21.11.
18. Elkin 1966 (1938):165.
19. Elkin 1966:188.
20. Grey 1841 vol. 2:228.
21. Durkheim 1965:110.
22. E. Macarthur to Kingdon, 7 March 1791 [*HRNSW* 11:502].
23. Collins 1975:465.
24. Phillip to Sydney, 13 February 1790 [*HRNSW* 11:310].
25. Tench 1793:202.
26. Collins 1975:465.
27. McCarthy 1967:19. The style of engravings could also identify clan territory.
28. Worgan 1978:21.
29. For example, by Dr James Kohen 1993:35.
30. Clark 1981:109.
31. Bradley 1969:98-9.
32. Collins 1975:455.
33. Collins 1975 (1802) vol. 2:41.
34. Gardiner 1791:77.
35. *SG* 6 October 1805, 2b.
36. 'Burra burra' here could refer to the burraburrigal or birrabaragal clan named for birra-birra, the Sow and Pigs rocks near the entrance to Sydney Harbour.
37. Simonov, quoted in Barratt 1981:47-8.
38. BT Box 53 (5:1789-90) ML [See Smith 1992:143].
39. Kohen 1993:77.
40. Returns of Aboriginal Natives, 1834-1843 [NSWAO 4/1133].
41. Proctor 1834:96-120.
42. 'Child Boy of Yuwarry { O-ring-gnouey g'nouey', Southwell 1787-93:58; 'Narrong nowey, The *Supply*', Hunter 1793:409.
43. *HRNSW* 11:192.
44. Bradley 1969 132-4.
45. Tench 1789:129.
46. Collins 1795:455.
47. Atkins, Journal, 11 April 1792.

15 EORA IN TOWN

1. Macarthur to Kingdon, 7 March 1791 [*HRNSW* 11:504].
2. Blackburn to Margaret Blackburn, 17 March 1791 [Norfolk Record Office, Reel 133/3].
3. Letter from John Harris, 21 March 1791 [A1597:858 ML].
4. Bradley 1969:245.
5. Collins Correspondence 1775-1810 [MSS 700 ML].
6. Phillip to Banks, 24 March 1791 [MS C213 ML].
7. Hunter 1793:205.
8. Hunter 1793:210.
9. Hunter 1793:527.
10. [William Dawes] 'Vocabulary of the language of N.S.Wales in the neighbourhood of Sydney (Native and English)'. MS 4165 (b), School of Oriental and African Studies, London. Referred to as Dawes 1790b.
11. Dawes 1790b:4.6.
12. Dawes 1790b:15.12.
13. Dawes 1790b:17.4.
14. Dawes 1790b:19.16.
15. Dawes 1790b:30.21.
16. Dawes 1790b:34.24.
17. Dawes 1790b:36.15.
18. Dawes 1790b:11.20.
19. Dawes 1790b:26.13.

20. Dawes 1790b:24.7.
21. Published in Francois Péron 1824. *Voyage de découvertes aux terres Australes* (2nd ed.: Paris). See Bonnemains, Forsyth and Smith 1988: Plates 20032.4, 20035.
22. Bradley 1969:231.
23. Collins 1975:451.
24. Tench 1793:122.
25. Kohen 1995:33-5; A. Capell 1970. 'Aboriginal Languages in the South Central Coast, New South Wales: Fresh Discoveries.' *Oceania* vol. 41, pp. 20-7.
26. King 1791:405.
27. Patyegarang to Dawes 1790b 1791:34.
28. Tench 1793:259, 296-7.
29. Capell op. cit.
30. J. Kohen 1993. *The Darug and Their Neighbours*, pp. 245-53; L. Threlkeld, 'Specimens of the Language of the Aborigines of New South Wales to the Northward of Sydney (Karee).' MS, ML, Sydney.
31. Return of Aboriginal Natives, Brisbane Water, 1833-42, NSW Archives.
32. J.F. Mann, *Daily Telegraph,* 31 March 1904; Smith 1992:148.
33. J.F. Mann, *SMH,* 1886 [Newspaper Cuttings, vol. 116:169, ML].
34. Collins 1975:49.
35. Bennelong to Dawes 1790b 2.12.
36. Hunter 1793:545.
37. Patyegarang to Dawes 1790b 33.12; Warreweer to Dawes 1790b 33.21.
38. Mahroot 1845 to Select Committee of the New South Wales Legislative Council.

16 EXPEDITION TO THE WEST

1. Tench 1793:112.
2. Tench 1793:114 (footnote).
3. Tench 1793:117; 'Gna-mo-roo – a Compass (so called by the Natives Gna to see & moroo a path)', Anon. 16.16.
4. 'Booroowunne – the name of a man a stranger', Anon. 12.9; 'Bur-ro-wun', Anon. 40.2.
5. Hunter 1793:512-25 (Chapter XXI); Tench 1793:112-27 (Chapter XIV).
6. Tench 1793:116-20 – 'an eater of human excrement' in Tench's translation.
7. Anon. 13.18;5.3.
8. Watling 75 NHM London; Smith and Wheeler 1988: Plate 48.
9. Hunter 1793:520-1.
10. Collins 1975:492; 2:47.
11. Anon. 41.1.
12. Phillip to Banks, 3 December 1791 [Banks Papers, ML A81:34-44].
13. Collins 1975:506.
14. Hunter 1793:527-9.
15. Pandal – Dawes 1790b:35.9; Bundell – see Smith 1992:116.
16. Tench 1793:107.
17. Bradley 1969:245.
18. Tench 1793:107.
19. Collins 1975:147-8.
20. 'Piyidyinina white-mana ngyinari Pandalna, Pundunga } A white man |beat us three – we three|Pandal, Poondah & myself understood', Dawes 1790b35.9 ... 'obtained 27 Novr by Patyegarang ... speaking to me', Dawes 1790b:35.16.
21. *British Journal,* 21 April 1791 [BP Box 58:301].
22. D.D. Mann, 1811:47. The Present Picture of New South Wales (London).
23. Chapman to his mother, 17 October 1791 [Chapman Papers A197].
24. King to Banks, 25 October 1791 [Banks Papers A78 ML].
25. Johnson to Fricker, 4 October 1791, quoted in Cobley: 1965:122.
26. Parker 1795:102.
27. Gardiner 1791:76.
28. Phillip to Banks, 3 December 1791 [Banks Papers A81:34-44 ML].
29. Collins 1798:464.
30. Gardiner 1791:83.
31. Collins 1975:159.

17 BALLOODERRY

1. Based on Collins 1975:137-9, 146, 465, 499-503 and Hunter 1793:532-4, 539-40.
2. Gardiner 1791:82.
3. Smith 1992:143-4.
4. Watling Collection, Natural History Museum, London. See Bernard Smith

(ed.) 1988 *The Art of the First Fleet* (Melbourne: Oxford University Press).

5. Meggitt 1962:322.
6. 'the boy Nan-bar-ry, or Bal-der-ry' – Hunter 1793:167.
7. Collins 1975:504.
8. Collins 1975:502.

18 WOMEN'S BUSINESS

1. Watling 51, 59, 42, 42, 43, 52, 68. Smith and Wheeler 1988: Plates 32, 33, 34, 42, 43, 44, 46.
2. Bennett 1865:84, also reprinted in C.H. Bertie 1924. 'Captain Cook and Botany Bay', *JRAHS*, vol. 10, part V. Bennett quoted a Sydney 'gentleman', who had collected stories from several Botany Bay elders.
3. Maiden 1889:435. George Caley gave the inland dialect (Darug) name as banga'ly (see 'Caley's Eucalypts' in Webb 1995: Appendix D).
4. 'Port Jackson Painter' in Watling 64; Smith and Wheeler 1988: Plate 50.
5. Troy 1993a:42.
6. Tench 1789:119.
7. Dawes 1790b:42.8.
8. 'The Banksiad which bears ye bottle washer} – Wa-tang-gre'; 'The Sceptre flower – War-ret-tah'; 'a low tree bearing a fruit like the Wa-tang-gre} Weereagan', Anon. 20.14, 18; 'Wattangurry – Honeysuckle', Caley 1807. See Keith Smith and Irene Smith, *Grow Your Own Bushfoods* (New Holland, 1999).
9. Bradley 1969:232b.
10. Caley to Banks, October 1807 [DTC.17:168-198 BL].
11. Collins 1975:462; H.W.H. Huntington in the *Northern Suburbs Echo*, 9 August 1902, said Dr J.D. Lang included: 'Honey – Shuger-bage' in his vocabulary of Aboriginal words (c.1830).
12. Warreweer to Dawes 1790b:42.11.
13. Patyegarang to Dawes 1790b:34.26.
14. 'Scarlet & Yellow bell flower – Ga-de-gal-ba-die-ree', Anon. 20.14.
15. Anon. 3.6; 20.11.
16. 'Fig Tree – Tam-mun', Anon. 20.9.
17. White 1790:191.
18. Bradley 1969:76.
19. 'Gur-gy, The fern root', Hunter 1793:409.
20. Phillip to Sydney, 15 May 1788 [HRA 1:30-1].
21. Tench 1793:24 (footnote). See Arabanoo.
22. Collins 1975:487.
23. Hunter 1793:479-80.
24. Tench 1793:200.
25. Southwell 1787-1793:57. 'Barring-an the name of a very handsome girl', Anon. 11.1; 'Co-ro-by – a native's name', Anon. 5.14.
26. Hunter 1793:497. The boy was probably Yemmerrawanne.
27. James Campbell. Letter to Dr Farr, Plymouth, Sydney Cove, 24 March 1791 [Doc 1174, ML].
28. Hunter 1793:503.
29. Collins 1975:465.
30. E. Macarthur to Bridget Kingdon, 7 March 1791 [*HRNSW* 11:504].
31. Collins 1975:459. 'Pin-niee-bool-long. The name of Colebe's Child', Anon. 11.13. Possibly a compound of kani burnt and boola two.
32. Anon. 23.1.
33. White 1790:204.
34. Phillip to Sydney, 13 February 1790 [*HRNSW* 11:300].
35. Collins 1975:458.
36. Kohen 1993:34, quoting G. England 1976:42.The Coffs Harbour Story.
37. Hunter 1793:510.
38. Hunter 1793:205.
39. Collins 1975:458.
40. Hunter 1795:205.
41. Tench 1793:111.
42. Collins 1975:504.
43. Collins 1975:502-3.
44. Smith & Wheeler 1988:30, 32.
45. Collins 1975:483. Collins took these teeth, including one from Nanbarry (Daringa and Colby's nephew), back to England.
46. Tench 1793:55.
47. Bradley: 1969:187.
48. Southwell to Butler, 27 July 1790 [Southwell Papers, Reel M1538, PRO, London].

49. *HRNSW* 11:718.
50. Hunter 1793:477.
51. Hunter 1793:468.
52. Hunter 1793:475.
53. Hunter 1793:476.
54. Collins 1795:503.
55. Phillip in Hunter 1793:480.
56. Barangaroo to Dawes 1790a:26.3-6. Perhaps Dawes also shaved Pemulwuy, who was in Sydney at about that time.
57. Hunter 1793:544-5.
58. McGrath 1996:233.
59. Ibid.
60. Collins 1795:465.
61. Barangaroo to Dawes 1790b:2.6-9.
62. Phillip in Hunter 1793:543.
63. Tench 1793:200.
64. McGrath 1996:241.
65. Collins 1798:605-6.
66. Collins 1798:545.
67. Southwell to his mother (from Batavia), 7 September 1791 [*HRNSW* 11:731].
68. Collins 1975:502-3.
69. Collins 1975:490.
70. Collins 1975:502.
71. Tench 1793:21. Tench thought Boorong was about fourteen years old.
72. Bradley 1969:171.
73. Tench 1793:184. 'Bir-rong A star', Collins 1975:507; 'Boorong, a star', Daniel Paine (1795).
74. King Journal, 9 April 1790:408.
75. Johnson to Fricker, 19 April 1790.
76. King Journal, 9 April 1790.
77. Blackburn to his sister Margaret, Batavia, 19 August 1790.
78. Tench 1793:186.
79. Dawes 1790a:8.2, dated 17 November 1790.
80. Historians and anthropologists who have said that Governor Phillip had no native informants from the inland areas were wrong, because Boorong, Ballooderry and Warreeweer Wogul-Mi were all from Parramatta.
81. Yeranibe to Dawes 1790a:4.11.
82. Ballooderry to Dawes 1790a:10.2.
83. Tench 1793:64-6.
84. Dawes 1790a:6.18.
85. Collins 1975:275.
86. Watling 57, NHM London; Smith and Wheeler 1988: Plate 49.
87. Collins 1975:305.
88. Phillip in Hunter 1793:475.
89. Phillip in Hunter 1793:479.
90. Tench 1793:185.
91. Watling 62; Smith and Wheeler 1988: Plate 27.
92. Johnson to Fricker, 18 March 1791 [quoted in Cobley 1965:31-2].
93. Collins 1975:464-5.
94. Patyegarang to Dawes 1790b:21.7. Domine, here meaning Chaplain Johnson, referred to a schoolmaster in the reformed churches. Dawes 1790b:5.17 gives the phrase: 'At Domine's house'.

19 AMITY ... AND REVENGE

1. Collins 1975:174.
2. Thompson Journal [*HRNSW* 11:797-8].
3. Tench 1789:57-8.
4. Atkins Journal, 11 April 1792 [Typescript, Macquarie University Library].
5. 'Punangan', Dawes 1790b.32.2.
6. Collins 1975:492.
7. Collins 1975:488-9.
8. Atkins Journal, 27 May 1792.
9. Collins 1975:460-1.
10. 'Gonangulye', Dawes 1790b.8.18; 'Gonan-goolie – name of a little girl', Anon. 3.1; 'Go-nan-goo-lie', Anon. 43.6.
11. Dawes 1790b:8.17; 30.6,13.
12. Collins 1975:489.
13. Collins 1975:461.
14. Fowell 1988:93.
15. Hunter 1793:67.
16. J. Kohen in Kohen, Knight and Smith 1999:32, 34.
17. Atkins Journal, 18 May 1792.
18. Collins 1975:178.
19. 'State of the Settlements at Sydney, Parramatta, and Norfolk Is.' [*HRNSW* 11:676-7].

20 THE SKILFUL GAME

1. Thomson 1949:70-81.
2. Malinowski 1970 [1922]:39-45.

3. Lechte 1994:26.
4. Marcel Mauss 1923-4 (1990). *The Gift: The Form and Reason for Exchange in Archaic Societies*. Trans. W.D. Hale (London: Routledge).
5. Cook, quoted in Beaglehole 1967:380.
6. Beaglehole 1967:1141.
7. Beaglehole 1967:1182.
8. Bowes Smyth 1788:106.
9. PRO London CO 201/2 [*HRNSW* 11:53].
10. Admiralty Account Book [*HRNSW* 11:388].
11. Beaglehole 1974:230.
12. In the minds of the invaders the dispossession of the inhabitants was obviously taken for granted.
13. Tench 1783:53; Worgan 1978:4.
14. King 1980:32.
15. Tench 1793:54.
16. Rev. J. McEncroe, letter to Rev. Dr Douglass, *SMH*, 27 April 1868, quoted in Charles H. Bertie 1924. 'Captain Cook and Botany Bay', *JRAHS*, vol. 10, part V:236-8.
17. King 1980:34-5.
18. Collins 1975:12.
19. Worgan 1978:19.
20. Bradley 1788:82.
21. Clark 1790:109.
22. Quoted in A.E. Komter (ed.) 1996. *The Gift: An Interdisciplinary Perspective* (Amsterdam University Press).
23. Tench 1793:57-8.
24. Hunter 1793:471.
25. Thomas 1996:145.
26. *Gentlemen's Magazine*, London, March 1789.
27. Thomas 1991. *Entangled Objects: Exchange, Material Culture, and Colonisation in the Pacific* (Cambridge, Mass.: Harvard University Press).
28. *London Chronicle*, 4-7 April 1789.
29. E. Macarthur to Kingdon, 7 March 1791 [*HRNSW* 11:502].
30. Collins 1975:122.
31. Caley to Banks, 1 June 1802 [Banks Papers, vol. 8:108 ML].
32. Barratt 1961:62-3.
33. W.R. Govett 1836. 'Sketches of New South Wales', *Saturday Magazine*, London.
34. T.L. Mitchell 1848:325. Journal of an Expedition ... (London).
35. Gillen to Spencer, 29 July 1901. Mulvaney, John (ed.) 1997:342. 'My Dear Spencer'. The Letters of F.J. Gillen to Baldwin Spencer (Melbourne: Hyland House).

21 A HEAD FOR SIR JOSEPH

1. Blumenbach to Banks, January 1791 [Add. MS9097:362-3 BL].
2. Phillip to Sydney, 15 May 1788 [CO 201/3 PRO London].
3. Phillip to Banks, 26 July 1790 [BP A1787 ML].
4. Phillip to Banks, 26 March 1791 [CY Reel 3002/102 ML].
5. Phillip to Banks, 17 November 1791 [CY Reel 3002/113-18 ML].
6. Phillip to Banks, 3 December 1791 [BP V.18.MLA81:36 ML].
7. Blumenbach to Banks, 1 November 1793 [Add. MS8089:116-17 BL].
8. J. Bronowski 1976 (1973):367. The *Ascent of Man* (London: BBC).

22 SAILING

1. Collins 1975:211.

APPENDIX

1. Caption: 'Portraits [sic] of Ben-nil-long, Wo-lar-ra-bar-ray, Wo-gul-trow-e, Boin-ba, and Bun-de-bun-da' in Collins 1798 'List of Engravings'. There was only one portrait – of Bennelong.
2. Caley to Banks, 16 February 1809. Caley said he was told by the natives that the name of 'Bannylongs' was Wallerbio. This is very close to wallibah, a wallaby.
3. Hunter 1793:168. More likely to have been the names of ancestors, as the Eora were forbidden to speak the names of those who had recently died.
4. Bennelong to Collins 1978:464.

BIBLIOGRAPHY

PRIMARY SOURCES

PRINTED WORKS

[Bowes Smyth, Arthur] 1979, P.G. Fidlon and R.J. Ryan (eds). *The Journal of Arthur Bowes Smyth: Surgeon, Lady Penrhyn, 1787-1789.* Sydney: Australian Documents Library [MSS 955 ML].

Bradley, William. 1969. *A Voyage to New South Wales: The Journal of Lieutenant William Bradley RN of HMS Sirius, 1786-1792.* Facs. reprint, Sydney: Trustees of the Public Library of NSW.

[Clark, Ralph] 1981. *The Journal and Letters of Lieutenant Ralph Clark, 1787-1792.* Paul G. Fidlon and R.J. Ryan (eds). Sydney: Library of Australian History [ZIC 221 ML].

Collins, David. 1975 [1798]. *An Account of the English Colony in New South Wales ...* London: T. Cadell Jun. and W. Davies, in *The Strand.* Vol. 2. published 1802 (1975).

[Easty, John] 1965. *Memorandum of the transaction of a voyage from England to Botany Bay, 1787-1793: A First Fleet journal by John Easty.* Trustees of the Public Library of New South Wales.

[Fowell, Newton] 1988. N. Irvine (ed.). *The Sirius Letters: The Complete Letters of Newton Fowell ...* Sydney: The Fairfax Library.

Hunter, John. [A. Phillip. and P.G. King] 1793. *An Historical Journal of the Transactions at Port Jackson and Norfolk Island ... Including the Journals of Governors Phillip and King, and of Lieut. Ball.* London: John Stockdale.

[King, Philip Gidley] 1980. P.G. Fidlon, and R.J. Ryan (eds). *The Journal of Philip Gidley King, Lieutenant, R.N., 1787-1790.* Sydney: Australian Documents Library.

Nagle, Jacob. 1988. J.C. Dann (ed.). *The Nagle Journal: A Diary of the Life of Jacob Nagle, Sailor, From the Year 1775 to 1841.* New York: Weidenfeld & Nicolson.

[Phillip, Arthur] 1789. *The Voyage of Governor Phillip to Botany Bay; with an Account of the Establishment of the Colonies of Port Jackson & Norfolk Island ...* compiled from authentic papers ... London: Stockdale.

[Scott, James] 1963. *Remarks on a passage to Botany Bay, 1787-1792: A First Fleet Journal by James Scott.* Sydney: Trustees of the Public Library of New South Wales. [MSQ43 DL].

Tench, Watkin. 1789. *A narrative of the expedition to Botany Bay; with an account of New South Wales, its productions, inhabitants, &c ...* London: J. Debrett.

Tench, Watkin. 1793. *A complete account of the settlement at Port Jackson, in New South Wales, including an accurate description of the colony; of the natives; and of its natural productions ...* London: G. Nicol and J. Sewell.

White, John. 1790. *Journal of a Voyage to New South Wales* ... London. Reprint 1962. Alec H. Chisholm (ed.). Sydney: Angus & Robertson. Fasc. New York: Arno Press and the *New York Times* [1971].

[Worgan, George Bouchier] 1978. *Journal of a First Fleet Surgeon*. Sydney: Library Council of NSW.

MANUSCRIPTS

Atkins, Richard. Journal of a Voyage to Botany Bay. Typescript. Macquarie University Library, Sydney.

Blackburn, David. Lieutenant HMS *Supply*. Letters. Blackburn Papers, Ab163 ML.

Campbell, James. Letter to Dr. Farr, Royal Naval Hospital, Plymouth. Sydney Cove, 24 March 1791. Doc 1174, ML. Original in British Library, London (4–140C).

Collins, David. 1775-1810. Correspondence. MSS 700 ML.

Gardiner, John. 1791-2. Account of the voyage of HMS *Gorgon*. MS 1 1-120 DL.

Harris, John, 1791 A1597 ML.

King, Philip Gidley. Journal, 1786-1790. MS C115 ML.

Kohen, J.L., A. Knight and K.V. Smith. 1999. Uninvited Guests: An Aboriginal Perspective on Government House and Parramatta Park. Sydney: Report prepared for the National Trust (unpublished).

Proctor, William. Journal on John Craig, 1834-5. CY1518 ML.

Return of Aboriginal Natives, 1834-43, NSW Archives, Sydney.

Southwell, Daniel. Extracts from journals in BL, 1787-91; Correspondence, 1787-93. Southwell Papers [*HRNSW* 11:668 et. seq.].

Surgeon's Log, *Britannia* 1793. MS Q36, DL.

REFERENCE WORKS, NEWSPAPERS AND PERIODICALS

Australian Dictionary of Biography 1966-81. Melbourne: Melbourne University Press.

Historical Records of Australia. 1914-22. Series 1. Canberra: Library of the Commonwealth Parliament.

Historical Records of New South Wales, 7 vols. 1892-1901. Sydney: Government Printer.

Journal of the Royal Australian Historical Society: Journal and Proceedings, Sydney, vol. 1, 1906 to date.

Sydney Gazette. Sydney, 1804-1834.

Sydney Morning Herald, relevant dates.

THE SYDNEY LANGUAGES

PRINTED WORKS

Kohen, James. 1993. 'Dictionary of the Coastal Darug (Eora) Language.' In *The Darug and Their Neighbours*. Blacktown: Darug Link/Blacktown and District Historical Society.

Kohen, Jim. 1995. 'Mapping Aboriginal Linguistic and Clan Boundaries in the Sydney Region.' *The Globe*, Journal of the Australian Map Circle, no. 41, pp. 32-9.

Mathews, R.H. 1901. 'The Dharruk Language.' *Journal of the Royal Society of NSW*, vol. 35, pp. 155-60.

Troy, Jakelin. 1992. 'The Sydney Language Notebooks and Responses to Language Contact in Early Colonial Sydney.' *Australian Journal of Linguistics*, vol. 12, pp. 140-70.

Troy, Jakelin. 1993a. *The Sydney Language*. Canberra: Australian Institute of Aboriginal and Torres Strait Islander Studies.

Troy, Jakelin. 1993b. 'Language contact in early colonial New South Wales 1788 to 1791.' In *Language and Culture in Aboriginal Society*. M. Walsh and C. Yallop (eds.). Canberra: Aboriginal Studies Press, pp. 33-50.

MANUSCRIPTS

Anon. n.d. [1790-1] [Probably A. Phillip and D. Collins] Vocabulary of the language of N.S. Wales in the neighbourhood of Sydney (Native and English, but not alphabetical. MS. 41645 (c), School of Oriental and African Studies

Blackburn, David. List of native names, with English equivalents. Blackburn Papers, Ab163 ML.

Dawes, William. 1790a. Grammatical forms of the language of N.S. Wales, in the neighbourhood of Sydney, by – Dawes, in the year 1790. MS. 4165 (a), Marsden Collection, School of Oriental and African Studies, University of London, London.

Dawes, William. 1790b. Vocabulary of the language of N.S. Wales in the neighbourhood of Sydney. Native and English, by – Dawes. MS. 4165 (b), Marsden Collection, School of Oriental and African Studies, London.

ANTHROPOLOGY AND ETHNOGRAPHY

Berndt, R.M., and Catherine Berndt. 1988 (1964). *The World of the First Australians*. Canberra: Aboriginal Studies Press.

Durkheim, Emile. 1965 (1915). *The Elementary Forms of the Religious Life*. Trans. Joseph Ward Swain. New York: The Free Press.

Elkin, A.P. 1966 (1938). *The Australian Aborigines: How to Understand Them*. Sydney: Angus & Robertson.

Flood, Josephine. 1990. *The Riches of Ancient Australia*. St Lucia: University of Queensland Press.

Grey, G. 1841. *Journal of Two Expeditions of Discovery in North-west and Western Australia*. London: T. and W. Boone, 2 vols.

Jones, R. 1968. 'The Geographical Background to the Arrival of Man in Australia and Tasmania.' *Archaeology and Physical Anthropology in Oceania*, vol. 3, pp. 186-215.

Kohen, J.L., and Lampert, R. 1987. 'Hunters and Fishers in the Sydney Region.' In Mulvaney, D.J., and White, J.P. (eds). *Australians to 1788*. Broadway, NSW: Fairfax, Syme & Weldon, pp. 343-65.

Kohen, James. 1988. 'The Dharug of the Western Cumberland Plain: Ethnology and Demography.' In R. Jones and B. Meehan (eds). *Archaeology and Ethnology: An Australian Perspective*. Canberra: Australian National University.

Kohen, James. 1993. *The Darug and their Neighbours*. Blacktown: Darug Link/ Blacktown and District Historical Society.

Kohen, James L. 1995. *Aboriginal Environmental Impacts*. Sydney: University of New South Wales University Press.

Langton, Marcia. 1997 [1993]. 'Rum, Seduction and Death: "Aboriginality" and Alcohol.' In G. Cowlishaw and B. Morris (eds.). *Race Matters*. Canberra: Aboriginal Studies Press. pp. 77-94.

Lechte, John. 1994. *Fifty Key Contemporary Thinkers: From Structuralism to Postmodernity*. London: Routledge.

McBryde, Isabel. 1989. '"To Establish a Commerce of this Sort" – Cross-Cultural Exchange at the Port Jackson Settlement.' In John Hardy and Alan Frost (eds). *Studies from Terra Australis to Australia*. Canberra: Australian Academy of the Humanities, pp. 169-82.

McCarthy, Frederick. D. 1967 (3rd ed.). *Australian Aboriginal Rock Art*. Sydney: Australian Museum.

McGrath. 1996. 'Birthplaces Revisited.' In Ross Gibson (ed.). *Exchanges: Cross-Cultural Encounters in Australia and the Pacific*. Sydney: Historic Houses Trust of New South Wales, pp. 219-42.

Mauss, Marcel. 1990. *The Gift: The Form and Reason for Exchange in Archaic Societies. Essai sur le Don* (1923-4). Trans. W.D. Hale. London: Routledge.

Meggitt, M.J. 1974 (1962). *Desert People*. Sydney: Angus & Robertson.

Thomas, Nicholas. 1991. *Entangled Objects: Exchange, Material Culture, and Colonialism in the Pacific*. Cambridge Mass.: Harvard University Press.

Thomas, Nicholas. 1996. 'Tabooed Ground.' In Ross Gibson, (ed.). *Exchanges, Cross-Cultural Encounters in Australia and the Pacific*. Sydney: Museum of Sydney.

Turbet, Peter. 1989. *The Aborigines of the Sydney District Before 1788*. Kenthurst: Kangaroo Press.

ART AND HISTORY

[Anderson, G.] 1811. *The History of New South Wales, from its first discovery to the present time, By a Literary Gentleman*. Newcastle-upon-Tyne.

Backhouse, James, and G.W. Walker. 1841. *A Narrative of a Visit to the Australian Colonies*. London.

[Banks 1963] J.C. Beaglehole (ed.). 1963. *The Endeavour Journal of Joseph Banks, 1768-1771*, 2 vols. Sydney: Angus & Robertson.

Barratt, Glynn. 1981. *The Russians at Port Jackson 1814-1822*. Canberra: Australian Institute of Aboriginal Studies.

Bennett, Samuel. 1865. *The History of Australian Discovery and Colonisation*. Sydney.

Bonnemains, J., E. Forsyth and B. Smith. 1998. *Baudin in Australian Waters*. Melbourne: Oxford University Press.

Brodsky, Isadore. 1973. *Bennelong Profile: Dreamtime Reveries of a Native of Sydney Cove*. Sydney: University Co-Operative Bookshop Ltd.

Cobley, John. 1963 (1962). *Sydney Cove, 1788*. London: Hodder and Stoughton.

Cobley, John. 1963. *Sydney Cove, 1789-1790*. Sydney: Angus & Robertson.

Cobley, John. 1965. *Sydney Cove, 1791-1792*. Sydney: Angus & Robertson.

[Cook, James] J.C. Beaglehole (ed.) 1967 (1955). *The Journal of Captain James Cook on his Voyages of Discovery*. 4 vols & portfolio. Hakluyt Society. Cambridge: At the University Press.

Currey, J.E.B. (ed.). 1966. *George Caley: Reflections on the Colony of New South Wales*. Melbourne: Landsdowne Press.

Frost, Alan. 1987. *Arthur Phillip, 1738-1814: His Voyaging*. Melbourne: Oxford University Press.

Gillen, Mollie. 1989. *The Founders of Australia*. Sydney: Library of Australian History.

Kenny, John. 1973. *Bennelong First Notable Aboriginal*. Sydney: Royal Australian Historical Society.

McBryde, Isabel. 1989. *Guests of the Governor: Aboriginal Residents of the First Government House*. Sydney: Friends of the First Government House Site.

McCormick, Tim, et al. 1987. *First Views of Australia, 1788-1825: A History of Early Sydney*. Sydney: David Ell Press.

[Mahroot 1845] 'Report from the Select Committee on the Condition of Aborigines'. *Votes and Proceedings*, NSW Legislative Council. Sydney.

Maiden, J.H. 1889. *The Useful Native Plants of Australia*. Sydney: The Technological Museum of New South Wales.

Parkinson, Sydney. 1784. *A Journal of a Voyage to the South Seas, in his Majesty's Ship The Endeavour* ... London.

Smith, Bernard, and A. Wheeler (eds). 1988. *The Art of the First Fleet and Other Early Australian Drawings*. Melbourne: Oxford University Press.

Smith, Keith Vincent. 1992. *King Bungaree: A Sydney Aborigine Meets the Great South Pacific Explorers, 1799-1830*. Kenthurst: Kangaroo Press.

Smith, Keith, and Irene Smith. 1999. *Grow Your Own Bushfoods*. Frenchs Forest: New Holland.

[Threlkeld, L.] Neil Gunson (ed.). 1974. *Australian Reminiscences and Papers of L.E. Threlkeld, Missionary to the Aborigines, 1834-1859*, 2 vols. Canberra: Australian Institute of Aboriginal Studies..

Webb, Joan. 1995. *George Caley: Nineteenth Century Naturalist*. Chipping Norton: Surrey Beatty & Sons.

Willey, Keith. 1985 (1979). *When the Sky Fell Down: The Destruction of the Tribes of the Sydney Region 1788-1850s*. Sydney: Collins.

INDEX

EORA

Life and culture of the Sydney area Aborigines and their 'contact with Europeans in the period 1788–1792 (includes Aborigines, Indians, indigenous people, natives)

PEOPLE

PLACES

74, 76–7, 79, 82, 84, 90,
99, 104, 106, 110, 119–
21, 123, 127, 129–30,
133, 143–4, 150–1, 153,
156
Brick Fields (Haymarket) 26,
30, 33, 121
Broken Bay 8, 19, 23, 26,
38, 52–4, 58, 65, 89,
105–6, 110–11, 119, 123
Calcutta 118–20
Camp Cove 16, 37
Cape of Good Hope 30, 37
Cape Town 107
Circular Quay 137
Cockle Bay (Darling Harbour)
32
Curracurrang 9
Darling Harbour (Long
Cove) 27, 29
Dawes (Spectacle) Island 26
Dawes Point (Tarra) 27, 29,
31, 72, 93–4, 129, 135,
138, 145
Eltham (Kent) 98
Endeavour River 20
Farm Cove 67, 132, 153
Garden Island 25, 123
George Street 4
George's River 82, 88
Goat Island 64
Governor Phillip's house
32, 39, 45, 51, 54, 63,
65–6, 69–71, 75–8, 80–1,
93, 96, 98, 116, 120–1,
123, 130, 132–5, 143, 153
Governor's; farm (Botanic
Gardens) 4, 26; garden
37, 121, 124–5, 135–7;
hut (Parramatta) 82–4,

120, 145; portable canvas
house 31, 151; wharf 65;
158; yard 93, 95–6, 116
Hawkesbury River 38, 110–
11, 113–16, 124, 129, 149
Hospital (The Rocks) 27,
29, 35, 76–8, 84, 94–5,
123, 134
Hyde Park 4, 105, 144
Kirribilli 105, 155
Kissing Point 120, 138
Kuringgai 110–11
Ku-rin-gai National Park 58
Lake Macquarie 21
Lane Cove 104
Lane Cove River 110, 152
Looking Glass Point 152
Look Out (South Head) 45,
52, 86, 95, 158
Lord Howe Island 41
Manly Cove (Kayeemy) 11,
15, 16, 23, 24, 31, 33,
39, 52–5, 57–8, 60, 69,
71, 100, 108, 119, 120,
123, 137, 152
Middle Harbour 15, 38
Middle Head 77
Nepean River 7, 22
Norfolk Island 33, 47, 59,
86, 107, 117–19, 135, 138
North Head 15, 20, 23
Northern Boundary 145
Parramatta (Rose Hill) 20,
27, 29, 46–7, 60, 62–3,
72, 79, 82, 84, 95, 106–7,
110, 113–16, 146, 155
Parramatta River 27, 29, 74,
106, 129, 145
Peacock Point 27
Pitt Water 111

Plymouth 118, 130
Port Jackson (see Sydney
Harbour)
Portsmouth 4, 140, 150
Prospect Hill 47, 145–6
Queen Charlotte Sound 157
Raiatea 41, 79
Richmond Hill 113
Rocks, The 158
Rose Bay 45, 52, 132, 144
Rose Hill (see Parramatta)
Rushcutters Bay 26, 27
South Head 15, 45, 52–4,
86–7, 95, 158
Spring Cove 23
Sydney Cove (Warrane) 16,
17, 20, 23, 25, 27, 30–4,
37, 39, 41, 44, 45, 51–4,
56, 58, 62–4, 66–6, 71–7,
74–5, 81–3, 88, 90, 93,
95–6, 98–9, 105–10,
113–14, 118–20, 121,
123–5, 127–8, 130, 134,
137, 143, 114–16, 148–9,
151–3, 156, 158
Sydney Harbour (Port
Jackson) 3, 4, 15, 16, 19,
21, 23, 25, 27, 29, 34,
41, 47, 106, 111, 117,
139, 143, 158
Sydney Opera House 4
Tahiti 41, 148, 156
Tank Stream 4, 144
Timor 96
Toongabbie 145
Trobriand Islands 147
Walsh Bay 128
Warrane (see Sydney Cove)
West Head 58, 111
Wooloomooloo 27

SHIPS

Alexander 26
Atlantic 118, 157–8
Bathurst 118
Brittania 52
Borrowdale 28
Discovery 148
Endeavour 4, 41, 150–1, 157
Fishburn 16
Friendship 16

Gorgon 7, 105, 109, 119–
20, 145, 146
Guardian 47
Lady Penrhyn 17, 24, 26,
148
Mary Ann 117
Pitt 119–20
Queen 119
Raven 105

Resolution 149
Scarborough 17
Sirius 4, 5, 7, 25, 28, 30, 37,
41, 45, 47, 52–3, 57, 59,
63, 67, 77, 104, 106, 138
Supply 16, 30, 33, 35, 41,
47, 72, 76, 117–8, 139
Waaksamheyd 107
William and Ann 105